D1126068

THE PURSUIT OF
ABSOLUTE INTEGRITY

Studies in Crime and Justice
A Series Edited by James B. Jacobs

The
Pursuit of
Absolute Integrity

How Corruption Control Makes
Government Ineffective

Frank Anechiarico
and James B. Jacobs

For Mike —
a true professional
and a great guy

with affection

Jim Jacobs

Nov '96

THE UNIVERSITY OF CHICAGO PRESS
CHICAGO AND LONDON

Frank Anechiarico is Maynard-Knox Professor of Government and Law at Hamilton College.   **James B. Jacobs** is professor of law and director of the Center for Research in Crime and Justice at New York University.

The University of Chicago Press, Chicago 60637
The University of Chicago Press, Ltd., London
© 1996 by The University of Chicago
All rights reserved. Published 1996
Printed in the United States of America
05 04 03 02 01 00 99 98 97 96   5 4 3 2 1

ISBN (cloth): 0-226-02051-7

Library of Congress Cataloging-in-Publication Data

Anechiarico, Frank.
    The pursuit of absolute integrity : how corruption control makes government
ineffective / Frank Anechiarico and James B. Jacobs.
        p.   cm. — (Studies in crime and justice)
    Includes bibliographical references (p.   ) and index.
    ISBN 0-226-02051-7 (alk. paper)
    1. Political corruption—United States.   2. Corruption investigation—United
States.   3. Civil service reform—United States.   4. Whistle blowing—United
States.   5. Government productivity—United States.   I. Jacobs, James B.
II. Title.   III. Series.
JK2249.A6225   1996
364.1'323—dc20   96-15863
                                                                      CIP

From FA to Linda and Mike Anechiarico and to my son, John

From JBJ to John Sexton, friend, colleague, and incredible law school dean

Contents

Acknowledgments

As we began sketching preliminary ideas and drafting some early papers, it became clear that we needed to carry out a good deal more empirical research. We are indebted to Dean John Sexton of the New York University School of Law, to the Law School's Center for Research in Crime and Justice, and to Eugene Tobin, then dean and now president of Hamilton College, for making it possible for Anechiarico to spend the 1991–92 academic year as a senior research fellow at the Center. During that year he conducted interviews with over two hundred city officials. In addition, we combed the municipal archives and agency libraries for internal and external studies, and for reports on corruption and corruption control over the course of the century.

Our research developed through the preparation of a series of articles. In various places throughout this book, we draw upon these articles, although on a number of points and in a number of ways our views have evolved since their publication. We are grateful for the assistance of the editors and reviewers of *Urban Affairs Quarterly* ("The Continuing Saga of Municipal Reform: New York City and the Politics of Ethics Law," 27 [June 1992]: 580–603); *Criminal Justice Ethics* ("Blacklisting Public Contractors as an Anti-Corruption and Racketeering Strategy," 11 [Summer/Fall 1992]: 64–76); *Public Administration Review* ("Visions of Corruption Control and the Evolution of American Public Administration," 54 [September/October 1994]: 465–73); *Crime, Law & Social Change* ("Panopticism and Financial Controls: The Anti-Corruption Project in Public Administration," 22 [January 1995]: 361–79); and *The New York Law School Law Review* ("Purging Corruption from Public Contracting: The Solution Is Now the Problem," 40 [Fall 1995]: 143–75).

David Garland, Milton Heumann, Charles Kuhlman, Eugene Lewis, David Paris, Ellen Schall, Ross Sandler, Dennis Smith, Michael Smith, David Wasserman, and Lynn Zimmer read the complete manuscript and offered invaluable criticisms and suggestions. A number of people read chapters in various forms, including Linda David, Lawrence Fleischer, Graham Hughes, Stacy Kinnamon, and Tony Tinker. To all these colleagues, we owe more gratitude than we are able to express.

We also benefited from outstanding research assistants. Janet Wieder spent the entire summer of 1994 and much of the 1994–95 academic year working on the manuscripts; she was always thorough, accurate, and precise. In the late fall of 1994 Kimberly Potter assumed the role of production manager, keeping track of holes to fill, tracking down hard-to-find sources, holding us to deadlines, and generally guiding the manuscript to completion. We owe her an enormous debt of gratitude. At various earlier points in our work, we benefited from research assistance from Kit Chu, Coleen Friel, Jessica Henry, and Stephen Reynolds. In the late stages of the work, Jessica Henry served as our copy editor. We also thank Judy Geissler for her efficient secretarial assistance.

We have the greatest respect for the men and women in public agencies who grapple daily with difficult questions that we have the leisure to contemplate. We hope that our work will bring clarity to problems of corruption control in public administration and stimulate a revitalized discourse that will generate creative solutions to the twin problems of corruption and corruption control.

Frank Anechiarico, Hamilton College
James B. Jacobs, New York University School of Law

PREFACE

> In governmental organization the costs of preventing or reducing corruption
> are not balanced against the gains with a view to finding an optimal invest-
> ment. Instead corruption is thought of (when it comes under notice) as
> something that must be eliminated no matter what the cost.
>
> Edward C. Banfield, "Corruption as a Feature
> of Governmental Organization"

Government reformers throughout the twentieth century have been animated by a vision of corruption-free government; each new generation has
contributed its own anticorruption laws, strategies, and institutions. Since
Watergate, there has been an eruption of anticorruption sentiment and activity. To an increasing extent, the laws and energy of federal, state, and local
governments focus on the surveillance and control of officials rather than
doing the business of government. This book analyzes the political and administrative campaign to combat official corruption in New York City, specifically, and the United States, generally, over the course of the twentieth
century. We call these government efforts the *anticorruption project,* by
which we mean the laws, regulations, and organizational policies aimed at
identifying, preventing, and punishing official corruption. Over the years,
the anticorruption project has been driven by cycles of corruption and reform. The trend is inexorable, but the term *anticorruption project* is not
meant to imply a disciplined movement. The absence of scandal is attributed to the success of existing strategies and institutions, while the occurrence of scandal is put forward as proving the need for additional laws and
strategies.

While official corruption has received a good deal of attention from political scientists and urban specialists, much less attention has been paid to
the political and administrative reactions to corruption and its impact on
governing. Most empirical and theoretical studies of urban public administration hardly recognize, much less emphasize, the extent to which gov-

ernment is absorbed in self-regulation in order to prevent bribery, embezzlement, nepotism, favoritism, and conflicts of interest. This is a serious oversight. Public administration scholars, the media, and the general public increasingly denounce government as inefficient, wasteful, and unresponsive. While many factors are responsible for the current crisis in public administration, we argue in this book that the pursuit of corruption-free government by means of more rules, procedures, and organizational shuffles is also an important contributing factor. It should not be assumed, as it often has been, that all corruption controls further or even coincide with governmental efficiency and effectiveness, or that such measures actually reduce corruption.

Typically, anticorruption reforms are instituted for "political cover" after a scandal or in response to pressures from the media or moral entrepreneurs. The impacts of such reforms on the "corruption rate" or on administrative efficiency and effectiveness are never evaluated and rarely considered. Eventually, however, many such reforms come to be viewed as another set of hurdles for government officials to get over and around.

Recognizing that the gradual accumulation of anticorruption apparatus is a key dynamic of public administration should deepen our understanding of why large government units are organized and operated the way they are. As Peter Self, a public administration scholar, has astutely observed, "The tensions between the requirements of responsibility or accountability and those of effective executive action can reasonably be described as the classic dilemma of public administration."[1]

The seeds of this book were planted during the mid-1980s when we collaborated with the New York State Organized Crime Task Force on an exhaustive study of corruption and racketeering in the New York City construction industry. The Task Force's determination to mobilize government in an all-out drive against corruption kindled our interest in the effects of the anticorruption project on public administration.[2] The field research for this book took place from 1991 to 1993. We interviewed over two hundred current and former officials in dozens of municipal, state, and federal agencies located in New York City.

While our empirical research was carried out in New York City, we would probably have found the same anticorruption dynamics in other cities. Some readers may be predisposed to think of New York City as uniquely corrupt. While there is no reliable methodology for making intercity comparisons regarding degrees of corruption, we do not believe New York City is special in this regard. Lincoln Steffins, in his 1902 classic muckraking expose of corruption in urban America, held up New York City as a national model of honest government.[3] To be sure, New York City has had its share of corruption, but so have most other American cities. For example, in the late 1980s, as a result of federal corruption probes, 5 percent of Cook County judges were indicted.[4] In Iowa, the chairman of the state liquor commission was convicted and imprisoned for extortion.[5] Former Oklahoma governor David Hall was convicted for bribing a state official, and ten New Jersey mayors were convicted for various types of official corruption.[6] As this book goes to press, it seems that practically the entire city government of Newark, New Jersey, is under indictment or investigation.[7] Official corruption cuts across all levels of government in all areas of the country: rural, suburban, and urban.[8]

Corruption is a problem and corruption control a constant challenge for all governments. Corruption undermines citizens' confidence in and commitment to the commonweal and can even destroy the legitimacy of the political system. Therefore, it is not difficult to agree with a phalanx of scholars and practitioners who argue that corruption must be controlled.[9] We part company with much of the mainstream literature on corruption in its unreflective acceptance of the reigning anticorruption project and its prescription for more of the same. This study of New York City shows that the mainstream anticorruption project imposes serious costs on public administration while failing to control corruption.

Whether or not New York City is distinctive for its corruptness, it is distinctive for the amount and intensity of anticorruption reform. Among the many reformers and reform groups who have achieved a place in New York City's anticorruption history are Seth Lowe, Raymond "Fearless" Fosdick, William Herlands, Robert Moses, Samuel Seabury, Thomas Dewey, Wallace S. Sayre and Herbert Kaufman, the Citizens Union, the Citizens Civic Committee, the Committee of One Thousand, the Bar Association of the City of New York, and the City Club, as well as contemporary keepers of the anticorruption flame like Michael Sovern, John Feerick, Kenneth Conboy, Rudolph Giuliani, and the *New York Times*. These prominent reformers passed the nation's first civil service law, invented the Department of Investigation, created a computerized database for all City contractors, established an inspectors-general system, enacted ethics and financial disclosure laws, and implemented myriad anticorruption strategies. The anticorruption project is embodied in the city's charter and in practically every nook and cranny of city government.

At various points throughout the book we draw on the federal government's anticorruption project. This is useful for at least three reasons:

1. In a number of cases (like auditing) the federal government's policies, rules, and regulations require the city to add to its anticorruption project.
2. In other cases (e.g., inspectors general) federal anticorruption strategies have been copied by the city.
3. In several areas (e.g., whistleblowers) the experience of the federal government provides useful support or contrast to the New York City experience.

The student of corruption and corruption control is bedeviled by the absence of data or indicators of the corruption rate. No one knows for sure whether official corruption has diminished over time and, if so, how much of that reduction, if any, is attributable to the anticorruption project. Former Attorney General Richard L. Thornburgh once stated, "There is no way to tell whether we have more corruption than we had 100 years ago."[10] No corruption rate has been calculated or even estimated for a number of reasons. First, corrupt transactions, such as bribery, are rarely reported to the authorities or survey researchers. Second, there are no statistics on the number of corrupt acts committed by public officials or the percentage of transactions or decisions tainted by official corruption. Third, the definition of corruption has changed over time to include more types of official and private conduct.[11] Because a corruption rate has never been calculated or even estimated, it is impossible to determine whether particular anticorruption campaigns and controls reduce corruption. Certainly, we cannot assume that because more corruption is brought to light, more corruption exists. According to federal judge and former law professor, John T. Noonan, Jr.,

> Nothing could be more fallacious. Greater activity indicates greater opposition to bribery [and corruption] and has no necessary connection with an increase in bribery [and corruption]. To take a contemporary American comparison, were the 1970s more corrupt than the 1950s? No one has done the work that can provide a rational answer to this question.[12]

This book offers a skeptical assessment of the effectiveness of anticorruption efforts. This hardly means that we are indifferent to the effects of corruption, any more than criminologists who question the efficacy of antidrug and antiviolence initiatives can be said to be indifferent to those crimes. We merely recognize what many students of corruption and white-collar crime have previously pointed out: that even the strongest enforcement efforts in these areas do not fulfill their goals.[13]

This book is not primarily about corruption, but about *corruption control.* Our thesis is that the anticorruption machinery has had profound, complicating, and often negative implications for the organization and operation of public administration. It constrains decision makers' discretion, shapes priorities, and causes delays that undermine efficiency. The irony of corruption control is that the more anticorruption machinery we create, the more we create bureaucratic pathology and red tape. In essence, both corruption and corruption control contribute to the contemporary crisis in public administration. State and local governments are less able to provide basic services and maintain infrastructure. In New York City, this deterioration of administrative capacity is epitomized by such debacles as the government's inability to rebuild the Central Park ice skating rink despite a decade of effort,[14] or to honestly and competently examine its schools for asbestos.[15] After pursuing the vision of corruption-free government for almost a century, we have the worst of both worlds—too much corruption and too much corruption control.

Our analysis emanates from three disciplinary perspectives: criminology, sociology, and public administration. As well as constituting a moral and a political problem, corruption is a crime problem. The reaction to it follows ideas and developments in law enforcement. In particular, the anticorruption project has been influenced by the growth and professionalization of prosecutorial and investigative agencies. Criminologists and sociologists like Michel Foucault, Stanley Cohen, Gary Marx, and David Garland have described a trend in social control characterized by more state power over more people and activities in more social contexts. Yet they have also shown that intensified social control does not necessarily work; it always breeds resistance and deviance. The natural reaction is to create additional control. The natural history of the anticorruption project reflects this general social pattern.

Political scientists and economists studying public administration have devoted substantial attention to the pathologies of bureaucracy and the need for organizational remedies. As early as 1904, political scientist Henry Jones Ford recognized that anticorruption goals could be incompatible with government effectiveness and efficiency:

> It is better that government and social activity should go on in any way than that they should not go on at all. Slackness and decay are more dangerous to a nation than corruption. . . . The graft system is bad, but it is better for city government to lend itself to the forces of progress even through corrupt inducements than to toss the management of affairs out upon the goose-common of ignorance and incapacity, however honest. Reform which arrests the progress of the community will not be tolerated by an American city.[16]

Even during the heyday of scientific administration in the late 1950s, there were scholars and practitioners who saw the anticorruption project as a possible drag on efficient and effective public administration:

> [W]aging this type of battle [against corruption] becomes a habit and tends to continue long after the enemy is routed or voluntarily retires. Since civil service appropriations tend to be limited in the first place, concentrating resources on combating an imaginary foe means neglecting the development and expansion of urgently required or highly desirable activities, such as more vigorous recruiting, personnel research and training.[17]

Similarly, Wallace Sayre and Herbert Kaufman, in their classic study of New York City government, recognized the importance and impact of the anticorruption project:

> The distrust of public officials, employees, and party leaders engenders complete and explicit rules to make sure that the boundaries of their jurisdiction are unmistakably demarcated and that the procedures they are to follow are clearly laid out. . . . When each grant of authority is carefully framed to avoid the possibility of abuse, and then surrounded by restrictions until little discretion is left to public officials, the volume of formal rules increases.[18]

While such revisionist statements can be found here and there in twentieth-century scholarly works, corruption *control* has only recently been treated as a problem by mainstream public administration scholars. For example, in 1991 political scientists James Fesler and Donald Kettl, in *The Politics of the Administrative Process,* considered the administrative costs of "control systems":

> Excessive controls can disrupt consistent administration and produce inequities. Excessive controls multiply requirements for review of proposed decisions, increase red tape, and delay action. So much energy can be spent attempting to control administrative activities, in fact, that little time or money is left to do the job at hand. Excessive controls, therefore, may dull administration's responsiveness to its public.[19]

Some contemporary rational-choice theorists in economics and political science have gone even further, arguing that corruption is sometimes efficient. For example, the barter of political influence for cash can produce social benefits:

> [P]ayoffs could be used for socially beneficial purposes. For example, they may be used to increase the quantity of useful information presented to voters by politicians or political parties. Even payoffs captured for politicians' personal use may permit paying lower public salaries than would otherwise be

required. The cost of encouraging behavior generally considered to be unethical must be set against any possible social benefits.[20]

Furthermore, pointing to the persistence of the moral themes that epitomized the Progressive Era's anticorruption reformers, James Buchanan and Gordon Tullock argue that reformers tend to emphasize ethical rules and regulations at the expense of ignoring the structural dilemmas that encourage corruption. Both the moral/political and the law-enforcement focus on "bad men," according to Buchanan and Tullock, undermine governmental effectiveness without significantly reducing corruption.[21] Philip Howard makes much the same point in his aptly titled book, *The Death of Common Sense: How Law Is Suffocating America.*[22]

Our goal is to flesh out the intuitions and insights of these revisionists by mapping the anticorruption project and attempting to discern its impacts. We argue that the present-day anticorruption project is committed to forms of disciplinary control that nurture and exacerbate bureaucratic pathologies and make fundamental public administration reform all but impossible. Part 1 provides background and context for the analysis that follows. In chapter 1, we argue that corruption is a socially constructed category which has expanded steadily throughout the century. Simply put, today there is more conduct that is considered corrupt than there was a generation ago. In chapter 2, we explain the historical evolution of the anticorruption project, summarizing the approaches to corruption control taken by the antipatronage reformers (1870–1900), the Progressives (1900–33), the scientific administrators (1933–70), and the panoptic reformers of our own time.

Part 2 illuminates three ways in which the government personnel system has been shaped by the anticorruption project. Chapter 3 deals with the civil service system, which is the first major anticorruption initiative and the foundation of public administration. While civil service has reduced the barter of public-sector jobs for political support or payoffs which characterized the patronage system, the price—a muscle-bound personnel system, has been very high. Chapter 4 examines conflict-of-interest and financial disclosure laws which aim to create civil servants who are autonomous, independent, and disinterested. The question we ask is whether that result is achievable and, if so, whether it is desirable. Chapter 5 examines legal initiatives to protect, and thereby encourage, whistleblowers. We identify the cost of whistleblower protections as the weakening of the authority of high-level managers.

Part 3 analyzes the anticorruption project's investigatory and punishment apparatus. Chapter 6 deals with the evolution of the New York City Department of Investigation, the nation's only full-scale municipal agency primarily dedicated to ferreting out corruption. Operating through its central staff and inspectors general, the agency casts a net of suspicion and sometimes fear over the city's 300,000 personnel. Chapter 7 describes the evolution of the prosecutorial machinery that mobilizes deterrence threats and state sanctions against official corruption. One of the most prominent trends of the past two decades is the proliferation and empowerment of federal, state, and local law-enforcement agencies with jurisdiction over matters of local corruption.

Part 4 shows the influence of the anticorruption project on two crucial government operations: contracting and accounting/auditing. Chapter 8 links competitive bidding and other checks and balances in public contracting to the anticorruption project and argues that these anticorruption strategies have contributed significantly to the unwieldy nature of government contracting. Chapter 9 argues that public-sector auditing agencies and financial control systems are evolving in the direction of law-enforcement investigations.

Part 5 deals with the implications of the anticorruption project for public administration. Chapter 10 explains why it would be wrong to conclude that the anticorruption project has reduced corruption. Chapter 11 draws on the previous chapters in identifying the negative effects of the anticorruption project on public administration and the prospects for fundamental public administrative reform. Chapter 12 analyzes alternative futures for the anticorruption project and public administration.

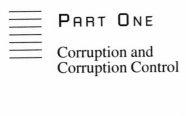

PART ONE

Corruption and
Corruption Control

 **ONE**

The Evolution of Corruption: From "Honest Graft"
to Conflicts of Interest

> Supposin' it's a new bridge they're going to build. I get tipped off and I buy
> as much property as I can that has to be taken for the approaches. I sell at my
> own price later on and drop some more money in the bank. Wouldn't you?
> It's just like lookin' ahead in Wall Street or in the coffee or cotton market.
> It's honest graft and I'm lookin' for it every day of the year.
>
> George Washington Plunkitt, as quoted in William L. Riordon,
> *Plunkitt of Tammany Hall*

To understand the evolution of the anticorruption project, it is necessary to
begin with some observations about corruption itself. This chapter deals
with four basic issues: the subjectivity of the definition of corruption, the
increasing gap between expectations of official behavior and actual behavior, the special politics of scandal and reform, and the difficulty of measuring corruption.

Defining Corruption

Corruption is neither a single form of behavior nor an obvious species of
conduct.[1] Corruption is the name we apply to some reciprocities by some
people in some contexts at some times. The popular use of the term does not
require that the conduct labeled corrupt be illegal; it is enough that the la-
beler thinks it is immoral or unethical. Since people's views about moral and
ethical conduct differ in important respects, corruption is often a contested
label. Indeed, these days public servants are admonished not only to adhere
to the skein of laws prohibiting a wide variety of conduct, but to avoid "the
appearance of corruption." Such a warning recognizes that the term *corruption* refers to more than just positive law, but fails to recognize that appearance of corruption is in the eyes of the beholder. When the beholder is a
mass audience and a muckraking press, it is a hard admonition to heed.

Even if the use of the term *corruption* is limited to conduct which has been expressly prohibited by law, much doubt and ambiguity remains. While the definitions of all crimes (even murder, rape, and theft) differ to some extent from time to time and place to place, there are major differences in what counts as corrupt conduct across different societies and over time in the same society. To begin, *corruption* itself is not a legal term of art and does not appear in the criminal code. All state criminal codes contain such offenses as bribery, extortion, and theft, but not all define them the same way and certainly not all have identically defined offenses of fraud, accepting unlawful gratuities, conflicts of interest, false statements, and illegal campaign financing and spending.

Bribery is the quintessential form of corruption.[2] People pay officials to exercise their authority and influence in a desired way. Sometimes the impetus for the bribe comes from the official (soliciting a bribe and extortion) and sometimes from a private individual who wants special favors (offering a bribe). Either way, money passes from private citizens to officials.

Payoffs can take different forms, some very complex; an envelope bulging with cash is the most crass example. Money, however, can be transferred to government officials as a gift, honorarium, or investment opportunity. Payoffs need not be pecuniary. They can involve sexual favors, campaign support, or promises of high-paying jobs or run-of-the-mill favors. The favor need not be bestowed on the official personally; it may be given to a member of the official's family or to a friend or lover. Accordingly,

> [t]he norms of a free enterprise, democratic society encourage wheeling and dealing and give and take. They support negotiation and persuasion. This can mean some persons back into committing technical violations without the intention to commit a crime. . . . For elected officials, the line between political contributions and buying favors and extortion can be thin.[3]

Consequently, there is a great deal of uncertainty involved in labeling some exchanges and reciprocities bribes and others lawful reciprocities or gifts.

Bribery is just one form of official corruption. Public officials, depending upon their positions, can convert public office into private gain in many ways.[4] Legislators can sell their votes. Bureaucrats sell their discretion over licenses, permits, franchises, and so forth. Procurement officers extract kickbacks. Inspectors solicit or extort payoffs.

There are many other types of corrupt conduct: thievery, for example. Government employees steal or misuse government property (computers, cars, furniture, food, etc.). They defraud the government and the taxpayers by arriving late, leaving early, doing private work on the job, or not working at all. Officials pad expense accounts, expropriate subordinates' labor for their private use, and make personal use of government cars, phones, and duplicating machines. Strictly speaking, every unauthorized phone call, expropriation of office supplies, private use of a government vehicle, and short working day is an act of corruption.

In all public and private organizations, certain derelictions are tolerated as *de minimis*. However, when a government agency is the focus of a corruption inquiry or scandal, *de minimis* is not a defense, at least not one accepted by the media and the general public.[5] Conduct which previously was tolerated becomes actionable, even indictable. Thus, abusing sick leave or using the agency computer for personal business become matters for investigation rather than for managerial action.

Public officials control the treasury, which derives revenue from taxes, licenses, and fees. Money can be siphoned off in numerous ways—simply embezzled, paid to dummy employees or contractors, paid to no-show employees or cronies who actually do not perform (or underperform) governmental business, paid to confederates or alter egos through phony invoices, and so forth.

Officials can enrich themselves by taking advantage of insider knowledge and opportunities; this is what Plunkitt meant by "honest graft." For example, they can purchase land that, in their official capacities, they expect later to condemn for a road or public building (at an exorbitant profit), or they can award lucrative government contracts to a company in which they have an interest. Some government and even political party officials can exploit their public offices via influence peddling, affiliating themselves with law firms, insurance brokers, or public relations firms. Not surprisingly, businesses and individuals assume that they are likely to get better results from the government if they hire firms that are "connected." With respect to being labeled corrupt, this kind of conduct still represents contested terrain.

This book focuses on *official corruption,* not on fraud by private citizens against the government, but these two species of crime are often connected. For example, officials may conspire with private parties to defraud government social welfare programs. Some anticorruption measures are implemented to prevent the government from being victimized either by private parties or by government officials.

Heightened Public Morality

Whether defined in terms of criminal law categories or ethical standards, the concept of corruption has expanded over the twentieth century to embrace more types of conduct. What political scientists Edward Banfield and James Q. Wilson identified as the moral values of the turn-of-the-century Protestant elite have become the prevailing public norms.[6] In the early decades of the century, Tammany Hall politicians in New York City bragged about their ability to use government power to help themselves and their friends flourish financially; indeed, they ridiculed the Progressives who demanded high standards of integrity for public office. In those days, certain forms of what we now regard as corruption were considered legitimate.

Over the course of some fifty years, there has been a big change. Much conduct that was legal a generation ago is now corrupt; yesterday's "honest graft" is today's illegal conflict of interest. An official of the New York City Department of Investigation explained that the Department's definition of corruption since the 1970s has included the "subversion of fairness, of distributive and common justice, and of equal opportunity." Under this definition, even acknowledged error leading to waste would be corrupt.

Most states have expanded the concept of bribery to cover gifts and payments to public officials whether or not there was an intent to corrupt or a provable quid pro quo (so-called antigratuity statutes). Politicians have been indicted for using their employees to provide personal services and even to work on their campaigns. Officeholders have been convicted for using campaign funds for personal use. Former public employees have been branded corrupt for engaging in lobbying and other private business after they left office. Low-level employees have been dismissed for petty thefts and even for doing personal business during work hours. Conflict-of-interest laws, supplemented by extensive financial disclosure requirements, have proliferated. Today, it is considered corrupt just to be in a decision-making role when one *could be* affected financially by the decision, regardless of the decision actually rendered.[7] Federal and other government officials face disciplinary action if they violate prohibitions against conduct that creates the "appearance of impropriety."[8]

Our entire political system is embroiled in a battle over the legal and moral status of campaign financing.[9] A generation ago, few people would have questioned the propriety of contributions to political candidates; the dominant belief used to be that those who felt strongly about electoral outcomes were entitled to contribute time, resources, and funds to get their candidates elected. Indeed, some theorists saw this as a unique strength of the American political system.[10] Public attitudes and norms have changed so much that politicians, for fear of appearing corrupt, are unwilling to acknowledge that large campaign contributors receive special favors or consideration. The politically correct position is that large contributors only obtain greater "access" to the candidate/politician. Sweeping "revolving-door" prohibitions now bar government officials from taking certain private-sector jobs *after* leaving government service. A whole regulatory regime surrounds campaign contributions: failure to follow procedures, to account for contributions, to make full disclosures, and so on are illegal. The Supreme Court has upheld the constitutionality of these measures on the ground that they serve the state's compelling interest in preventing corruption. For example, in *Austin v. Michigan Chamber of Commerce*,[11] the Supreme Court upheld a Michigan law prohibiting corporations from using corporate treasury funds to make independent expenditures in support of or in opposition to any candidate running for state office. The Court stressed the dangers of corruption stemming from "the corrosive and distorting effects of immense aggregations of wealth that are accumulated with the help of the corporate form and that have little or no correlation to the public's support for the corporation's ideas."[12] In dissent, Justice Scalia warned that "[u]nder this mode of analysis, virtually anything the Court deems politically undesirable can be turned into political corruption—by simply describing its effects as politically 'corrosive,' which is close enough to 'corruptive' to qualify."[13]

The trend toward ever-higher official conduct norms was discerned as early as 1964 with remarkable prescience by Bayless Manning, then Dean of the Stanford Law School. In "The Purity Potlatch," a splendid essay on emerging conflict-of-interest prohibitions, he wrote,

> To the extent that our politics partake of the nature of a Morality Play, they have inevitably required, and generated, a set of theatrical conventions as arbitrary, and as acceptable, as those of any dramatic form. The vocabulary of our politics conforms to its role as a national Morality drama. That vocabulary is formal, dogmatic, simplified, symbolic, repetitive and goal-setting; it is not descriptive and should not be thought of as being descriptive. And the actors in the political drama must, as in epic drama, appear as more than life-size, establishing, declaring, and appearing to live in accordance with standards that are not of this world. We therefore demand ultimate moral pronouncements from our parties and our officials.[14]

We know of no systematic scholarship devoted to explaining why norms about government ethics became stricter in the 1960s and 1970s in the United States and throughout the world.[15] Indeed, while we were writing this book, corruption scandals toppled the governments of Japan, Brazil, and Italy.

In the United States, the escalation of official morality is no doubt linked to wider cultural shifts: for example, the war on drugs, the rise of the religious right, and diminished public confidence in public officials.[16] In addition, the Watergate scandal (1972–73) triggered waves of media and public denunciations of "politics as usual" and demands to close the gap between what Michael Reisman calls the "mythical" and "operating" systems of government.[17] Congress responded to the scandal by passing the Ethics in Government Act of 1978,[18] the purpose of which was not only to "deter and punish exploitation of positions of public trust, but also to foster public confidence in the integrity of government employees."[19] Among other things, the Act established the Office of Government Ethics (OGE), which was given the task of developing ethical rules and standards of conduct and enforcing these standards for federal employees.[20] In a 1989 executive order outlining the principles of ethical conduct for government officers and employees, President George Bush mandated that federal employees "endeavor to avoid any actions creating the appearance that they are violating the law or the ethical standards promulgated pursuant to this order."[21] The OGE was assigned the task of issuing standards of conduct to help federal employees avoid the "appearance of impropriety." The purpose of both the 1978 Act and President Bush's executive order was "to ensure that every citizen can have complete confidence in the integrity of the Federal Government."[22] The 1978 Act, subsequently amended by Congress,[23] and the executive order stimulated a great deal of anticorruption activity by state and local governments.[24]

In the 1980s and 1990s, what Bayless Manning called a "purity potlatch" became more widely noticed. Suzanne Garment's 1991 book, *Scandal: The Culture of Mistrust in American Politics,* argued that there was an "overproduction" of political scandal:

> Still, our time is different from the decades preceding it. Political scandal has proliferated, and this proliferation reflects not so much an increase in corruption at the federal level as it does our growing capacity and taste for political scandal production.
>
> The resulting culture of mistrust has made the always difficult job of governing measurably harder. The climate of sensationalism has contributed to public cynicism and to the fact that symbolic issues and public funding for offensive art shoot more speedily than ever to the top of the public agenda.[25]

Political scientist Larry Sabato sees a new style of "attack" journalism reflecting and contributing to the new politics of scandal and reform:

> [S]candal coverage is no longer restricted to misuse of public office, incompetence in the exercise of public responsibilities, or some other inadequacy or

malfeasance in a *public* role; it extends to purely *private* misbehavior, even offenses, some of them trivial, committed long before an individual's emergence into public life.[26]

At times, according to Sabato, public officials become subject to a "feeding frenzy [whereby] . . . a critical mass of journalists leap to cover the same embarrassing or scandalous subject and pursue it intensely, often excessively, and sometimes uncontrollably."

We have created a system that is constantly on the lookout for scandals and susceptible to reform proposals. Perhaps this is the intent. Demands for higher levels of job-related and personal morality in public officials inevitably lead to disappointment, public accusation, scandal, hand-wringing, righteous indignation, and reform. One cannot help but think that such calls for morality serve a social function. Perhaps Americans derive some perverse satisfaction or sense of self-righteousness from exposing hypocrisy and dishonesty in government. Michael Reisman believes that periodic crusades and reforms bolster the power of elites who, in carrying out such rites, demonstrate that they adhere to the proper norms and that their authority is legitimate.

In any event, the expanded definition of corruption and the concomitant growth of the anticorruption project have not convinced the citizenry that government officials are more honest than their predecessors. Quite the contrary, as political scientist Norman Ornstein points out:

> One fact is unmistakable: To an overwhelming majority of Americans, our political process, especially in Washington and especially inside the first branch of government, Congress, is morally bankrupt in a fashion worse than at any time in recent memory.
>
> ABC News asked voters in mid-1992, "Do you think the overall level of ethics and honesty in politics has risen, fallen, or stayed the same during the past ten years?" A full 60 percent said it had fallen; only 9 percent believed it had risen. . . .
>
> These survey findings . . . show a high level of public hostility toward Washington, Congress, and politicians in general. Finding a public consensus on any major issue of public policy these days is difficult, but there is a clear consensus that Washington has lost its moral moorings, that public corruption is endemic, that the system is not working as it is supposed to."[27]

Scandal and Reform

Corruption, scandal, and reform have always counted in American politics and public administration.[28] According to Ornstein, focusing on corruption, immorality, and scandal is an American pastime, a time-honored tradition of the public, journalists, and political opponents. If we had scientific public opinion surveys for the eighteenth, nineteenth, and early twentieth centuries, chances are they would show that voters have always believed that corruption had reached its peak during their lifetimes.[29]

Allegations of corruption are a regular feature of American political campaigns; challengers to incumbents often define themselves as anticorruption reformers. Large numbers of Americans have always regarded politicians and police as corrupt, although tolerance for different kinds of corruption has varied over time and in different social groups.[30]

A comprehensive history of corruption in American government would require an encyclopedia,[31] and that would only cover corruption that had somehow been exposed, which is a mere fraction of all corrupt transactions.[32] Indeed, Walter Lippmann once stated that "[i]t would be impossible for an historian to write a history of political corruption in America. What he could write is the history of the exposure of corruption."[33] In the United States, the exposure of corruption dates back to the nation's formative years.[34] As early as 1795, our young nation was riddled with corruption scandals. Four companies, whose investors included high-ranking state and federal officials, judges (among them a Supreme Court Justice), and fathers of the Constitution, bribed Georgia legislators to pass a bill conveying title to 35 million acres of land known as the Yazoo River, and which today comprises Alabama and Mississippi. After the bribery came to light in a great scandal, the sale was revoked.[35]

Corruption pervaded the 1824 presidential election. Because neither candidate obtained a majority of the electoral votes, the House of Representatives had to choose between the three finalists—Andrew Jackson, John Quincy Adams, and William Crawford. Ultimately, it was a contest between Jackson and Adams because Crawford was debilitated by a stroke. Each state was allowed to cast only one vote. Adams met with key members of several state delegations in order to secure votes. Although it has not been proven, inferences that Adams bribed his way to the presidency can be drawn from entries in Adams' diary and by a letter written by Henry Clay, who initially opposed Adams.[36]

Even the passage of a revised Thirteenth Amendment, which abolished slavery, involved possible bribery. After the Amendment was defeated in the House in 1864, President Abraham Lincoln told his fellow Republican Congressmen that the two-thirds vote needed to pass the Amendment "must be procured." Supposedly, Congressman Ashley of Ohio was dispatched to secure the needed votes by whatever means necessary.[37]

During the twentieth century, the 1922 Teapot Dome scandal led to the conviction of the Secretary of the Interior, Albert Bacon Fall, for accepting a bribe from two companies to which he granted the rights to drill for oil in the Navy's oil reserves.[38] And in 1939, Judge Martin T. Manton was convicted of bribery for accepting payments from litigants to "fix" cases.[39]

Contemporary politics is punctuated by scandals like Watergate, Abscam, Operation Greylord,[40] the jailing of Syracuse Mayor Lee Alexander for taking kickbacks on contracts and all sorts of other schemes,[41] the imprisoning of Tennessee Governor Ray Blanton for selling pardons and paroles,[42] and the conviction of House Ways and Means Chairman Dan Rostenkowski for converting public funds to private use.[43] From 1970 through 1977, one thousand public officials, from county sheriffs to the Vice-President of the United States, were indicted or convicted.[44] During the eight-year Reagan administration, over one hundred federal officials were either indicted or convicted. Several members of President Clinton's administration (e.g., Agriculture Secretary Mike Espy and former Associate Attorney General Webster Hubbell) have seemingly been felled by charges of corruption.

Corruption is hardly a phenomenon unique to the national administration. Scandals occur in small towns, suburbs, and large cities in all areas of the country. Corruption is a fact of life in rural Oklahoma as frequent as in Boston, Newark, and Reading, Pennsylvania.[45] Nearly every day, the media carry a corruption story about federal, state, or local officials. A few of these stories blossom into national soap operas lasting for weeks and months.

The media play a crucial role in the politics of corruption reform. Corruption sells. Exposing hypocrisy and wrongdoing among those sworn to create, administer, or enforce the law makes for compelling reading or viewing. The higher the rank of the corrupt official, the greater the human drama and spectacle. Once the media get hold of a corruption story, they are reluctant to let it go, some journalists perhaps harboring the hope that they will uncover the next Watergate, "Keating Five," or Wedtech.[46] But journalists (as well as prosecutors and other investigators) are in a delicate position with regard to high-level corruption—they must proceed cautiously lest they antagonize the very establishment that they depend upon for news (or, in the case of prosecutors, for political and budgetary support).

The anticorruption project ebbs and flows with the politics of corruption and reform. During episodes of scandal, massive attention is devoted to formulating and implementing anticorruption innovations. As scandal recedes in memory, some recommendations go unimplemented, and those that are implemented become routine. Predictably, when the next scandal breaks open, leaders will label the existing anticorruption apparatus inadequate and urge more and better controls. Thus, there is an inexorable tendency to ratchet up the intensity and comprehensiveness of anticorruption strategies.

A frequent component of anticorruption politics is the impaneling of a "nonpolitical" independent commission to conduct an investigation and make recommendations for change; appointment of a nonpartisan blue ribbon panel is meant to calm public indignation and legitimate the authority of the government and political system with its integrity under attack. The commission, staffed by lawyers, often with prosecutorial experience, frames the problem in terms of inadequate rules and/or enforcement mechanisms. It inevitably proposes new laws to increase the costs of corrupt behavior and to make corruption more difficult to carry out. It often recommends the creation of new agencies or the reorganization of old ones.

Social problems increasingly are approached as puzzles to be solved through comprehensive legal strategies. Currently, these strategies include prohibiting innocuous activities that are believed to provide the means or stepping stones to corrupt behavior. When corruption recurs, failure is attributed to poor drafting and not enough law; typically the solution is "smarter" legal interventions. Some reformers have an extraordinary belief in the efficacy of legal threats to deter corrupt behavior; others cynically recognize that the best way to deal with scandals is to paper them over with ineffective laws that are not meant to be enforced.

In addition to being propelled by scandals, the anticorruption project is furthered by a good government constituency whose membership and power vary over time.[47] That constituency was quite powerful during the heyday of the Progressive Era, and it is again powerful today. As the anticorruption establishment has become more professionalized and self-conscious, it has generated its own momentum; in effect, it has become an interest group with components outside and inside government. Some politicians, anxious to appear morally pure, support dubious and cumbersome "reforms," regardless of the possible effects of those reforms on public administration. Moral entrepreneurs are likely to be so consumed with stopping corruption, or at least with appearing that way to the media and to the public, that they give slight, if any, thought to the costs of implementing their vision. In the aftermath of serious scandal, concerns about guaranteeing integrity and about the appearance of integrity trump efficiency. Rarely is the integrity/efficiency trade-off even considered. Anticorruption reformers, including prosecutors and journalists, are neither trained nor temperamentally inclined to be sensitive to problems in public administration that are inevitably complex, tedious, and seemingly intractable. In any event, it is convenient for anticorruption reformers to assume that the medicine which prevents or cures corruption must also nourish the processes and institutions of governing.

The politics of corruption and reform ensure that, over the long run, the trend toward a larger, more intensive anticorruption project is inexorable. The anticorruption project, like the law-enforcement apparatus itself, continues to spawn new techniques and strategies. It is more relentless than ever, even inventing scandal (e.g., the House of Representatives bank scandal) if none is conveniently available.[48]

Just as the criminal law and its corresponding law-enforcement machinery have expanded and intensified over the course of the century, so has the anticorruption project. At the same time that the criminal law has expanded into new areas, the anticorruption project has encompassed more aspects of official conduct. New offices, practices, and laws aimed at corruption control have been added. Some of these have been borrowed directly from law-enforcement agencies, and some have been invented as corruption-specific remedies. Furthermore, there has been slow but steady penetration of government by the law-enforcement establishment itself.

While the anticorruption project seems to expand over the long term, there are short-term contractions. Fiscal crisis and competition for scarce resources impose limits on the creation and maintenance of anticorruption mechanisms. However, scarce resources do not limit the proliferation of new laws and rules. It is always possible, and even advantageous, for politicians to throw law at a problem. By so doing, they can make a symbolic statement without expending significant resources. Agency reorganization has many of the same advantages.

In recent years, prosecutors have become an increasingly important force in exposing political corruption. In 1976, as a response to the Watergate scandal, the U.S. Department of Justice established its Public Integrity Section to counteract corruption at the local, state, and federal levels.[49] Many U.S. Attorneys' offices established similar units. Using mail fraud and other federal criminal statutes,[50] the federal prosecutors investigated and charged state and local officials who previously had little need to worry about being investigated because the leaders of local law-enforcement agencies were members of the same political party or machine.

The rise of a larger and more independent law-enforcement establishment has had an important impact on the politics of corruption control. Prosecutors can make their reputations by bringing down important political figures. Denouncing government has become politically popular. Even prosecuting low-level government officials can bolster a prosecutor's claim to be a corruption fighter and a person of the highest principle. Suzanne Garment has hypothesized, quite sensibly in our view, that the generation of prosecutors who came of age in the 1970s is more idealistic, more passionate about moral values, and more relentless than its predecessors.

Measuring Corruption

We undoubtedly will disappoint many readers by not offering an opinion on whether there is more official corruption today than there was in the past, or whether there is more corruption in New York City than in other cities. Unfortunately, there are no adequate crime statistics from which to draw such conclusions. When experts discuss the nation's crime rate, corruption is not considered. It is usually not seen or heard about by anyone other than the participants. Although suspected, it is rarely reported to the police. If it is reported, it is unlikely to be investigated, "solved," and punished.[51] Furthermore, in attempting to estimate the amount of corruption, we find no victim surveys or self-report studies on which to rely.

The difficulties in detecting corruption, coupled with the term's changing definition, make it unwise to speculate as to whether there is more official corruption today than there was in the past or whether there is more corruption in one city or county than in another. Simply discovering more corruption in a particular city at a particular time does not mean that corruption is on the rise; it may indicate only an increased effort to ferret out corruption in that place and at that time.[52] However, since we are so often pressed for an opinion on the matter, we wish to bolster our case for agnosticism by pointing out even more obstacles to comparing corruption over time or across jurisdictions.

What kind of statistic would we need in order to plot the corruption rate? Our first challenge would be to agree on a definition of corruption that could be held constant over time or across jurisdictions. As we have previously noted, the term *corruption* means something different today than it meant fifty years ago.

Assuming we could hurdle this definitional obstacle, we would need to measure the frequency of corruption. The kind of victim surveys that are used to count burglary and robbery would not work for corruption offenses (the victim may not see the behavior as corrupt); nor would self-reporting studies be feasible. We probably would have to look to arrest and conviction statistics that are very unreliable because so little corrupt behavior comes to the attention of law enforcement and because governmental units vary so much with respect to the resources they put into corruption investigation and enforcement.

Even if we could solve the empirical problem, it would make no sense to compare the *total amount* of corruption one hundred years ago with today's *total amount* because the nation, states, and cities are not the same as they were a generation ago. Government is larger today. It engages in far more activities and spends vastly more money. Thus, a comparison requires some kind of "normed" statistic—a percentage of corrupt government agencies or officials. But what would that mean? The percentage of government acts or decisions that are illegal? The percentage of governmental units or agencies in which there is (any? some? much?) corruption on any given day or over the course of some extended time period? The percentage of government officials who act corruptly (even once) each month, year, and so on? The percentage of government budget lost through corruption?[53]

Some readers, although by now perhaps convinced that it is impossible to come up with a hard statistical basis for determining or even estimating whether corruption in this generation is greater than in previous generations, might suggest that we compare the scandals of one time period with those of another. A moment's thought, however, reveals the infeasability of this suggestion. The occurrence of a scandal often depends upon chance. The magnitude and depth of a scandal depend upon the reactions of a whole range of actors, from reformers and the media to politicians and the police. All these players determine how a scandal is revealed and presented. The magnitude of a scandal is heavily dependent upon the resources committed to unearthing it. Moreover, as time passes, our perceptions of yesterday's scandals are profoundly affected by those journalists and scholars who have chosen to write about them. Each author presents a distinctive interpretation. Much of what we know about a particular scandal comes from the contemporaneous commissions, muckraking journalists, and reformers. However, years later, "revisionist" scholars sometimes question the motives and biases of those contemporaneous writers. For example, there is now a considerable difference of opinion about the nature and magnitude of corruption in the regime of Boss William Marcy Tweed during the 1870s.[54] Even a corruption scandal in our own day, such as the Parking Violations Bureau debacle that occurred during the regime of Mayor Edward Koch, is fraught with interpretational difficulties.[55] The only book on the subject was written by two long-time Koch critics, whose goal was to tie Koch (by action and inaction) to wrongdoing by officials, high and low, connected to New York City government and/or the Democratic Party. Writers sympathetic to Koch could have produced a much different book, emphasizing his strong support for professional administration and the anticorruption project.

Perhaps it will be suggested that we ought to focus on a city's reputation for corruption in different eras. But "reputation" is not easy to pin down. Reputation among whom? Reputation for what? As we have already seen, to some people patronage and large campaign donations are corrupt. Others equate corruption with diverse criminal offenses. Should we compare the reputation that *currently exists* about past corruption, or should we compare the reputation of one city for corruption according to opinions at one point in time with the reputation of another city for corruption according to opinions at a different point in time? If so, at what points in time?

We do not believe it possible to estimate reliably whether there is less official corruption today than in previous generations. If the corruption rate has fallen, it would run counter to the upward trend of most other crimes. Our operating assumption is that corruption, especially in light of the expanding definitions, remains a common phenomenon today that can be found in every level of government and (if one scratches hard enough) in practically every agency. In this book, we are interested in how policy makers and policy shapers define and react to corruption and the fear of scandal, the institutions they create for preventing corruption, and the impact of those institutions on the organization and operation of public administration. These responses to corruption are easier to measure, or at least to describe, than corruption itself.

Conclusion

Corruption is a social, legal, and political concept laden with ambiguity and bristling with controversy. Conceptions about what is corrupt are constantly evolving. In the last several decades, the public standard of morality has become much more strict, and the gap between the mythical system and the operating system much wider. Previously acceptable conduct (e.g., favors for campaign contributors) is now deemed unethical, and previously unethical conduct is now deemed criminal (e.g., taking certain private employment or lobbying after leaving government service). Consequently, the politics of corruption have become more unsettled, unpredictable, and intense.

Corruption is a major issue for politics. It is always advantageous for a political aspirant to stigmatize a politician or political candidate as corrupt and to raise the smell of scandal about an officeholder and his or her administration. The media and the public enjoy the sport of exposing hypocrisy among those who make and implement the law. Denunciation of corruption and calls for reform, ever-present features of American politics, become most salient when popular opinion becomes focused on a scandal.

Scandals vary in important ways. Some scandals are contained by politicians, while others are taken over by reformers who operate "outside the system." Sometimes reformers are fully or partially neutralized by being placed on commissions whose work product consists of comprehensive recommendations which, at most, are only partially implemented. At other times, however, reformers are able to force change on the government. Even when changes are imposed, however, there is no guarantee that they will be effective. To the contrary, they are frequently blunted, distorted, and subverted so that what remains is form rather than substance—government reorganization, agency reshuffling, new layers of oversight. Ironically, such reforms often generate incentives and opportunities for corruption.

Large governmental organizations, such as New York City's, are loaded with anticorruption mechanisms. As years pass, however, the origins and purposes of these mechanisms are forgotten; they become permanent features of the government and its bureaucracy and contribute very little, if anything, to the prevention or detection of corruption.

Two

The Evolution of the Anticorruption Project: From Virtue to Surveillance

> All sovereigns are suspicious of their servants. . . . How is suspicion to be allayed by knowledge? Trust is strength in all relations of life and, as it is the office of the constitutional reformer to create conditions of trustfulness, so it is the office of the administrative organizer to fit administration with conditions of clear-cut responsibility which will insure trustworthiness.
>
> Woodrow Wilson, "The Study of Administration"

The currently prevailing anticorruption project is the product of several generations of reform ideas and reform efforts. This history of anticorruption reform in public administration can be conceptualized in terms of four visions of corruption control—antipatronage, Progressive, scientific administration, and panoptic. By *vision,* we mean a paradigm or *weltanschauung* (worldview) that includes assumptions about human behavior and social control by government institutions. The first three visions of corruption control—antipatronage, Progressive, and scientific administration— correspond roughly to parallel stages in the history of American public administration theory, but the most recent vision of corruption control, the panoptic vision, deviates significantly from conventional wisdom about public administration. The political agenda of the antipatronage, Progressive, and scientific administration reformers addressed more than corruption control; these reform movements sought to transform and improve the efficient functioning of government. By contrast, the panoptic vision is not concerned with efficient governing, but with control alone. Each vision has built on those that have come before, and thus one ought to think of the process of reform as adding one coat of paint on top of another. Nonetheless, we think that distinguishing these visions as ideal types helps to explain the evolution of anticorruption reform over the last hundred years.

One other preliminary point is worth noting: The anticorruption project has never been monolithic. It does not represent a coherent, coordinated effort or platform of a single group, but the ideas and strategies of different interest groups. Some of these could be characterized as "moral entrepreneurs" predominantly concerned with governmental morality and some as administrative reformers predominantly concerned with making government more rational and efficient.

The Antipatronage Vision of Corruption (1870–1900)

The movement to end the spoils system[1] and to create an American civil service began during the Reconstruction Era. The spoils, or patronage, system was one of the hallmarks of "machine party politics," which flourished in urban areas during the late nineteenth and early twentieth centuries. Patronage involved the dominant political faction doling out jobs and benefits solely to friends and supporters. Political scientist James C. Scott described the political machine as

> a nonideological organization interested less in political principle than in securing and holding office for its leaders and distributing income to those who run it and work for it. . . . A machine may, in fact, be likened to a business in which all members are stockholders and where dividends are paid in accordance with what has been invested.[2]

The spoils system "was finely organized and articulated to maximize its electoral support."[3]

The attack on the spoils system was the second phase of a powerful movement that began with the drive to abolish slavery.[4] The reformers believed that replacing the spoils system with morally exemplary elected officials and public servants would revitalize democracy. To that end, "elections had to be freed from purchase or covert control and . . . government officials had to be made responsive to the public interest."[5] This revitalization would be brought about by a civil service merit system characterized by political neutrality, tenure in office, recruitment and appointment through special training or competitive exams, and standards for promotion, discipline, salary, and retirement.[6] Senator Carl Schurz's support for civil service reform makes this point:

> The question whether the Departments at Washington are managed well or badly, is, in proportion to the whole problem, an insignificant question after all. Neither does the question whether our civil service is as efficient as it ought to be, cover the whole ground. The most important point to my mind is, how can we remove that element of demoralization which the now prevailing mode of distributing office has introduced into the body politic?[7]

According to Schurz, "demoralization," or the debasement of the public sector due to patronage, made changing the nature of leadership in American government a moral necessity. Creating a civil service would "make active politics once more attractive to men of self-respect and high patriotic aspirations."[8]

Julius Bing, another important proponent of civil service reform, clearly saw the antipatronage campaign as a moral imperative:

> At present, there is no organization save that of corruption; no system save that of chaos; no test of integrity save that of partisanship; no test of qualification save that of intrigue. . . . we have to deal with a wide-spread evil, which defrauds the country in the collection of taxes on a scale so gigantic that the commissioners of revenue, collectors, assessors, and Treasury officers—at least those of them who are honest—bow their heads in shame and despair. We have to deal with an evil that is manifest here and there and everywhere.[9]

The mugwumps and other civil service reformers in the last quarter of the nineteenth century believed that government could be returned to honesty if run by virtuous officials motivated by the public interest rather than by patronage, cronyism, and graft. The reformers thought that patronage was inimical to everything public service should be and that it corrupted the moral fiber of government.

Corruption and graft, in the view of Carl Schurz and other civil service reformers, resulted from the party-dominated organization of public administration. In essence, corruption and patronage were synonymous. They believed that public service should be a "calling" and the repository and showcase of the highest moral principles, and that public servants should be exemplary citizens. According to civil service reformers, the ideal public servant "was a good citizen, loving liberty but preferring the public welfare to his private well-being. He put policy above party, and where virtue was at stake, maintained his independence. . . . He loved his country, desired security, and was content with a modest salary, since merit brought advancement."[10]

The Progressive Vision of Corruption Control (1900–1933)

The second stage of the anticorruption project was the Progressive reform movement, which dates approximately from the turn of the century to the New Deal, although the Progressive tradition remains powerful to the present day. To Progressives, the key to rooting out corruption was complete reform of the political system.[11] Corruption control was a condition precedent to government efficiency and democratic accountability. By studying European administration, scholars like Woodrow Wilson came to believe in the possibility of a system of public administration completely separate from party politics, the root cause of corruption.

Wilson and the Progressive reformers adhered to a vision of a politically independent, corruption-free administration, but they lacked a fully developed plan. As Wilson noted, "[t]he object of administrative study is to rescue executive methods from the confusion and costliness of empirical experiment and set them upon foundations laid deep in stable principle."[12] The details of human governance, great and small, would be filled in by wedding American democracy's moral superiority to European administration's scientific superiority. The result would be honest, democratic, and efficient administration.[13]

Wilson proposed integrity as the first principle of public administration. Similarly, Frank Goodnow, a professor of administrative law, argued that politics had debased administration and limited its efficiency. Professor Goodnow's solution was to separate politics from administrative functions and to centralize government so that procedures and rules of conduct might be standardized.[14] In other words, Goodnow wanted to take politics out of city government. These reforms, in his view, would make public administration responsive to the public interest rather than to party bosses.[15]

The Progressives aimed to establish an autonomous public sector by insulating administration from politics and staffing government with apolitical experts. Expert administrators themselves might be politically appointed, but their tenure was to outlast the appointing politician's term of office, and they were not to be removed without cause.

For the Progressives, corruption inhered in the cronyism of machine politics. In what was perhaps the first major expansion of the definition of corruption, the Progressives labeled as corrupt any practices or activities associated with the political machine, including public contracts awarded without competitive bidding, ward-level hiring of day laborers, and party control of police precincts.

The Progressive's professionalization agenda was never fully instituted. Public administration did not become professionalized like law and medicine. In the largest cities, reform was minimal. In New York, each reform administration was followed by the Tammany Hall machine's return to power.[16]

The Scientific Administration Vision (1933–1970)

Several decades of Progressive reform and municipal civil service did not eliminate corruption.[17] Repeated episodes of scandal undermined the belief that civil service personnel would be self-policing. The antipatronage and Progressive reform visions were supplanted, or at least supplemented, by a new vision that sought to control officials' behavior through scientific administration, which aimed to improve government by applying principles of economy and efficiency. Beginning around 1938, all sorts of organizations, from schools to hospitals, were influenced by the so-called scientific administration movement. In the public sector, efficiency was only one goal of scientific administration; another was corruption control.

The scientific administration reformers emphasized bureaucratic control over political reforms.[18] They considered the Progressives' strategies to be "outmoded and insufficient to meet the problems of an industrialized, urbanized world power."[19] They argued that corruption in complex administrative agencies could not be controlled by informal means and professional norms, and that peer pressure, which is so effective in small groups, could not be effective in bureaucracies.[20] They approached corruption as a problem in the structural design of organizations, rather than as a problem of politics or ethics. Public officials did not fail to act honestly and ethically because of faulty character, but because of failure in "the proper machinery of government."[21] The scientific administrators added an organizational dimension to the definition of corruption. They defined corruption to include waste and mismanagement, noting that a lack of hierarchy, standard operating procedures, and adequate supervision contributed to corruption. "Corrupt men stole money; moral men, in innocence and ignorance, wasted it. The difference could come to be negligible."[22]

The "science" of administration moved from theory to practice, as public administration emerged as a professional discipline. Professor Leonard White of the University of Chicago and Professor Frank Goodnow of Columbia University brought the principles of scientific administration to the public sector.[23]

The public sector embraced scientific administration theory, optimal spans of control, perfection of hierarchy, and new auditing and accounting techniques as means for corruption control.[24] They believed that government integrity would flow from sound organization. Their basic premise was that the correct deployment of administrative authority, coupled with comprehensive monitoring and evaluation, would prevent corruption or quickly bring it to light.

White expressed the scientific administration vision as follows:

> Out of reform, moral in its motivation, came reorganization, technical and managerial in connotation. Expertness, once assured its place, could continue a steady drive for better standards from within rather than from without.[25]

> [We] note the further development of the technique of large-scale management, especially overhead direction, long-range planning, and the effective coordination of the parts of a constantly expanding machine. Here government may learn from the methods of great industrial organizations, where similar problems exist.[26]

Of course, scientific administration had goals other than corruption control, namely, organizational efficiency and economy. Nevertheless, this vision was based on the belief that administrative integrity could be achieved through administrative control. Luther Gulick, a public administration scholar, expounded this belief:

> If government is to advance with modern science, if it is to keep pace with the efficiency of modern business, government cannot stand aside from the current of progress. . . . In public administration, not less than in other realms of human endeavor, we need to substitute for ignorance, competence; for the amateur, the professional; for the jack-of-all-trades, the expert; for superficial facility, increasing differentiation and specialization; and for the untutored novitiate, the systematically trained executive.[27]

Gulick argued for an administrative strategy called "external control,"[28] which he defined as investigative evaluation of government operations by specialized officials located in units outside the operating agencies. Gulick identified external control as a central component of scientific administration in his introduction to Harold Seidman's 1941 study of the New York City Department of Investigation. He praised the Department of Investigation as an agency capable of providing the kind of scrutiny and oversight required to ensure efficient government operations. Gulick and Seidman saw no contradiction between corruption control and efficiency; indeed they saw external control as a prerequisite for efficient public administration.

The Panoptic Vision (1970–present)

Since the early 1970s a *panoptic vision* has dominated corruption control. This vision assumes that officials will succumb to corrupt opportunities, and advocates comprehensive surveillance, investigation, and "target-hardening" strategies. It is built on one hundred years of ideology, rules, law-enforcement techniques, and reformist ideas. While the beefed-up

law-enforcement techniques that characterize the panoptic vision are a qual-
itative change from earlier anticorruption efforts, they build upon the goals
that were articulated by the Progressives and elaborated and expanded by
later reformers. Like its predecessors, the panoptic vision has critical implications for government organization and public administration. Indeed, its
implications are even more significant for public administration, because its
adherents urge a much broader definition of corruption and much greater
authority for corruption-control personnel, agencies, and institutions.

The panoptic vision regards public employees as akin to probationers in
the criminal justice system. Their routine is governed by a comprehensive
system of administrative/criminal laws and enforced by law-enforcement
agencies using a full array of investigative tools, including covert operations. This system is backed by threats and sanctions, including jail, fines,
and job and pension forfeiture. The panoptic vision has led to the expansion
of anticorruption institutions and strategies, and to enhanced authority for
anticorruption units and personnel.

Our use of the term *panoptic* is taken from Jeremy Bentham, who
envisioned a "panopticon" prison whose ingenious architecture featured a
control tower at the center of a circular cell house. From this tower, the
cells, inmates, and staff would be completely visible to the watchers. In
Discipline and Punish, Michel Foucault argues that the panopticon's architecture and operation were paradigmatic of a nineteenth-century vision of a
"disciplinary society" in which surveillance, monitoring, and control would
make undetected deviance impossible. The panopticon operates like a one-
way mirror; the controller can continuously monitor the prisoner, worker, or
subject, but these subjects do not know when the controller is watching,
since the tower is shaded or covered with louvers. The controller's omnipresence, according to Foucault, transforms mere organizational routine
into conformity. The pervasive gaze itself creates less need for coercive
control as subjects internalize the expectations of the controllers. Under the
panopticon, management and control merge. Each administrative routine
has its place in the scheme of observation. The business of control becomes
the everyday business of governing.[29]

Two major events strengthened the anticorruption project. First, the Watergate scandals sparked a round of federal anticorruption laws which, in
turn, led to the passage of similar state and local laws. New federal and local
prosecutorial units specifically devoted to corruption were created. Second,
the fiscal crisis of the mid-1970s in New York and other large cities added
fiscal accountability to the purview of anticorruption fighters. Incompetence, indifference, negligence, and nonfeasance came to be included under

the anticorruption mandate in the federal inspector-general law, which aimed to prevent "fraud, waste, and abuse." Command and control mechanisms of all types were strengthened; public managers became subject to stringent ethics laws and financial controls.

If the antipatronage reformers generated moral theory and scientific administrators engineered organizational structure, contemporary corruption controllers emphasize law-enforcement strategies and punitive sanctions.[30] They have gone beyond the political, legal, and institutional legacies of their predecessors, searching out corruption vulnerabilities that can only be addressed by comprehensive administrative, organizational, and law-enforcement initiatives. The contemporary reformers adopt or invent technologies, institutions, and routines to monitor public employees closely. The panoptic vision embodies a comprehensive system of control based on surveillance, massive information gathering, auditing, and aggressive enforcement of a wide array of criminal and administrative sanctions. While these techniques are clearly successors to external control and other earlier approaches, when taken together they constitute a wholly different regime of control. What is more important, the personnel who sponsor and operate these techniques constitute a self-conscious interest group within government.

Rather than theorists like Woodrow Wilson, or New York City Department of Investigation Commissioner William Herlands, the central figures in the contemporary war on corruption are prosecutors, inspectors general, corruption-vulnerability experts, auditors, and antifraud specialists. Their anticorruption project is extraordinarily ambitious; they have radically expanded the definition of corruption to include the appearance of conflict of interest, failure to disclose financial interests, misstatements on job applications, unauthorized use of government telephones, leaving work early, accepting favors and gifts, and entering into public contracts with morally tainted private companies.

With each scandal, the corruption-hunting cadre lobbies both for greater resources and for an expanded definition of its mission.[31] The inevitable result is that more corruption is uncovered. Thus, the panoptic vision of corruption control feeds on corruption scandals and generates initiatives that have profound effects on public administration.

According to the panoptic vision, corruption is not primarily attributed to incompetence, absenteeism, laziness, and partisan influence, or even to inadequate organization and administration, but to insufficient rules, controls, and deterrence.[32] This vision of corruption control de-emphasizes issues of governmental accountability, recruitment, and training. It views public officials, politicians, managers, and rank-and-file personnel as seekers of corrupt opportunities, and government as an organizational form that generates abundant opportunities for corruption.[33] Corruption is the norm, and all public employees are suspect.

The kind of organizational reforms associated with the panoptic approach should not be confused with the political reforms demanded by the Progressives or with the currently popular "reinventing government" movement. According to the panoptic vision, the purpose of administrative reform is to deter and prevent corruption via a system of thorough and efficient observation and surveillance, including accounting, auditing, and layers of oversight.

The Evolution of the Panoptic Vision: A Case Study of the New York City Department of Buildings

To demonstrate how the panoptic vision has built and expanded upon the earlier visions of social control and corruption control, it is useful to examine the way in which the anticorruption project has unfolded in an area where both corruption and anticorruption reform have persisted throughout the century: construction regulation in New York City. The panoptic approach to corruption control has not been applied to all parts of public administration at the same time and with the same intensity. While some innovations, like civil service regulation and program auditing, have been applied across the board, others, like internal investigations and contract regulation, have been applied selectively. We will see that one layer of anticorruption reform after another has been added to construction regulation until, at the present time, the whole process is so mired in monitoring, audits, investigations, and checks and balances that the basic regulatory mission has almost become ancillary to corruption monitoring and control.

State legislative hearings at the turn of the century revealed that Department of Buildings (DOB) officials were taking payoffs to ignore violations of building and sanitation codes.[34] The Progressives blamed the corruption on patronage and passed new legislation that aimed to replace party hacks with physicians and public health specialists.[35] They also implemented a series of anticorruption initiatives based upon technical expertise and professional discretion. Department of Buildings reports began to refer to the growing body of knowledge concerning health and safety issues in the construction and maintenance of housing. The reformers proclaimed success in transforming a city function that had been rife with corruption into a model of integrity and professional efficiency. Further, the reformed department added city planning and improving living standards to its mission.

In the 1930s, construction regulation was again the focus of scandal. Reformers, following the teachings of Frank Goodnow and Leonard White, responded by centralizing administration and implementing principles of scientific administration. The Department of Housing and Buildings would no longer rely on individual officeholders' professionalism and good moral character as a prophylactic measure against corruption.

Mayor Fiorello H. LaGuardia, who championed scientific administration in the fight against corruption, reformed the city charter and pushed through a modern municipal administrative code that sought to utilize procedure and routine to control opportunities for corruption in all areas of city government.[36] The comprehensive New York City Code covered such matters as the proper procedures for residential sewer connections, civil service grievances, and procedures for resolving disputes between contractors, vendors, or citizens and city agencies. Procedure and routine were designed to permit managers and administrators to monitor actively their subordinates' discretionary decisions.

To enforce the new administrative code and to ensure public probity, LaGuardia appointed William Herlands in 1938 to be commissioner of the Department of Investigation (DOI), an agency which was beginning to play a central role in the anticorruption project. With its investigatory and research capabilities and authority over all government agencies, the DOI epitomized the scientific administration reformers' ideal of an external control agency. Herlands, a former chief assistant to then United States Attorney Thomas E. Dewey in the racketeering investigations unit, focused on dishonesty, waste, inefficiency, and neglect of duty.

By the 1970s, when recurrent scandals revealed the same old corruption in the construction industry, the DOB became a laboratory for the panoptic vision of corruption control. DOI agents posing as contractors offered bribes to city inspectors to overlook violations or to expedite code approvals. Time and again the inspectors flunked these "integrity tests." The DOI promulgated scores of recommendations for reorganizing and administering the Department of Buildings; so did the New York State Comptroller and the New York State Organized Crime Task Force. The DOI suggested twenty specific "corrective actions," including everything from the establishment of an independent, professional reinspection unit, to increased staffing of the Department's disciplinary unit.[37] Similarly, the Organized Crime Task Force recommended an array of changes, including the wholesale reform and revision of the City Building Code, measures to encourage whistleblowers, and tougher administrative sanctions, especially pension forfeiture. Pursuant to the recommendations, the department instituted "double checks" and rotation of inspector routes. By the 1980s the top management in the Department of Buildings was thoroughly preoccupied with external criticism and corruption prevention.

The most recent anticorruption protocol, pursuant to a City Comptroller's audit, requires all field inspectors to return to borough headquarters at the end of the day, instead of leaving for home from the last inspection site. The policy is meant to ensure that personnel do not leave work early. While no one knows how much, if any, corruption has been prevented, there has been a nearly 30 percent reduction in inspector productivity because of the time consumed in returning to the office. This policy perfectly illustrates how the Progressive vision of virtuous public professionals has been superseded by panoptic control.

Conclusion

Over the course of the century, each new stage of the anticorruption project has served to proliferate corruption controls. Reformers cite each new corruption scandal as evidence that additional controls are needed. Likewise, reformers argue that the absence of scandal is proof that extant anticorruption controls are necessary. New corruption controls do not displace old ones; rather, they supplement them. Thus, public agencies are layered with organizational structures and roles, and with policies and procedures originally instituted to prevent corruption, or at least to create that impression.

Since the 1970s the panoptic vision of corruption control held by prosecutors, inspectors general, and other law- enforcement and quasi-law-enforcement personnel has become the dominant approach in municipal governments like New York City's. This anticorruption vision currently has unprecedented influence on public administration. Under the panoptic vision of corruption control, investigating, preventing, and deterring corruption have become ends, rather than means, to more effective governing.

The panoptic vision of corruption control does not parallel the dominant paradigm in public administration, which emphasizes systems. Rather, panoptic corruption control focuses on people, investigations, multiple layers of monitoring, and masses of rules and regulations. While many modern public administration specialists advocate an antibureaucratic philosophy of public administration that includes downsizing, privatization, and a reduction of internal regulations, the managers of the anticorruption apparatus recommend more command and control, even at the expense of administrative efficiency.

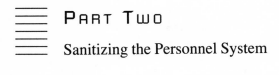

Part Two

Sanitizing the Personnel System

THREE

Civil Service and the Anticorruption Project: Bondage to a Principle

> The truth of the matter, I think, is that an entirely objective view of political life at its base where political organization is in direct contact with the population, would show that corruption in some form is endemic. I do not mean that everybody is bribed. I do mean that the exchange of favors is the elemental and essential motive power which operates the semi-private machinery inside the political parties which in their turn operate the official machinery of government. . . . [O]rganizations like Tammany, which bind together masses of people in a complex of favors and coercions, are the ancient form of human association. They might be called natural governments.
>
> Walter Lippman, "A Theory about Corruption"

Since the last quarter of the nineteenth century, patronage has been widely defined as a species of corruption for which the civil service system is the antidote.[1] This was not always the case. Earlier in the nineteenth century, the moral status of patronage was less clear. President Andrew Jackson extolled the patronage system as a democratic alternative to an insulated governing elite unrepresentative of the majority of citizens and unresponsive to the wishes of the electorate and its representatives.[2]

In the view of its opponents, there was nothing democratic about patronage. To the contrary, they believed that patronage produced politicians and administrators who placed their parties' interests and their own self-interest above the public interest. According to the mugwumps, patronage was corrupt in itself. Moreover, it caused other forms of corruption: the election and appointment of self-serving officials who embezzled taxpayer money and looted the public coffers; a contracting system marked by favoritism for party potentates and their friends; a personnel system which made government jobs dependent upon party sponsorship and the job seeker's willingness to work for and contribute to the party.[3]

This chapter sketches the growth of the civil service movement in New

York City, culminating in the fascinating case study of the "Talent Bank" scandal of the 1980s. The development of the civil service movement and the modern-day Talent Bank scandal demonstrate that abhorrence of patronage distorts analysis of critical issues of efficiency in public administration.

The Evolution and Expansion of Civil Service in New York City

The first municipal civil service system in the United States was established in New York City shortly after passage of the Federal Civil Service Act of 1883. The New York law envisioned "a personnel system in which comparative merit or achievement governs each individual's selection and progress in the service, and in which the conditions and rewards of performance contribute to the competency and continuity of the service."[4] In practice, it proved to be no easy matter to implement a merit-based personnel system, in part because of the staying power of the political machine, which (to some extent) was able to incorporate civil service into the patronage system.[5]

Mayor Fiorello LaGuardia (1934–45) instituted the main components of the modern civil service system in New York City. In 1934 he established a new job classification system, reorganized the Civil Service Commission, and reduced the number of noncompetitive positions and jobs exempt from civil service.[6] Because LaGuardia believed that recruiting college graduates would make city government more honest and efficient, he established a scholarship for civil servants wishing to study at City College.

In spite of LaGuardia's reforms, a 1946 commission on management, created by Mayor William O'Dwyer (1946–50), concluded that administrative personnel were deficient in quantity and quality. The commission recommended that a personnel officer be assigned to each operating agency. Instead of a Civil Service Commission responsible for both rule making and administration, the commission proposed that one agency deal with the rule-making functions, and another agency handle the administration of the civil service.[7]

During the administration of Mayor Vincent R. Impellitteri (1950–53), outside management consultants were hired to evaluate the efficacy of the personnel administration. A study done by Richardson, Bellows, Henry & Company, Inc. concluded that the Municipal Civil Service Commission was underfinanced, understaffed, and generally ill equipped to carry out the duties of personnel administration effectively. They recommended new examinations, repeal of the Lyon Law (a 1937 residency requirement), and a salary increase to make city jobs competitive with private-sector jobs. Professor Wallace Sayre and Herbert Kaufman, in another study, recommended that the Civil Service Commission be abolished and replaced with a personnel advisory board, a municipal council, and a labor relations bureau, which would also advise the mayor's office on personnel matters. They also recommended that the city develop relationships with local universities to recruit managers.[8] None of these recommendations was implemented.

Under Mayor Robert Wagner (1954–65), the Civil Service Commission's Personnel Department became the City Department of Personnel, which was controlled by the mayor's office. Mayor Wagner also implemented some of the recommendations made during the Impellitteri years. First, he created the office of personnel director, which was placed under the control of the mayor's office and usurped some of the Civil Service Commission's power. Further, a Personnel Council was established to promote the coordination of personnel information among agencies and to review common personnel management problems. A Labor Department, which replaced the Division of Labor Relations, was charged with hearing grievances, settling employment disputes, and making recommendations to the mayor's office.

At the same time, the rise of public employee unions and public-sector collective bargaining units shook the entire personnel system to its core. In effect, the unions created a second personnel system overlapping and often conflicting with civil service.[9] In 1958, Mayor Wagner issued Executive Order 49, which granted collective-bargaining rights to employees represented by unions. The unions began to play a major role in determining salary levels and in defining the relationship between salary and job functions. A decade later, the New York State legislature passed the Public Employees' Fair Employment Act (the Taylor Law), establishing public employees' rights to bargain collectively and to "form, join and participate in, or to refrain from forming, joining or participating in an employee organization of their choosing."[10] The Taylor Law reinforced the independence of civil service from managerial control and effectively fortified it against significant challenges or reforms.

The Talent Bank Scandal

In reaction to the scandals in the Koch Administration, Governor Mario Cuomo appointed a blue-ribbon panel to determine the causes of corruption in city government and to recommend preventive strategies. In 1987 the commission began investigating City Hall personnel operations, campaign financing practices, the city's contracting process, the use of public authorities, and other practices and operations of city and state government. In conformity with tradition, the members of the commission were chosen for their ethical credentials rather than for their expertise in public administration. The commission was chaired by John Feerick, Dean of Fordham Law School, and included a civil rights attorney, two former prosecutors, a former judge, an Episcopal bishop, and a former U.S. Secretary of State (Cyrus Vance). The commission's primary concern was the "degradation of public service by the wrongdoing of public servants and party leaders,"[11] (i.e., corruption), not the deplorable state of New York City government, which by the 1980s seemed incapable of efficiently delivering services or maintaining the infrastructure.

Based on a whistleblower's tip, the commission began investigating the Talent Bank, a job-referral office created by Mayor Koch in 1983 to recruit minorities and women into city government. The investigation revealed that the office was a conduit for patronage in an administration that publicly shunned patronage politics.

The Feerick Commission spent a great deal of time and resources investigating the Talent Bank, examining dozens of witnesses under oath, collecting thousands of documents, and conducting public hearings in January and April 1989 that dominated the coverage of city politics for weeks. The commission concluded that the Talent Bank, directed by special mayoral assistant, Joseph DeVincenzo, had been transformed from an affirmative action job bank into a "patronage mill." According to the commission, the Talent Bank controlled several hundred positions over which the mayor had discretionary appointing authority (in effect, patronage positions) and several hundred "provisional," or temporary, appointments. DeVincenzo, known around City Hall as "Joe D," reputedly exercised great influence over hiring and promotions. While virtually unknown to the general public, Joe D was "the man to see if someone wanted a City Hall office painted or a parking sticker for the City Hall lot."[12] The commission found that he had final authority over hiring, promotion, transfer, and termination of discretionary and provisional personnel. Witnesses testified that a "Joe D" letter was commonly required before an agency could fill a vacancy.[13] Further, DeVincenzo and his staff purportedly pressured agencies to hire Talent Bank applicants referred by politicians, and required an agency to submit a written explanation if it did not hire the politically referred applicant.[14]

During the hearings, whistleblower and former Talent Bank director, Nydia Padilla-Barham testified that computer printouts of politically referred Talent Bank resumes were kept in a binder called the Black Book, which indexed the pending and hired referrals according to political sponsor.[15] Resumés were placed in color-coded files representing political sponsors—"hot" or important political referrals were kept in red folders; pink folders denoted political referrals of less importance; and green folders held "street," or unsolicited, resumés.[16] DeVincenzo and his assistant, James G. Hein, denied knowledge of the Black Book. Hein explained that colored files had been adopted to boost morale because employees "were tired of filing the same drab folder."[17] Witnesses testified that in February 1986, Hein, carrying out instructions from DeVincenzo, ordered Talent Bank employees to purge the computers of all references to political sources and to destroy the colored files and resumés containing the names of political sources. Both Hein and DeVincenzo testified that purging stale resumés was routine and not a cover-up of patronage. Following an eleven-count perjury indictment, DeVincenzo admitted he lied to the commission. Michael Cherkasky, head of the Manhattan district attorney's investigation unit, explained that "[w]hile patronage itself is not illegal and there exists in this case no underlying crime, the grand jury found that DeVincenzo lied to cover up the patronage system."[18]

The Feerick Commission treated the Talent Bank as an instance of gross corruption. The commission and the media expressed shock and indignation over the revelation that political influence played any role in filling government positions, even non–civil service positions explicitly within the mayor's discretion. The voice of the Feerick Commission echoed those of previous generations of reformers, especially the Committee of Seventy (the Tweed Ring scandals) and the Seabury Commission (the scandals of Mayor Jimmy Walker's administration). The commission affirmed the moral necessity of civil service and demanded that it be extended to more city employees.

> By injecting ulterior and illegitimate influences in place of formal standards and procedures, patronage impairs the integrity of government. Involving as it does the deploying of public resources to serve private political objectives, patronage though it may not be unlawful or invidious in intent, is itself a breach of the public trust. It simply has no legitimate place in a personnel system.[19]

The media's moral indignation over the Talent Bank scandal surpassed that of the Feerick Commission. The *New York Times* demanded that the commission press its investigation to the very top of city government.

> Why not hear from Koch administration members who had responsibility for the Talent Bank, including First Deputy Mayor Stanley Brezenoff, John

LoCicero, a political adviser who has only testified in private, and the Mayor himself?[20]

In a classic "feeding frenzy," the *New York Times* printed the names of those public employees who allegedly had obtained their jobs through the Talent Bank.[21] This attack on the character of public employees against whom there were no allegations of incompetence or venality indicates how pernicious the *Times* editors considered the Talent Bank scandal. The following letter to the editor of the *New York Times* from Brooke Trent, deputy commissioner of the Human Resources Administration, whom the *New York Times* named as a Talent Bank appointee, clearly illuminates the politics of the scandal.

> The fact is, I got my job through the *New York Times*. I guess Nathan Leventhal, then a Deputy Mayor, put the resume I sent him (during a job search) in the Talent Bank, but that did not get me the position; the resume I sent in response to a June 21, 1981, ad in your paper did.
>
> But what if I had got that job through the Talent Bank? By 1981, I had 12 years of public sector experience—federal, state, and city. I entered city government in Mayor John V. Lindsay's administration and took a Civil Service exam for that job. As a manager, I have occasionally tapped the Talent Bank for resumés of qualified candidates, particularly women and minority-group members, and I also place ads in your paper and others, remembering my own story. I have told it many times to encourage qualified people to come into government, assuring them that you don't have to 'know someone.'
>
> I guess you have destroyed my credibility and that of others. Too bad for government, whose professionals and managers seem relentlessly and often inaccurately criticized by the news media, further discouraging talented people from entering its ranks and staying.[22]

The Talent Bank scandal drove mayoral aides James Hein and Joe DeVincenzo from office for having made "contradictory" statements at public hearings. DeVincenzo was sentenced to five years probation after pleading guilty to one count of perjury based upon misstatements to the Feerick Commission. Hein was demoted and testified against DeVincenzo before the grand jury under a grant of immunity. Mayor Edward Koch was blamed for not knowing about the patronage mill and for not accepting blame for his ignorance. Shortly thereafter, he dismantled the Talent Bank. Nevertheless, the scandal was a major blow to his reelection efforts. Patronage was equated with corruption. The Koch administration was criticized as the most "corrupt" since Jimmy Walker's. The mayor lost the Democratic primary.

In its final report, the Feerick Commission urged that "[t]he [New York City] personnel system must be structured so as to prevent personnel decisions based on politics."[23] It therefore recommended expanding and strengthening the civil service system and "drastically reducing" the number of discretionary and provisional employees because political control of these nonmerit appointments often resulted in unsuitable or incompetent people being placed in important administrative and staff positions. This conclusion was based upon the antipatronage ideology that has been embraced by reformers for a century, but it certainly was not based on the record. There were no studies even purporting to compare the competence and performance of political appointees with merit appointees. The practical superiority of civil service as a mechanism of personnel administration is simply an article of reformist faith.

The Impact of Civil Service on Public Administration

Decades of civil service reform, including more coverage, centralization, and job security, reinforced in the 1960s by the implementation of public-sector collective bargaining, have severely constrained government efficiency and severely limited the capacity to innovate.[24] Commissioners cannot hire their subordinates nor can they promote them, give them pay raises, or discipline and fire them. In short, they do not control their personnel and therefore their agencies. This alone would lead one to expect a crisis in public administration.[25] Indeed, more than thirty years ago, a Brookings Institute study of New York City's personnel system concluded that New York City faced a civil service crisis. The Brookings study criticized civil service hiring and promotion because it "divorces personnel responsibility from program responsibility."[26] It also criticized the so-called merit selection and promotion system as slow, inflexible, and ineffective, and as one which "in many ways impedes recognition of true merit."[27]

A recent study of the "constraints and opportunities" of the New York City civil service system by the Columbia University Program in Politics and Public Policy found that civil service reform has rendered city government ineffective and, ironically, subject to political manipulation—the worst of both worlds.[28] Many of the same problems highlighted by the 1963 Brookings Institute study were once again raised by the Columbia study in 1993. The Columbia study surveyed managers of all ranks in three agencies and found uniform negativism about the personnel system. Criticism centered on five major problems:

- *Hiring takes too long.* It can take from months to years to fill a position. The complex process of testing and audits done by various agencies leaves the hiring agency without needed personnel for extended periods. The audits proceed in three stages. First, the Department of Personnel conducts an audit to assure that the agency has complied with all relevant state and local laws and regulations. Second, the Office of Management and Budget conducts a fiscal audit to certify that adequate funds are available to pay salary and benefits. Third, the Mayor's Office of Operations conducts a final audit of all procedures, and issues certification for employment.

• *Testing does not assess relevant abilities.* The tests are antiquated, uniformly too easy, and do not provide grounds for distinguishing among candidates. It would be better in most cases to award jobs on the basis of a lottery, according to one manager. Most managers consider themselves better judges of candidates than the testing process.

• *Promotion is not controlled at the agency level and so deprives managers of a basic incentive.* The civil service promotion tests are given on an erratic schedule. In some agencies the waiting list for the promotion exam is 5–10 years old. Even when a position opens up, those wishing to compete for it must wait for the depletion of a preference list of those laid off from similar positions.

• *Job descriptions are so technically and narrowly written that a minor internal transfer becomes a major bureaucratic issue.* Managers found that the obvious talents of employees were being wasted because of confining definitions of duties.

• *Discipline, punishment, and removal have been made all but impossible by civil service protections.* Protections written into the civil service law serve to shield unproductive workers. Managers admit that the cumbersome and lengthy process required to remove poor performers makes it unlikely that they will do so. "He [the Inspector General] asked each of the four ACs [Assistant Commissioners] to identify their ten worst employees—a total of 40 out of 4,000. . . . When their files were pulled, not one of them had a single unsatisfactory performance evaluation."[29] When the protections afforded by union contracts are added, managers found that there was too much job security in the civil service.[30]

More than half of the high-level officials surveyed by the Columbia group favored complete elimination of promotional and hiring exams. When managers mentioned patronage, it was to suggest that they be given some of their own so they could override the civil service system to recruit and develop a staff that was competent, efficient, and motivated.

Our own interviews reinforce the Columbia team's findings and conclusions. The commissioners and assistant commissioners whom we interviewed regarded the Talent Bank as a tempest in a teapot. They opposed the idea of centralized hiring and personnel administration because it empowers persons other than agency heads to select, promote, and make disciplinary decisions concerning agency employees. In their view, reformers have a simplistic view of patronage. More than any other component of the anticorruption project, civil service limits and prevents public-sector managers from implementing their policies and improving their operations.

Counterreforms and Adaptations

The negative impact of civil service on competency, efficiency, and flexibility, and the inability to reform the system that itself stands as the quintessential reform in the history of public administration have inspired some theorists and politicians to propose reforms and end runs around civil service. No mayor since World War II has proposed eliminating or even limiting mayoral appointments to any significant extent. Mayor John V. Lindsay (1966–73) argued that the mayor's patronage was necessary in order to assert governing authority over a large and fractious government. For Mayor Lindsay, who was without ties to a political machine, the amount of patronage available was too small, and he criticized the so-called merit system as an impediment to the mayor's achieving control over the bureaucracy.

The 1975 Charter Revision Commission's studies of the civil service system concluded that "many features of the system, as it is now structured, do not promote 'merit and fitness' in city service. Rather they fuel a negative philosophy and practical rigidities that make it difficult for the City to manage its multi-billion dollar operations."[31] The commission highlighted the need to move beyond the traditional negative rationale for personnel management—to insulate public administration from political manipulation and patronage. Specifically, the commission proposed that the charter should (1) delegate substantial responsibilities to operating agencies for personnel administration; (2) create a Management Service to bolster the middle-management corps; and (3) make the Civil Service Commission an affirmative force in personnel management. The commission also proposed new roles for the personnel director, the Civil Service Commission, and the agency heads. The personnel director was to be separated from the Civil Service Commission and was to assume administrative duties and rule-making authority. The director was given sole responsibility for position allocation and classification, severely restricting the Bureau of Budget's role in personnel classification. All of these proposals were implemented.[32]

The agency heads obtained enhanced responsibilities for personnel management functions such as position classification and assignment, appointments, performance evaluation, disciplinary actions, merit increases and incentive awards, equal opportunity, and record keeping. Personnel functions such as examination, recruitment, and training were delegated to task forces, creating such groups as the Criminal Justice Task Force, the Task Force on Urban Affairs, and the Environmental Protection Task Force.

Mayor Edward Koch (1978–89) urged the legislature to pass laws that would have prohibited supervisors from belonging to the same unions as workers, expanded exempt classes, established a one-in-ten rule (rather than the one-in-three) which would permit agency heads to choose from among the ten highest scorers on the civil service exams, granted authority to transfer personnel without their consent, established the assignment of more quantitative weight for performance evaluation than for seniority in layoff decisions, given all new starting employees the same equal seniority, expanded city control over all municipal employees, consolidated bargaining units, and implemented a no-bargaining clause for management rights. City personnel and their unions opposed Koch's civil service "reforms," and these laws were never enacted.

Some revisionists have even come to believe that patronage ought to be tolerated and accepted, to some extent, as "the grease that keeps the machinery of government working,"[33] and "a staple of American politics."[34] In their view the idea that patronage can and should be completely eradicated is unrealistic and unwise. One modern-day proponent of patronage explained that "[p]olitical appointees are often necessary to build the kind of public consensus that any effective government needs. A trusted friend in a key post may also be able to get the ear of the mayor in important policy disputes. Problems arise only when patronage appointments are excessive, incompetent, or outrageously camouflaged."[35]

Robert Moses and Civil Service

Robert Moses (1888–1981), New York City's master builder, started his career as a good government reformer and civil service crusader. When it came to implementing vast public works projects in the New York metropolitan area, he employed creative techniques to bypass the civil service system, which he in part helped to create.[36] The man whose organizational genius created dozens of parks, bridges, tunnels, highways, dams, beaches, and stadiums began his public career at age twenty-five as Mayor John Purroy Mitchel's (1914–17) expert consultant on civil service reform. Having written a doctoral thesis at Columbia University on the civil service in Britain and the potential for a professional, efficient public workforce in the United States, Moses was a logical choice for the job.[37] In his *Detailed Report on the Rating of the Efficiency of Civil Service Employees, Excepting*

Members of the Uniformed Forces in the Police and Fire Services and in the Lower Ranks of the Street Cleaning Service, he proposed plans for classifying and standardizing job titles and salary grades, and centralizing control of competitive exams for appointment and promotion, job descriptions, merit system protection, and uniform pay scales. After being disowned by the mayor and comptroller and amended dozens of times by the Board of Aldermen, parts of the plan were enacted in 1916, only to disappear the following year, after the election of a Tammany slate headed by Mayor John Hylan (1918–25).

Eventually, the reformers were to have their day. Fifteen years later, after Moses had moved on, a majority of his proposals were implemented by Mayor Fiorello LaGuardia. According to historian Wilbur C. Rich, "LaGuardia's administration was a high point in the history of public service. The mayor used the momentum of the New Deal, the instability of Tammany leadership, and the renewed enthusiasm of academic reformers to impose new standards on the city's civil service."[38] Political scientist Wallace Sayre viewed the major principle of LaGuardia's civil service effort as "the elimination of 'spoils' patronage, the extension of the merit system, and the development of a career service in New York City."[39] LaGuardia hoped to achieve these objectives by (1) extending the merit principles; (2) reducing the number of exempt personnel; (3) increasing the number of competitive personnel and decreasing the number of noncompetitive personnel; (4) reorganizing the classification system into a series of new career services; (5) implementing modern and more scientific recruitment and examination procedures; and (6) widening promotion opportunities.

Ironically, while LaGuardia was embracing the ideas of civil service reformers, Moses was becoming disenchanted with them. In 1934, Moses, then the first commissioner of a citywide Parks Department, had responsibility for directing a massive and unprecedented repair and building plan. In order to complete more than fifteen hundred major projects in his first year—including 10 golf courses, 6 golf houses, 240 tennis courts, 3 tennis houses, 51 baseball diamonds, and 2 zoos, he required the service of six hundred architects and engineers.[40] Using civil service pay grades and hiring procedures would have stalled the plan for months because incumbents of these job classifications could not be paid more than $30 per week. After Moses threatened to quit, city and federal officials relented and exempted Moses' projects from the civil service rules.

As Parks Commissioner, Moses learned how to avoid rigid civil service requirements for hiring and salary, but these ad hoc end runs around civil service were time-consuming and sometimes controversial. Ultimately, he came up with the idea for a new form of governmental unit: the "public authority," which as a public service corporation would be exempt from civil service and other intragovernmental regulations.

With Moses' prodding, the legislature established the Triborough Bridge Authority (TBA), which became an independent colossus that built roads and bridges virtually anywhere in the metropolitan area. Not only did the TBA have unlimited bonding authority, it was also permitted to retain and reinvest the enormous revenues generated by tolls on the Triborough and later the Whitestone and Throgs Neck bridges. Moses had a secure stream of funds, independent control over the TBA's agenda, and freedom from burdensome regulatory requirements like those of the civil service. He defined jobs to suit his needs, set pay scales to attract the best talent, and hired and fired whom he pleased, all in the name of "getting things done." He did not need to eliminate the civil service; he just made it meaningless for his purposes.[41] Moses, frequently regarded as the most successful administrator in New York City history, was successful largely because he circumvented civil service.

The Feerick Commission even attacked the use of public authorities (like the TBA) on the ground that they provided inadequate protection against patronage, despite the time-proven ability of these public authorities to "get things done." The commission argued that "[t]he proliferation of these bodies with fragmented, weak or non-existent oversight, has important implications for the integrity of government. . . . This is a situation with potential to breed favoritism, abuse of power, and even corruption."[42] The commission recommended that lawmakers impose "the same ethical standards and oversight on all governmental bodies," including

> at a minimum, public disclosure of their transactions; contracting based on procedures designed to ensure competition; employment decisions based on merit and fitness; decision-making by leaders who are not subject to conflicts of interest; documentation of all decisions, sound internal controls, and periodic audits of their books and records.[43]

Conclusion

Civil service reform was founded on and is still driven by an antipatronage ideology that equates patronage with corruption. Many reformers' abhorrence of patronage is so strong that it blinds them to the needs and complexities of public administration. Reformers strove unceasingly to expand and strengthen the civil service in order to break the patronage system that was the backbone of the political machine which they despised and called "corrupt." In spite of their excellent motives, the reformers' neglected the needs of public administration. Civil service historian Paul Van Riper's critique of the reformers' overarching emphasis on destroying patronage also applies to the Feerick Commission:

> It is quite clear that only secondarily . . . were the reformers interested in efficiency and economy. . . . They mentioned these things, but they almost invariably referred to the "greater" moral issues. . . . [E]fficiency in administration was but a corollary to [their] major purpose: the achievement of a new morality in public affairs.[44]

A similar point is made by political scientist William Munro:

> In implementing and perfecting a comprehensive civil service system, reformers believed that they were creating a professional government service with high standards of ethics and integrity. . . . Unfortunately, it has not turned out that way. Civil service reform has rendered a great service in debarring the clearly unfit from appointive office, and the merit system probably offers the most practicable method of getting the best men into *some* administrative positions; but to insist that it is the only practicable method of securing competent men for *all* appointive posts, whether high or low, and irrespective of the qualities needed—to press the point thus far is to give a typical example of the reformers' bondage to principle.[45]

This principle is as strong (if not stronger) today as it ever was. The Feerick Commission viewed the Talent Bank as an example of rank corruption, and made public hearings on this scandal the centerpiece of its work. A whiff of patronage constituted a scandal. That the Talent Bank dealt with merely several hundred discretionary appointments in a municipal workforce of almost 400,000 made no difference in the social construction of that scandal. The mainstream media define morality, not administration, as the most important priority of governing.

While the Feerick Commission railed against the Talent Bank, it did not offer any criticism of civil service; indeed, it enthusiastically recommended its expansion. This view starkly contrasts with the Columbia study's indictment of civil service for its negative impacts on New York City government. The Columbia group found that public managers were deeply dissatisfied with the personnel system. But managers cannot change things under current regulations. Advocating overthrow of civil service is not only regarded as heresy, but as being soft on corruption. Thus, managers must struggle to gain control over agencies with incompetent employees whom they cannot fire, demoralized and underpaid professionals whom they cannot reward, and vacant positions which they cannot fill unless they are fortunate enough to get approval to hire "provisional" employees.

Managers, not surprisingly, search for ways around this dilemma. In New York City, a major end run around civil service is the proliferation of provisional employees, whose appointments are only temporary but can be renewed indefinitely, and who can be fired for any lawful reason. The ability to appoint such employees provides administrators with much-needed flexibility. Nevertheless, the Feerick Commission predictably denounced provisional employment and recommended that practically all positions be swept under the civil service umbrella. An even more striking illustration of a civil service end run, as we saw in the example of Robert Moses, is the creation of public authorities, which are completely exempted from civil service rules.

Competency, efficiency, and motivation cannot simply be assumed. Managers need authority and incentives to manage their agencies. Instead of recognizing the political and problematic nature of administration, as successful private-sector organizations have, civil service reformers have tried to bury politics.

FOUR

Conflicts of Interest and Financial Disclosures: The Pursuit of Absolute Integrity

> Today's appearance ethics so richly compensates correct appearances (e.g., by advancing careers) and so harshly punishes incorrect ones (e.g., by killing careers), that the easiest, safest, and most rewarded strategy for career advancement is to devote far more of one's efforts to maintaining appearances than to actually doing one's job.
>
> Peter W. Morgan, "The Appearance of Propriety: Ethics Reform and the Blifil Paradox"

Laws prohibiting conflicts of interest and requiring disclosure of personal finances and investments aim to prevent government officials from having their decision making distorted by the potential for personal gain or loss.[1] Conflict-of-interest and financial disclosure laws constitute a specialized administrative/criminal code that applies only to public officials. Laws prohibiting conflicts of interest consist of a list of "shall nots." Conflicts of interest are created simply by *being* a public official and, at the same time, a stockholder, someone's daughter, or a member of the board of a charitable organization. Financial disclosure provisions constitute affirmative obligations analogous to the reporting requirements of the Internal Revenue Code. Together, the two sets of rules envelop public officials in a fog of potential liability.

At the end of the nineteenth century and the beginning of the twentieth century, corruption was not understood as embracing certain types of exploitation of public office for private gain. The colorful George Washington Plunkitt openly bragged that he sought opportunities for "honest graft." Likewise, some government officials have steered insurance and law business to firms in which they or their family members are owners or partners, and some have awarded contracts to companies in which they hold an interest or at least an expectation of future employment. Patronage—hiring supporters, friends, and relatives—constitutes a conflict of interest that has been acted upon.

It is important to note that some instances of self-interested wheeling and dealing do not necessarily involve an economic loss to the government entity. The government, for example, may get insurance coverage for a reasonable price even when a high-level official gets a kickback. Nevertheless, by today's standards, such conduct is deemed corrupt because all private gain from public service is said to be at least unethical and to undermine the public's confidence in the integrity of government.

The definition of corruption includes placing oneself in a conflict-of-interest situation, even if one's decision has not yet been rendered or has been rendered contrary to self-interest. The most recent major extension of the anti-conflict-of-interest norm is the prohibition of the *appearance* of conflict of interest or the *appearance* of impropriety. In 1989 President Bush issued an executive order adopting appearance of propriety as a standard of conduct for federal employees, and authorized the Office of Government Ethics (OGE) to promulgate rules incorporating this standard.[2] As President Bush's Commission on Federal Ethics Law Reform put it, situations "that create the appearance of a conflict of interest do undermine public confidence in the integrity of government, and we thus suggest that the avoidance of appearances of impropriety remain as one of the broad principles of government ethics."[3] Thus, conflict-of-interest laws aim to increase the public's confidence in the integrity of government. "[D]emocracy is effective only if the people have faith in those who govern, and that faith is bound to be shattered when high officials and their appointees engage in activities which arouse suspicions of malfeasance and corruption."[4]

Conflict-of-interest and financial disclosure laws have their work cut out for them. Public opinion polls reveal that most Americans have little confidence in public officials. A 1989 *USA Today* poll found that 54 percent of the public believe that one out of every three members of Congress is corrupt.[5] Similarly, a 1989 *Washington Post*-ABC News poll found that more than 50 percent of the public believe that members of Congress profit improperly from their office.[6]

The Association of the Bar of the City of New York explained the need for conflict-of-interest regulation as follows:

> The evil . . . [of conflicts of interest] is risk of impairment of impartial judgment, a risk which arises whenever there is temptation to serve personal interests. The quality of specific results is immaterial. . . . Like other fiduciaries . . . the public trustee has a duty to avoid private interests which cause even a risk that he will not be motivated solely by the interests of the beneficiaries of his trust. Properly conceived, conflict-of-interest regulation does not con-

demn bad actions so much as it erects a system designed to protect a decision-making process.[7]

Financial disclosure requirements are meant to reinforce conflict-of-interest prohibitions. As late as 1969, only eleven states required public financial disclosure. By 1977, more than 38 states had such laws.[8] In 1978, the federal Ethics in Government Act mandated financial disclosure for a significant proportion of federal employees.[9] The disclosure requirements are an anticorruption measure one step removed from actual corruption. They focus on perception, that is, the appearance of impropriety. Disclosure requirements and conflict-of-interest laws are preventive and prophylactic. They aim not to detect and punish wrongdoing, but to provide "safeguards which lessen the risk of undesirable action."[10] Generally, financial disclosure forms oblige designated public employees to list (and make public) all their own (and their family's) financial assets and obligations as well as their organizational memberships and affiliations. The theory is that such disclosure will (1) deter them from placing themselves in conflict-of-interest situations, and (2) focus their attention on organizing their financial arrangements to avoid inadvertent conflicts of interest. Withholding or distorting information on the forms is itself a criminal offense.

This chapter first details the development and operation of ethics laws and financial disclosure requirements as they apply to public officials in New York City. Second, it examines the impact of these laws on corruption and public administration.

Background

The antipatronage and Progressive reformers believed that the elimination of patronage and the creation of a professional, merit-based civil service would eliminate the use of public office for private gain as a serious problem; professional public servants could be relied upon to police their own behavior. They would pursue the public good without regard to the effect of their decisions on their own self-interest, financial and otherwise.

The scientific administration reformers emphasized optimal "spans of control" and enhanced auditing and accounting. They believed that government integrity would flow from sound organization. Correct deployment of administrative authority, coupled with comprehensive monitoring and evaluation, would prevent corruption or quickly bring it to light. Because they believed that scientific administration itself would prevent corruption, the 1930s reformers did not propose comprehensive ethics codes to regulate public employees' financial affairs.[11]

During the 1950s, reformers began proposing more elaborate conflict-of-interest laws as a strategy of corruption control. The National Municipal League produced a Model State Conflict of Interest and Financial Disclosure Law, which required disclosure to a superior of a situation that could "cause financial benefit or detriment to [the public official]."[12]

The 1960s and especially the 1970s saw the triumph of comprehensive ethics codes supplemented by comprehensive financial disclosure laws. These codes are not simply hortatory; they are made up of prohibitions and sanctions that resemble criminal law. Indeed, New York City's financial disclosure law makes it a misdemeanor to fail to file or to misstate assets and liabilities, and it imposes a $100 fine for a late filing. These laws demonstrate the panoptic vision of corruption control that relies heavily on rules, threats, surveillance, and coercion. Law professor Robert Vaughn has noted that the result of equating ethics with respecting criminal prohibitions is to undermine the concept of ethics.

> Too great a reliance on legal regulation can have side effects, like a drug too frequently used. By converting ethical problems into legal ones, the law becomes the sole judge of propriety. What can be done becomes what should be done. If what is legal continues to seem improper, additional conduct is made illegal, reinforcing the perception that what is legal constitutes what is proper. Soon ethics has limited significance apart from legal command and enforcement structures and sanctions become increasingly important.[13]

The Politics of Current New York City Ethics Laws

There was nothing subtle about the politics that led to passage of recent ethics legislation. A particularly egregious conflict of interest brought to light during the Parking Violations Bureau (PVB) scandals involved Bronx party boss, Stanley Friedman, who pushed the PVB and the Board of Estimate to award a contract for hand-held computers to Citisource, a company with no assets and one employee. Friedman, the largest stockholder of Citisource, became a millionaire virtually overnight when the value of Citisource stock increased as a result of its contract with PVB.[14] Mayor Koch attempted to distance himself from the scandal that was enveloping his administration by stating, "I am embarrassed, I am chagrined, I am absolutely mortified that this kind of corruption could have existed and that I did not know." The columnist Murray Kempton suggested that "I am shocked" ought to be made the city motto since Mayor Koch said it so often.[15] In the wake of the scandal, city and state politicians competed over who could most strongly express moral indignation and outrage toward corruption, including conflicts of interest.

The U.S. Senator from New York State, Daniel Patrick Moynihan, declared, "[P]ublic corruption is more than a crime; it is betrayal and is contemptible and unforgivable."[16] Governor Mario Cuomo demonstrated his concern by appointing two blue-ribbon commissions: The New York State-City Commission on Integrity in Government (the Sovern Commission), and the New York State Commission on Government Integrity (the Feerick Commission). Both commissions waxed indignant about corruption and generated recommendations to close the legal loopholes that allowed corruption to breed. These recommendations included financial disclosure, prohibitions against participating in decisions from which the public servant stood to benefit financially, and the establishment of a commission to enforce ethics legislation.[17] While neither commissions' recommendation was immediately enacted, in 1987 a new state ethics law emerged as a hard-fought compromise between the governor and the legislative leadership.[18] Some provisions seemed to impose stringent ethical requirements on state employees, but others arguably weakened prior standards. According to one critic of the Act,

> [t]he conflict of interest provisions enacted by the new ethics code fail to regulate a wide range of conduct that would appear to constitute a conflict between a state official's or legislator's public duty and her private interest. For example, while a public official cannot receive compensation for appearances or services rendered before state agencies, the Act *expressly* allows any firm, association or corporation of which the public official is a member to charge fees for such appearances or services, provided the public official does not share in the net revenues. This restriction does not eliminate the rewards that may accrue to a public official for improperly influencing an agency or the Legislature.[19]

Overall, the 1987 Act significantly bolstered New York's ethics laws by requiring financial disclosure, prohibiting appearances or lobbying by a public servant on behalf of a private individual or entity doing business with the government, and regulating the receipt of gifts by public servants.

In New York City, ethics reform followed a path that did not involve the legislative process. The main forum for debate over anticorruption reform was the Charter Revision Commission, which Mayor Koch appointed in 1981 after a federal court declared the city's upper legislative chamber, the Board of Estimate, to be in violation of the constitutionally required principle of "one person, one vote."[20] After the PVB corruption scandals erupted, however, the Charter Revision Commission gave anticorruption reform top priority. The Charter Revision Commission's recommendations did not have to go through a legislative process of compromise or revision; they became law via referendum.

Like most other New York City anticorruption reforms of the modern era, the Charter Revision Commission's ethics provisions were not cut wholly from new cloth. Many key provisions were based on a body of national conflict-of-interest legislation and jurisprudence that had developed since Watergate. They enjoyed the vigorous advocacy of good-government groups and scholars around the country.[21] The commission sought advice and testimony from organizations such as the Citizens Budget Commission and the Institute for Public Administration, and from scholars like political scientist Aaron Wildavsky.

Conflict-of-Interest Laws

The 1989 New York City Charter's Ethics Code (Chapter 68) establishes comprehensive standards and prohibitions for public employees' financial conduct and relationships that occur on and off the job. It also outlines behavior, activities, and relationships appropriate for public servants' spouses and minor children. Violation of these rules is punishable by both civil and criminal sanctions, including forfeiture of office, fines, and incarceration.[22]

This comprehensive web of prohibitions is applicable to all city employees and elected and appointed city officials (including former officials). The prohibitions address a wide variety of self-dealing, including investments in or ties to companies doing business with the city, spousal interests in businesses doing business with the city, receipt of gifts worth more than fifty dollars, volunteer or paid work with not-for-profit organizations, and restrictions on employment following government employment.

Further, Chapter 68 prohibits council members or *any salaried city employees* from having a direct or indirect financial interest in any business dealings with the city or its agencies; nor can a council member or any city employee act as an attorney, agent, broker, or consultant for any person, firm, corporation, or other entity interested directly or indirectly in any business dealings with the city. In short, it is illegal for public officials to profit in any way from city contracts.

Chapter 68 attacks the patronage system that enabled Donald Manes, Queens party boss and Queens Borough President, to function as a power broker who could convert influence to cash, by prohibiting elected officials (except for city council members) and some appointed officials from holding high political party offices. Similarly, Bronx party boss Stanley Friedman wielded enormous political control without holding any public office which would have required him to comply with conflict-of-interest and financial disclosure laws. The state's 1987 Ethics in Government Act sought to change all that by expanding the scope of conflict-of-interest and financial disclosure provisions to cover party leaders. Further, party leaders in New York City are prohibited from doing business with the city, except bidding for contracts, and from representing clients before city agencies.[23]

In another provision, Chapter 68 aims to protect public employees from being forced to donate to political parties by making it unlawful for any public servant to compel, induce, or request any person to pay any "political assessment," or kickback. It is also an offense to solicit or receive a "political assessment."

The conflict-of-interest rules also regulate employment following government service. Former city officials, such as agency heads, are barred for three years from private employment with companies involved in matters in which they worked while in city government.[24] Further, for one year after leaving the government, public employees may not appear before their former agencies,[25] and elected officials and other specified appointed officials are barred from appearing before the entire branch in which they served.[26]

In addition to prohibiting specific conflicts of interest, Chapter 68 contains several catch-all prohibitions:

> No public servant shall engage in any business transaction or private employment, or have any financial or other private interest, direct or indirect, which is in conflict with proper discharge of his or her official duties.[27] No public servant shall use or attempt to use his or her position as a public servant to obtain any financial gain, contract, license, privilege, or other private personal advantage, direct or indirect, for the public servant or any person or firm associated with the public servant.[28]

Public officials are also prohibited from entering into a business or financial relationship with superiors or subordinates while employed by the city.[29] These provisions cast a long shadow over public service. What counts as using one's position to "secure an advantage," directly or indirectly, for a friend or child? What about a call to another government employee to enquire about an agency opening for a friend, or what about a letter of recommendation? Can public officials be confident that in their financial arrangements and in all their actions, public and private, grounds will not be found to charge an illegal conflict of interest?

Each year the Conflict of Interest Board responds to approximately four hundred formal requests for opinions and one thousand phone calls seeking informal confidential advice. This indicates that many public employees are anxious about and confused by the rules.[30]

Indeed, anxiety and paranoia may plague city employees trying to grapple with potential conflict-of-interest situations because, as one employee of the Conflict of Interest Board explained, "substantively it's a good ethics law [Chapter 68], but no one can understand it. It's completely unintelligible." As a result, public employees who would rather be safe than sorry may feel compelled to check with the board before their spouses start a business or accept a job offer, engage in volunteer work, or accept part-time teaching positions.

As illustrated by the board's advisory opinions, Chapter 68's reach could be interpreted to extend far beyond concerns about self-dealing and corruption. A city employee checked with the Conflict of Interest Board before attending (for free) an annual golf and tennis outing sponsored by an organization which does no business with the public servant's agency. The board permitted the public servant to attend the golf outing, even though several firm members of the sponsoring organization did business with the city, including the public servant's agency.[31] Employees of a city agency, concerned that a possible conflict of interest might arise, checked with the board before soliciting donations "from firms engaged in a trade that falls within the agency's jurisdiction" on behalf of a colleague who was seriously injured in a car accident.[32] Similarly, employees of the Police and Fire Departments inquired whether their children could apply for merit scholarships awarded by a not-for-profit trade association whose for-profit member companies were subject to some safety monitoring by the Fire Department. The board ruled that the public servants' children could apply for the scholarships.[33]

Even where Chapter 68 prohibits certain conduct, the board may in some circumstances issue a waiver if it finds that the conduct would not conflict or interfere with the effective performance of official duties. In order to obtain a waiver, however, the employee's agency head must provide written approval stating in detail why the conduct would not conflict with official duties. Typically, waivers are sought where a public servant wants to teach a course at a college or university which has financial transactions with the city. Without a waiver, compensation for teaching would violate Chapter 68 §2604a(1)(b), which provides that no employee whose primary employment is with the city may have an interest in a firm which the employee knows does business with the city. The board issues "bucketfuls" of waivers for public servants who want to teach, as long as the course does not concern subject matter "which directly involve[s] his official duties."[34] This is certainly an odd caveat since the public servant's specific expertise is likely to be what the college finds attractive. Given the increasing demand for advice by the board, delay is inevitable, despite the routine nature of these waivers. Thus, Chapter 68's broad reach probably discourages public servants from seeking out adjunct teaching positions.

Financial Disclosure Requirements

New York City enacted its first financial disclosure requirements in 1975[35] and expanded them in the 1980s to cover more public employees and require more extensive disclosure.[36] In addition, many city employees are also covered by the financial reporting requirements of the 1987 New York State Ethics in Government Act.[37] The consequence is that some employees have to fill out a number of disclosure forms when they first take a city job and then on an annual basis ever after. In order to prevent conflicts of interest from even arising, the ethics law regulates the economic life of not only the covered employees, but also members of their nuclear families as well.

One city official told us that when he joined city government at a senior level, he had to fill out three sets of disclosure forms: (1) a terms and conditions-of-appointment form for the New York City Department of Investigation (DOI), complete with fingerprints, photos, tax returns, and a twenty-five-page questionnaire; (2) a disclosure form for the Conflict of Interest Board comprising sixteen pages of requests for financial information; and (3) an annual financial disclosure form amounting to a twenty-four-page questionnaire plus requests for receipts. These intimidating forms demand comprehensive financial information and require the disclosing individual to trace his or her job history back to high school. The amount of time and effort required to fill out disclosure forms, in itself, may act as a disincentive for qualified individuals.

New York State's Ethics in Government Act requires government employees to do the following:

- List any office, trusteeship, directorship, partnership, or position of any nature including honorary positions, if known, held by the reporting individual, his or her spouse or unemancipated children. If the entity had any significant business or activity with a state or local industry, the reporting individual must name the agency.

- List the name, address, and description of any occupation, employment, trade, business, or profession engaged in by the reporting individual, his or her spouse or unemancipated children. If such activity was licensed by or had business or had matters before any state or local agency, name the agency and describe the matter.

• List any interest in excess of $1000, excluding bonds and notes, held by the reporting individual, such individual's spouse or unemancipated minor child in any contract made by a state or local agency and include the name of the entity which holds such interest and the relationship of the reporting individual, spouse, or child to the entity.

• List any position the reporting individual held as an officer of any political party.

• If the reporting individual practices law, is a real estate agent, or other licensed professional, describe the principle subject areas undertaken by the individual.

• List the name, address, and general description or the nature of the business activity of any entity of which the reporting individual or the individual's spouse had an investment greater than $1000 excluding investments in securities and interests in real property.

• List the identity and value of each interest in a trust or estate or other beneficial interest.

• List the amount and nature of any income in excess of $1000 from each source for the reporting individual and the reporting individual's spouse.

• List the sources of any deferred income in excess of $1000 to be paid at the end of the calendar year for which this disclosure statement is filed.

• List the type and market value of securities held by the reporting individual or such individual's spouse from each issuing entity at the close of the taxable year.

• List the location, size, general nature, acquisition date, market value, and percentage of ownership of any real property in which any vested or contingent interest in excess of $1000 is held by the reporting individual or the reporting individual's spouse.[38]

The demand for so much detailed financial data makes it likely that many forms will contain purposeful or inadvertent misstatements, errors, inaccuracies, and omissions. Intentional misstatements or omissions are punishable by imprisonment for up to a year, a fine not to exceed $1,000, or both. One former New York City commissioner told us that, throughout her tenure in office, she regarded the financial disclosure forms "as a way of holding us hostage." In other words, an investigating agency that wanted to "get" a particular individual but couldn't find evidence of serious corruption could comb the disclosure reports for a conflict of interest or for a distortion or omission that could be used to force the official from office or at least place the taint of corruption on him or her.

Despite the millions of dollars spent on setting up the financial disclosure apparatus in New York City, only *three* public officials have ever been caught for intentional violations! The ritual performance of filling out disclosure forms on an annual basis has become a symbolic act. Due to budget cuts, the Conflict of Interest Board does little more than babysit the filed disclosure forms, which accumulate at the rate of two million pages per year.[39] Of the more than 12,000 forms filed in 1994, only 1,000 were reviewed for conflicts of interest. Critics of annual disclosure claim that even a substantive review of all forms would not necessarily reveal any conflicts of interest, because there is no database of companies that do business with the city to which the completed forms may be compared. According to Professor Joseph Little, a critic of financial disclosure,

> [t]he general goal [of financial disclosure] is honest service. The specific plan is to prevent corruption in governmental decisions and operations, to promote neutrality in these activities, to make government decisions and operations more credible in the eyes of the governed people, and to enhance the accountability of those in service to the electorate. Financial disclosure is ill equipped to serve any of these purposes.[40]

Campaign Finance and Conflict of Interest

The New York State Ethics in Government Act of 1987 imposes upon candidates for elected office another layer of financial disclosure: campaign finance laws. These laws regulate who may make contributions, when contributions may be made, how much money can be donated, and when campaign contributions must be disclosed. They are animated by the same concerns over self-dealing and improper influence that are deployed in behalf of financial disclosure and conflict-of-interest laws. The Feerick Commission nicely summarized these concerns:

> [T]he political action committees and businesses which pour money into state [and city] elections see their contributions, not as an expression of ideological support, but as a way of influencing elected officials, who are expected to favor contributors out of either appreciation for past contributions or a desire for future ones.[41]

It has become increasingly common for charges of corruption in campaign financing to make newspaper headlines following elections. During the 1993 elections, incumbent city comptroller, warrior in the anticorruption battle, and former Brooklyn District Attorney Elizabeth Holtzman was accused by the DOI of being "grossly negligent" in failing to ensure that a $450,000 loan from Fleet Bank to finance her unsuccessful campaign for United States Senate did not create a conflict of interest.[42] Although Holtzman complied with campaign finance laws and there were no allegations that she had violated them, conflict-of-interest problems arose when it was discovered that Fleet Financial Group (FFG), a subsidiary of Fleet Bank, had done business with the city and had recently been awarded a bond underwriting contract.[43]

Holtzman denied knowledge of awarding the contract to FFG, and she stated that a subordinate, who was unaware of the campaign loan by Fleet Bank, recommended FFG as the most qualified underwriter (FFG had sold more city bonds in the previous two years than any of the other companies that applied for the contract). In order to save face and possibly save her reelection campaign for city comptroller, Holtzman apologized, saying she made a "mistake" when she permitted her office to award the contract to FFG. Although there were never any allegations that the city or the taxpayers had been cheated, or that FFG was unqualified or had received a sweetheart deal or unreasonable compensation, the mere hint of favoritism was enough to cast the shadow of scandal over Holtzman's campaign. She was soundly defeated in the primary.

Impact on Corruption

Do the conflict-of-interest and financial disclosure laws reduce bribery, criminal frauds, conflicts of interest, and influence peddling? There are no data to answer this empirical question, but we believe that with respect to hard-core criminality, the answer is probably no. Bribery and fraud have long flourished despite their being illegal and subject to severe punishment. The ethics laws do not enhance sanctions against the most venal and corrupt forms of behavior, which are already prohibited and punished by the criminal code. Nor do ethics laws substantially enhance the risk of getting caught; public employees who are willing to solicit or accept bribes will probably have no compunction about lying on financial disclosure forms. In theory, perhaps those lies would be detected by investigators who routinely scrutinize the forms. In practice, however, there are no such routine investigations. The completed forms are only examined when an individual is under scrutiny for some other reason. Even if forms were audited, only conflicts that were apparent on the forms themselves would be discovered; lies and omissions would not be detectable without substantial investigation. The accumulation of tens of thousands of financial disclosure forms that will never be read is an example of the overreach of the panoptic vision of corruption control.

Although the ethics laws are comprehensive, they are only minimally enforced. In the first instance, enforcement is assigned to a three-member Conflict of Interest Board and the DOI. However, the board is essentially not an enforcement agency, but focuses on policy making, issuing interpretative guidelines and advisory opinions, and overseeing the publication and dissemination of the ethics rules. Indeed, the board views its primary purpose as education, not enforcement.

The board is authorized to receive complaints of misconduct against public servants, to refer appropriate cases to the DOI's commissioner of investigation, and when probable cause exists, to hold hearings to determine whether the conflict-of-interest rules have been breached. The board, however, has only three unpaid (except for per diems) commissioners, four attorneys, and four other staff, but no auditors or investigators.

> The Board's tasks include, among other things, preparing and distributing 12,000 report forms annually, collecting and filing those reports, identifying late-filers and no-filers, considering late-filer's requests for waivers of fines, collecting fines, tracking public servants' appeals of their agency's determination that they must file, filing amendments to reports already on file, initiating enforcement proceedings against non-filers, evaluating filer's privacy requests and responding to disclosure requests from the media and others. . . .
>
> [T]he Board each year receives complaints from others of possible violations of Chapter 68, including referrals from other agencies such as the Department of Investigation. Fifty such complaints have been received since the Board's inception: 8 in 1990; 20 in 1991; and 22 in 1992. Of the 50 complaints, 24 were dismissed as unsupported by evidence or not stating a claim; one was disposed of by stipulation; 18 are under active investigation; seven are the subject of enforcement proceedings.[44]

Perhaps the ethics law has the potential to have a greater effect on Plunkitt's "honest graft"—those kinds of previously lawful self-dealing and opportunity-taking that flowed from governmental position and insider knowledge—than on hard-core graft. Two types of public employees might be affected: (1) those who previously lived by the credo that everything is permissible except that which is clearly prohibited, and (2) those who did not realize that there was anything wrong with personally benefiting from economic opportunities that arise in the course of public employment. The process of filling out the financial disclosure forms will force, or at least provide an opportunity for, both types of public employees to think about conflicts of interest and the legality of their financial arrangements and dealings.

Undoubtedly, there are public servants who, though unwilling to solicit or take bribes, are willing to cut corners or turn a blind eye to ethical norms as long as their wheeling and dealing is not explicitly prohibited. However, public employees who fall into this category will continue to look for loopholes, just as some taxpayers look for loopholes in the tax code. To close every possible loophole is impossible and even undesirable, because it would make public administration more muscle-bound.

A second category of public employees, those who previously were confused about the boundary between the permissible and impermissible and who may have inadvertently violated ethical standards, will now be alerted that something is or may be wrong with a contemplated business arrangement or transaction. They may change their financial relationships accordingly.

Impacts on Public Administration

Ethics legislation represents an effort to translate the "mythical code" of governmental integrity into a positive code that governs day-to-day conduct. This genre of legislation, in the words of Bayless Manning, is "prescriptive, not descriptive."[45] It sends a message from legislators to their constituencies that the government abides by the highest standards of morality, much higher than the standard to which private employees would normally be expected to adhere.

To suggest that governmental ethics legislation must be understood in terms of symbolic politics is not to deny its impact on the real world. The 1989 New York City Charter includes a complex personnel code that has practical consequences for the lives of tens of thousands of New York City employees and for public administration. If an account of such consequences were possible, it would probably show that these administrative consequences are more significant than the impact of the ethics laws on reducing corruption.

Comprehensive ethics legislation will surely prevent some qualified people from entering public service. Some individuals, especially those with substantial wealth, do have financial holdings and relationships that raise actual or potential conflicts of interest, especially when conflicts of interest are broadly defined. In particular, the New York City Charter increases the probability that a conflict of interest will arise by defining the public official's "interests" to include his or her spouse's and unemancipated children's personal finances, economic activities, memberships, and investments.

Ethics legislation may do more than discourage qualified individuals from entering public service. In some circumstances it may force qualified individuals to resign. Chapter 68 provides that a public servant may not have an "ownership interest" in a firm that does business with the city. An ownership interest is defined as managerial control over the firm or an interest held by the public servant, his spouse, or unemancipated children which exceeds $25,000 or 5 percent of the firm. The practical consequence of this provision is that if a public servant's spouse is promoted from an employee to a partner in a firm that does business with the city, even if the spouse is not directly involved in city business, the public servant is left with a Hobson's choice—either the public servant must resign because of the so-called conflict of interest, or the spouse must resign in order to eliminate the conflict of interest (of course, they could divorce). The language of Chapter 68 does not permit the board to grant a waiver or an order requiring the public servant to recuse himself from matters involving the spouse's firm.

The stringent conflict-of-interest rules also create governing problems for public officials. A good example is the 21 April 1990 disqualification of the mayor and city council president from voting on renewal of a cable television franchise for Manhattan. The Conflict of Interest Board barred Mayor David N. Dinkins and City Council President Andrew J. Stein from voting on the renewal because their relatives owned stock in companies that were partners in separate ventures with Time Warner, the media giant that owns interests in the two competing firms. The city's chief lawyer ruled that the two officials could delegate others to vote "independently" in their place. Despite doubts about how anyone in his employ could be independent, Mr. Dinkins named his Deputy Mayor for Public Safety to act in his stead. Mr. Stein began searching for an outsider with no conflict, but he struck out on his first five tries. Floyd Abrams, the noted First Amendment lawyer, declined because his firm represented *The American Lawyer,* a magazine owned by Time Warner. Cyrus R. Vance, the former Secretary of State, passed because his firm represented a Time Warner competitor. Joan Ganz Cooney, the creator of *Sesame Street,* was ruled out because a relative had previous dealings with Time Warner. John Brademas, the president of New York University, was ineligible because some NYU board members and friends had ties to Time Warner. Stein's fifth choice, Michael I. Sovern, the president of Columbia University, declined because Time Warner contributed to Columbia. "The problem," Mr. Stein said, "is Caesar's wife didn't have to run New York." He added, "I'm still searching."[46]

Successful citizens working in the private sector, who constitute a valuable pool from which to recruit commissioners and other key personnel, are especially likely to have real or perceived conflicts of interest. If such individuals are disqualified or scared away from public employment by the disclosure requirements and the "revolving-door" restrictions, public administration will lose a valuable source of recruits. This is especially true of individuals asked to serve on important boards which are not remunerated at all (e.g., the Civilian Review Board).

Further, it would not be surprising if many people decided not to seek or accept a tour of duty in the public sector because they objected to revealing their family's investments, bank accounts, and organizational affiliations.[47] The added burden of being forced to divest an ownership interest (a spouse may have to resign from a partnership or sell a business) presents another disincentive to public service.

After New York City passed its first financial disclosure requirements in 1975, some public employees filed a class action, challenging the law as an invasion of privacy. The trial court held that the disclosure requirements could not pass constitutional muster as long as they failed to provide a way for the disclosing employee to claim an exemption from disclosure of a particular item on privacy grounds. The New York Court of Appeals affirmed.[48]

Following this litigation, the City Council passed an amended disclosure law which, while requiring full disclosure to the board, permits the disclosing employee to flag certain items as arguably exempted from disclosure to the public; the board must rule only if and when there is a request from a member of the public to see the disclosure form. In response, a group of fire fighters went to court arguing that requiring financial disclosure by public employees with little or no policy-making authority adversely affects privacy while serving no substantial public purpose. In *Slevin v. City of New York,* Judge Abraham Soafer upheld the requirement that disclosure be made to the Board of Ethics, but struck down a portion of the law permitting members of the public to see the disclosure form.[49] In a companion case brought by New York City police officers, the Second Circuit Court of Appeals reversed Judge Soafer and upheld the public disclosure requirement. The Second Circuit explained that in light of the extensive police corruption revealed by the Knapp Commission, "the City's interest in public disclosure outweighs the possible infringement of plaintiffs' privacy interests."[50]

On the federal level, the Supreme Court recently struck down as unconstitutional a portion of the 1989 Ethics in Government Act which prohibited high-level federal executive branch employees from accepting compensation for any speeches or articles, even if unrelated to their work.[51] Justice Stevens criticized the law as a "crudely crafted" piece of legislation riddled with arbitrary distinctions (a public official may accept compensation for poems, but not a speech about poetry), and unsupported by any evidence of conflicts of interest or impropriety by public officials. The plaintiffs in the suit included a Food and Drug Administration microbiologist who is also a dance critic, a Goddard Space Flight Center engineer who also lectures on black history, and a Nuclear Regulatory Commission attorney who also writes about Russian history. The Court could not identify how this "blanket burden on the speech of nearly 1.7 million Federal employees" served the goals of preventing corrupt or unethical behavior.

The increasingly stringent restrictions on what jobs public officials can take after they leave public service is bound to have negative effects on both recruitment and retention of individuals. Passage of a New York State ethics law in May 1991 precipitated a rash of resignations among local officials all over the state (except in New York City, which had its own law). The New York State Association of Counties reported over one hundred resignations from county government positions, especially from county health boards, zoning and planning commissions, and community college boards.[52]

Even if these laws do not deter people from seeking or accepting public office, public administration may still suffer if ethics legislation negatively affects morale or if it makes decision making more defensive and slower. The negative impact of ethics laws on morale has been discussed by commentators who argue that public employees perceive comprehensive ethics legislation as presuming their venality and guilt until (continually) proven otherwise.[53] It would hardly be surprising if public employees who feel this way were unenthusiastic and ineffective in carrying out their responsibilities. In addition, the large and increasing number of requests to the Conflict of Interest Board for opinions has led to a significant case backlog; months can go by before the inquiring employee gets an answer, which in itself entails costs. An individual waiting for a decision from the Conflict of Interest Board prior to accepting an offer of employment from the city may decide the hassle is not worth the price and seek opportunities elsewhere. Additionally, a public servant may forfeit an opportunity to teach, lecture, or do volunteer work because of delays in receiving advisory opinions.

Conclusion

The modern-day panoptic reformers view public officials as seekers of corrupt opportunities and government as an organizational form that generates rich opportunities for corruption. Consequently, the panoptic approach to controlling corruption treats public employees like probationers in the criminal justice system. Their routine is governed by increasingly comprehensive administrative/criminal laws, backed by threats of sanctions, including jail, fines, and job and pension forfeiture. These laws have expanded the definition of corruption to cover a broad spectrum of conflicts of interest and even the appearance of conflicts of interest. Moreover, codes restrict nongovernmental employment opportunities and investment decisions. The companion financial disclosure requirements seek to deter conflicts of interest by opening up public officials' financial affairs to public scrutiny.

According to the modern-day architects of the anticorruption project, financial disclosure by public officials must be exhaustive and ongoing. Review must be entrusted to an agency situated outside operational lines of authority. Rather than relying on credentials or professional norms, the crime-control strategy relies on deterrence, surveillance, and investigation.

New York City's ethics legislation has profound implications for public employees and public administration. Some qualified people will be deterred from taking government jobs. Perhaps more important, financial disclosure undermines trust in public administration and public officials. Instead of strengthening public service, ethics legislation might negatively affect morale. Public officials may resent legislation that they perceive to be directed at them or because they have to expose their family finances to public scrutiny. Indeed, they are likely to feel as if others regard them as potential criminals who seek opportunities to enrich themselves and their friends, rather than as trusted public servants who have made financial sacrifices to serve the public.

FIVE

Whistleblowers: Uncovering Wrongdoing at Any Price

> The Congress must also weigh the objective of stronger protection for whis-
> tleblower disclosures against the objectives of management authority and
> accountability. Unrestrained whistleblowing could raise levels of dissidence
> and insubordination to the point where efficiency could be affected.
>
> Comptroller General's Report, Hearings Before
> the House Subcommittee
> on Civil Service, 15 May 1985

Encouraging public employees to disclose information ("blow the whistle")
to officials outside their own agencies, to politicians, or even to the media
about their supervisors' corruption and misfeasance is another important
component of the modern day anticorruption project. A strategy for encouraging "whistleblowing" emerged in the 1970s; it was predicated on the belief that public employees could and would expose a great deal of corruption
and other wrongdoing if they were guaranteed protection from reprisals by
their supervisors. Consequently "whistleblower laws" seek to protect employees who disclose wrongdoing to persons outside the bureaucratic chain
of command by giving outside investigators and agencies the power to look
into the employees' complaints and to prevent the employees from being
disciplined or disadvantaged in any way. While the contribution of whistleblowers to detecting corruption is not measurable, they certainly have direct and indirect effects on public administration; most important, they
undermine the disciplinary authority of agency heads and supervisors over
their subordinates.

Since the early 1980s, twenty-one states have enacted whistleblower
protection laws. The proliferation of these anticorruption laws serves two
purposes: (1) to encourage disclosure of wrongdoing; and (2) to act as a deterrent. According to the Feerick Commission, new whistleblower rules and
regulations help to create an environment in which opportunities and incen-

tives for public officials to abuse the public trust are reduced.[1] The deterrent purpose neatly supports the panoptic vision of corruption control—public officials will be less likely to behave corruptly if they fear that any colleague or subordinate is a potential whistleblower.

The Federal Whistleblowing Initiative

The federal Civil Service Reform Act of 1978 (CSRA) marked the emergence of the whistleblower protection movement. The CSRA created three new organizations: the Office of Personnel Management (OPM), the Merit System Protection Board (MSPB), and the Office of Special Counsel (OSC). The OPM is the general administrator of the civil service system and has no direct responsibility for enforcing whistleblower protections. The MSPB is authorized to hold hearings and appeals of federal employees' grievances. The OSC, an external control agency, is charged with investigating whistleblower allegations of waste, fraud, and abuse, and complaints by federal employees claiming to have suffered reprisal for

> the lawful disclosure of information that the employee reasonably believed evidenced: (1) a violation of any law, rule, or regulation, or (2) mismanagement, a gross waste of funds, an abuse of authority, or a substantial and specific danger to public health or safety.[2]

The law protects the whistleblowing employee from such negative personnel actions as demotion, termination, and transfer, and also from negative inactions such as failure to promote. Proponents of increased whistleblower protection argue that more law is required because it is not unusual for whistleblowers to experience adverse consequences following a disclosure. Lobbying for a more comprehensive whistleblower law, Senator David Pryor stated that "in the cruel world of the bureaucracy, most Government whistleblowers can expect extraordinary efforts by their own agency to shut them up, to discredit them, or to eliminate them."[3]

A decade later, Congress held hearings on the effectiveness of the Civil Service Reform Act's whistleblower protections. Many people, both for and against increased whistleblower protections, testified, including members of Congress, whistleblowers, OSC and MSPB officials, and representatives of organizations like the Whistleblower Coalition and the Government Accountability Project. Some witnesses charged that the CSRA provided inadequate protection to whistleblowers. Most of the blame was laid at the OSC's doorstep. Senator Carl Levin called the attitude of former special counsels "lackadaisical," claiming that one of them warned potential whistleblowers, "[u]nless you are in a position to retire or are independently wealthy, don't do it. Don't put your head up because it will be blown off."[4] Moreover, Harold Hipple, a former Veteran's Administration employee who claimed he had been fired after blowing the whistle on a supervisor, testified that it took the OSC four months to schedule an interview. Hipple stated that the OSC took no written statements during his interview and interviewed no witnesses to the police brutality he had alleged.[5] Witnesses from the Government Accountability Project and the Whistleblower Coalition offered similar examples of OSC apathy.

The OSC representative admitted that the agency had not yet lived up to expectations, but attributed its shortcomings to inexperience. OSC Special Counsel William O'Connor urged Congress to maintain the status quo now that the OSC had become "a properly disciplined investigative and prosecutive force. . . . More law is not what makes the country work better."[6]

There was never any doubt that the hearings would result in a recommendation for greater whistleblower protections. Supporters of increased protections cited a 1983 MSPB study which found that 37 percent of federal employees would not blow the whistle for fear of reprisal.[7] Opponents of stronger whistleblower laws questioned the importance of the study:

> It's in the nature of all of us to be reluctant to come forward, and I suspect whatever bill is passed, if you go out and take a survey of the federal workforce, or a corporate workforce for that matter, you're going to get probably the same minimal percentage of people saying they are concerned about coming forward. I don't know that you can ever address that legislatively.[8]

Nonetheless, the Whistleblower Protection Act of 1989[9] strengthened the whistleblowing machinery in five ways:

1. It made the OSC more independent of the MSPB so that it would be an advocate for self-proclaimed whistleblowers, rather than a watchdog for the merit system.
2. It permitted whistleblowers the option of bypassing the OSC entirely and taking their complaints directly to the MSPB.
3. It lowered the standard of proof necessary to make out a case of protected whistleblowing. The employee must show that his or her disclosure of information was "a factor" (rather than the *predominant or motivating factor*) in the subsequent negative personnel action or inaction.
4. It provided that once an employee showed that the disclosure was a factor in the negative personnel action or inaction, the burden of proof shifted to the agency, which must prove that it would have taken the same personnel actions regardless of the disclosure.
5. It authorized lawyers' fees in the event that the whistleblower prevailed before the MSPB.

The apparent premise underlying the 1989 Act is that whistleblowers' allegations are generally true. Therefore, the OSC must operate under the assumption that any change in employment status or the work environment following a disclosure is more likely than not a reprisal.

In 1994, the Senate introduced a new anticorruption law (the Anticorruption Act) designed to expand the federal government's role in punishing and preventing public corruption at the federal, state, and local levels.[10] One section of the proposed Act provided for greatly expanded whistleblower protection, which significantly departed from current state and federal whistleblower laws. Most existing whistleblower laws contain a reporting requirement, which specifies to whom the whistleblower must report wrongdoing, whether agency heads or supervisors must be notified of the wrongdoing before an external agency can be notified, and the standard of wrongdoing covered by the law (e.g., gross mismanagement, waste, abuse of authority, or "reasonable belief" that the law has been violated). The proposed Anticorruption Act contained no reporting requirement. Furthermore, while most existing whistleblower laws provide for backpay and reinstatement, the proposed Act authorized *treble* backpay and *up to five years imprisonment* for retaliating employers.

The proposed expansion of whistleblower protections ignores the importance of management control and efficiency in the workplace. Some public employees facing layoffs or legitimate discipline will surely be tempted to claim whistleblower status. An employee may report accusations regarding virtually anything (use of government word processors for personal matters) to virtually anyone (a tabloid), and, in the event of a disciplinary retaliation, he or she obtain substantial damages. The proposed Act provides no safeguards, such as reverse attorney fees or penalties, to prevent bad-faith whistleblowers from flooding the OSC, the Department of Justice, or other government agencies with information about insignificant, lawful, or fabricated managerial "retaliation."

New York City's Whistleblower Law

The federal legislation in 1978 and 1989 triggered a slew of state and local whistleblower laws.[11] New York City's whistleblower law[12] was passed in 1983 in the wake of a small scandal involving disciplinary action against an analyst who reported mismanagement of the city's medicare program. When the media exposed this retaliation, it triggered a call for remedial legislation. Mayor Koch reinstated the employee and proposed an ordinance patterned after, but even stronger than, the federal whistleblower law. One extraordinary provision, which did not pass, would have *required,* on pain of dismissal, city employees to report any evidence of corruption or conflicts of interests that came to their attention.[13] This proposal would have gone far toward institutionalizing the kind of pervasive monitoring and reporting that Foucault anticipated.[14]

The New York City whistleblower law prohibits retaliatory personnel actions against employees who disclose information to the Department of Investigation or the City Council about "corruption, criminal activity or conflict of interest by another city officer or employee, which concerns his or her office or employment, or by persons dealing with the city, which concerns their dealings with the city." This law was designed to encourage city employees who previously were afraid to come forward with evidence or suspicion of corruption, or who were reluctant to take complaints outside the agency's chain of command in order to communicate directly with the Department of Investigation.[15]

While other cases are investigated by the DOI's inspectors general (IGs), who are assigned to specific agencies and are therefore reasonably familiar with agency procedures and operations, whistleblower cases are investigated by the DOI's central staff. Most DOI personnel, and almost all central staff investigators, are recruited from outside city government. It is almost inevitable, and in fact part of the law's design, that there will be an adversarial and even hostile relationship between the DOI and the executive agencies in whistleblower cases.

Once a city employee claims to have suffered retaliation for whistleblowing, the DOI *must* investigate.[16] As a matter of course, DOI personnel interview the whistleblower's supervisor and colleagues. When the investigation is completed, which can take months, the DOI issues its report and recommendations to the whistleblower's agency head. The agency head must accept or reject the findings of the investigation without benefit of the interview transcripts. While the DOI cannot compel an agency head to follow its recommendations, it may be professionally risky to reject a DOI recommendation that favors the whistleblower, since this could be interpreted as "being soft on corruption" or, even worse, as corrupt in itself.

One New York City department's experience with whistleblower cases illustrates the kind of tensions that this anticorruption strategy can generate. G. P. (not the individual's real initials), accused coworkers of corruption at around the same time that the agency attempted to fire him for poor work. Because the complaint of corruption came first, the DOI investigated the situation and declared the employee a whistleblower. The agency's case against G. P. included a long list of complaints from citizens about arbitrary and abusive treatment. The agency also had considerable documentation of G. P.'s poor work record. According to the commissioner, his productivity was less than half of the average for workers in his job category.

The DOI investigators sought to determine who, if anyone, was responsible for unlawfully retaliating against G. P. Once the DOI became involved, the operating agency had to suspend its disciplinary action against G. P.; it could neither remove nor transfer him while the investigation was pending. The DOI's investigative posture presumes retaliation and shifts the burden of proof to the agency to show a legitimate reason for the negative personnel action. Because interview transcripts and other evidence are not available to the agency, the DOI's presumption of retaliation is difficult to rebut. In the G. P. case, it took the DOI *four years* to close its investigation and approve his termination. By this time, the agency head refused to act for fear of triggering criticism. According to an agency administrator, "paranoia was pervasive. DOI was running scared because of its reputation in the 1980s, and our commissioner was afraid of appearing to approve of retaliation, even after DOI relented." It took *two more years,* a change of leadership in the agency and in the DOI, and a full hearing by the Office of Administrative Trials and Hearings (OATH), to finally remove G. P. In the meantime, the productivity of other employees in G. P.'s unit plummeted. Morale, a supervisor noted, hit an all-time low.

A second case in the same agency involved P. P., who reported an incident of corruption to the agency IG. The IG found the allegation baseless. P. P. then falsely told his coworkers that he had filed corruption complaints against them. When his supervisor reprimanded him for spreading disinformation, P. P. again complained to the DOI, which now labeled him a whistleblower. He began skipping work and neglecting duties. The agency head demoted him. P. P. filed yet another complaint with the DOI. More than six months later, the DOI agreed with the agency and withdrew the whistleblower designation. Then P. P. sued the city for violating its whistleblower law. The corporation counsel decided that fighting even a defrocked whistleblower would look bad and agreed to a monetary settlement.

In yet a third incident involving this same agency, an investigator in the agency's disciplinary unit correctly anticipated that he was about to be fired. He told the DOI that personnel in his unit had covered up certain cases that would have embarrassed the agency. During the investigation, which dragged on for two years, the disciplinary unit all but ceased to function. Its managers spent much of their time consulting lawyers about DOI's investigation. Finally, the DOI withdrew the presumption of retaliation and the cover-up charge.

A top DOI official estimates that not more than a dozen employees a year lodge complaints with the DOI about retaliation for whistleblowing,[17] but nobody at the DOI or any other city agency has tried to determine what percentage of whistleblower cases have produced credible information about corrupt or other illegal activity. That fact alone testifies to the failure to integrate corruption control with public administration.

Effects on Public Administration

The Senate Committee which drafted the 1989 federal whistleblower law recognized that protecting whistleblowers *could conceivably* provide a cover for incompetent employees who might falsely claim whistleblower protection in order to fend off legitimate disciplinary action.

> The section should not be construed as protecting an employee who is otherwise engaged in misconduct, or who is incompetent, from appropriate disciplinary action. If, for example, an employee has had several years of inadequate performance, or unsatisfactory performance ratings, or if an employee has engaged in an action which would constitute grounds for dismissal for cause, the fact that the employee "blows the whistle" on his agency after the agency has begun to initiate disciplinary action against the employee will not protect the employee against such disciplinary action.[18]

While the Senate Committee spotted the problem, it offered no remedies for avoiding it. Rather, the senators simply reasserted their confidence in the value of this anticorruption control.

> Protecting employees who disclose government illegality, waste, and corruption is a major step toward an effective civil service. In the vast federal bureaucracy it is not difficult to conceal wrongdoing provided that no one summons the courage to disclose the truth. Whenever misdeeds take place in a federal agency, there are employees who know that it has occurred, and who are outraged by it. What is needed is a means to assure them that they will not suffer if they help uncover and correct administrative abuses.[19]

Inevitably, some disgruntled, incompetent, or otherwise poorly performing employees will file whistleblower claims in order to keep their jobs as long as possible or simply to harass their supervisors. Interestingly, when an evaluation showed that the OSC rejected the vast majority of whistleblower claims for being ill-founded, Congress interpreted this as a failing on the part of the OSC rather than as evidence of complainants' misuse of the whistleblower machinery. Thus, the whistleblower law was amended to further protect complainants, and the OSC was reorganized into an agency whose sole mission is to protect whistleblowers, rather than to protect the integrity of the civil service merit system. Further, the law was amended to remove almost completely the agency head from participation in the investigation. Thus, Congress has indicated its belief that top officials in the executive branch not only refuse to take seriously complaints of wrongdoing and mismanagement in their agencies, but commonly retaliate against those who make such allegations.[20]

It is worth asking whether and to what degree the encouragement of whistleblowing undermines authority and efficiency in public agencies.[21] Top public-sector managers worry about the consequences of firing or otherwise disciplining disgruntled employees.[22] The employee may level spurious charges against her supervisors, claim that the disciplinary action is a reprisal for whistleblowing, and at no expense to herself can generate a time-consuming and resource-draining investigation that will drag on for months or even years.[23] During this time her supervisors' authority over her will be very limited. If the disciplinary action is ultimately reversed on the grounds that it was retaliatory, the supervisor loses face and authority, while the agency suffers from lowered productivity and morale. This may deter the agency's managers from attempting to discipline poorly performing employees in the future.

A New York City agency administrator, a former IG, assessed the whistleblower program as follows:

> The whistleblower laws are so broad and give investigators so much power that they are easily abused, and they have been abused. There are simply no checks. In all areas of litigation, lawyers will pore over materials to be sure that there is nothing they might have missed that will be picked up by the other side. In whistleblower proceedings there is no other side, so it has not been necessary for the DOI to be very careful about who it backs or what kind of evidence allegations are based on. There's a real need for some neutral arbiter in the process. It is commonplace, currently, for people's reputations to be impugned in press releases before those people have had a chance to respond or are even aware of what's been said about them.

Whistleblower rules reinforce centralized public administration. By definition, whistleblowing calls the honesty and legitimacy of agency management into question. Creating mechanisms by which employees can lodge complaints and charges outside the chain of command may bring to light more high-level corruption, but the evidence is inconclusive. Of practical concern is whether managers will be deterred from enforcing discipline. The three cases discussed above are widely known and serve as cautionary tales for New York City managers. It has become rational for a manager to tolerate an ineffective or abusive employee, given the enormous trouble that will result if the employee impugns the manager's honesty with a whistleblower complaint. Without speedier determination of the validity of whistleblower claims, false claimants will remain on the job poisoning the atmosphere and undermining the manager's authority.

Conclusion: The Politics of Whistleblower Legislation

Anticorruption reformers focus on the corrosive effects of corruption on governing; they do not deal with, or even admit, the negative impacts of anticorruption controls on public administration. The politics of corruption and reform inevitably spawns proposals for more and tougher anticorruption controls. Yet there has been a steady stream of recommendations to pass legislation that is increasingly protective of the whistleblower. For example, Elizabeth Holtzman, New York City comptroller from 1989 to 1993, labeled the city's law totally inadequate and recommended legislation that would create a new corruption-fighting agency, the Office of Special Counsel (OSC), which "would not be controlled by anyone." Holtzman's proposals are similar to the federal Anticorruption Act, which has been considered and rejected by Congress each year since 1991. They are also consistent with many contemporary proposals to create completely independent monitoring agencies. According to Holtzman's vision, "the OSC would investigate allegations of retaliation, defend whistleblowers against retaliation at no cost to them, and receive and investigate disclosures of improper government actions from public employees."[24] She proposed that public employees be authorized to make disclosures of "misdeeds" to law enforcement agencies *or the media,* not just to the DOI and the City Council as current law provides. Moreover, under Holtzman's proposal, if the disclosure results in a cost savings to the public, the whistleblower is eligible for a $2,000 reward.

The Feerick Commission pointed out that the Talent Bank (discussed in chapter 3) might never have been uncovered had not a courageous public employee come forward to the commission. According to the commission, this showed the critical importance of mobilizing rank-and-file public employees to help control corruption.

> Having been struck by the frequency with which public employees evinced concern that they would be punished for undertaking what the Commission regarded as an important civic responsibility—namely, the disclosure of possible government misconduct to the appropriate public authorities—we

turned our attention to the New York State whistleblower law. We examined
the law to determine whether it is adequate to discourage and remedy wrongful
retaliation against those who disclose misconduct by government officials (or
whether, to the contrary, the widespread concern of public employees is reasonable). We have concluded that the protection provided to public employees
who reveal wrongdoing is too limited to reduce the legitimate fear of reprisal
that employees experience.[25]

Although it had no empirical information on reprisals against state employees who disclosed evidence of fraud, waste, and abuse to their supervisors or others, the commission offered sweeping recommendations
similar to Holtzman's. The Feerick Commission advocated: permitting public employees to complain directly to an outside agency rather than trying to
resolve the matter through agency channels; freezing any adverse employment action from the time a complaint is lodged until the investigation is
completed; and expanding the type of "improper governmental actions"
covered by the whistleblower laws.[26]

The protection and encouragement of whistleblowers is one facet of the
emerging panoptic vision of corruption control. It encourages all employees
to be investigators and activists in the anticorruption project. The whistleblower machinery itself is a good example of the entrenchment of external control mechanisms. This machinery is predicated on the belief that
the bureaucracy cannot effectively police itself. It assumes that anticorruption responsibility can only be effectively discharged by those who are independent of and have no stake in the target agency's reputation. However,
such people are also likely to have little information about the agency's operations and no interest in whether the agency achieves its goals. Furthermore, this whistleblowing machinery empowers the rank and file at the
expense of their managers and encourages an agencies' most disgruntled
employees to come forward with even spurious complaints. Undoubtedly,
some of the whistleblowers' complaints will have merit, but the overall
value of this corruption control must be weighed against the direct and indirect costs to effective public administration.

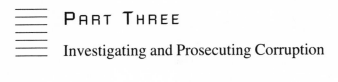

PART THREE

Investigating and Prosecuting Corruption

Six

Internal Government Investigation:
The Panopticon in New York City

> True, the Department [of Investigation] as presently organized is one of the finest examples of a staff agency applying the scientific method to the problem of public administration. . . . Here lies the fundamental challenge of the Department of Investigation. How far can we apply the methods of intelligence, in this case the technique of scientific reform, to problems of government? To what extent should such methods be applied within the framework of a representative government responsive to the popular will?
>
> Commissioner of Investigation William Herlands, Preface
> to Harold Seidman's *Investigating Municipal Corruption:*
> *A Study of the New York City Department of Investigation*

> In May 1980, the primary mission of the Department was simply affirmed as, "to protect the integrity of City government." . . . The Commissioner of Investigation was no longer the fact-finder, the "eyes and ears" of the Mayor, who was as concerned with governmental efficiency as with criminality. Rather, the detection and deterrence of criminal activities was the paramount function of the Department.
>
> Richard S. Winslow and David W. Burke, *Rogues, Rascals, and Heroes:*
> *A History of the New York City Department of Investigation*

No component of the anticorruption project better illustrates the triumph of the panoptic vision of corruption control than the New York City Department of Investigation (DOI). New York City is unique among government entities in the United States in having a large executive agency whose primary mission is to investigate and prevent official corruption. This chapter examines the evolution of the Department of Investigation from an agency specializing in good government and administrative reform to an agency which, augmented by an inspectors-general system, specializes in a law-enforcement style of anticorruption investigation. The DOI's transformation illustrates the evolution of the anticorruption project, demonstrating the extent to which, under the panoptic vision, corruption control has become an end rather than a means to more effective governing.

The Evolution of the Department of Investigation

The DOI's origins can be traced to 1873 when the state legislature created the Office of the Commissioners of Accounts (OCA) in response to the scandals surrounding Boss Tweed's ring, which extorted and swindled money from legislators, businessmen, contractors, clergymen, lawyers, and a host of others.[1] Initially, the City Charter issued a narrow mandate to the OCA to act as a fiscal check on the comptroller and chamberlain, two centers of theft and corruption during Tweed's reign.[2] The legislature envisioned the OCA addressing both corruption and administrative problems in public administration, primarily by auditing the books and accounts of city agencies to make sure employees were not looting the city's funds. The early commissioners quickly expanded their inquiries beyond quarterly examinations of the comptroller's and chamberlain's books, and began examining the accounts of many city agencies.[3]

The OCA served a staff function for the mayor, who could call upon its investigative resources to "ferret out the facts" on such matters as "sanitary conditions in bakeries and meat stores, standards of measure in the retail milk business" or the nefarious activities of a borough president.[4] Rather than waiting for the next scandal to arise, the OCA sought to identify areas of waste, abuse, and inefficiency and recommended measures that would promote governmental effectiveness. However, its recommendations were mostly ignored.[5]

In 1898, after issuing a report excoriating waste and fraud on a Fifth Avenue repaving project, the OCA established an Engineering Bureau to monitor contract specifications, bidding procedures, and the entire public works process. The bureau fulfilled these responsibilities so competently that, within a decade, it was recognized as an outstanding contributor to civil engineering; other cities adopted a number of its findings on the fitness of building materials and techniques.[6]

Corruption detection and prevention was just one part of the OCA's multifaceted responsibility to make government more effective. Mayor George B. McClellan (1904–9) characterized the OCA as "an active agency for carrying out the program of research and investigation which will show where the government of the city should be strengthened and its efficiency increased."[7] Similarly, the OCA commissioners of the Progressive Era regarded corruption as a symptom of underlying problems in agency administration and operations, and they looked to organizational and administrative reforms as the predominant remedial strategies. Thus, the 1901 New York City Charter required that at least one of the OCA's commissioners be a certified public accountant.[8]

Commissioner John Purroy Mitchel (1907–9) changed the focus of the OCA from accounting and bookkeeping review to "investigating all phases of municipal government."[9] Under the leadership of Commissioner Raymond "Fearless" Fosdick (1909–12), Mitchel's successor, the OCA reached its pinnacle as a stimulator of administrative reform.[10] Fosdick, who described the OCA as the "Mayor's eye," earned the nickname "Fearless" as a result of investigations targeting police corruption.[11] Continuing the work begun by Mitchel, Commissioner Fosdick pursued not only corruption, but "studied consumer protection and other public problems and attempted to set up standards of governmental efficiency."[12] Fosdick and his talented staff operated the OCA as if it had a general mandate to improve city government. In his own words:

> There is probably no other branch of the City government which possesses greater possibilities for the support of an efficient administration. . . . The potential power and utility of this Commission and the fact that it was designed for a broader purpose than technical audits, have only been recently brought prominently to notice. Its exceptionally far-reaching inquisitorial powers, and the broad use to which they may be put by the Mayor in the furtherance of efficient administration are developments of the last two or three years. With its double powers of audit and investigation, this Commission is peculiarly fitted not only to detect official misconduct and incompetency, but to suggest new methods and systems to prevent waste and inefficiency. Furthermore, it is in an excellent position to collect in authoritative and official form all possible information concerning the conduct of public business.[13]

Fearless Fosdick turned his attention to whatever harmed the public or undermined government efficiency. For example, he reported that by eliminating overstaffing and poor scheduling in the Bureau of Ferries, the city could save $150,000 a year. Other Fosdick investigations and recommendations led to centralized probation, placing the Board of Elections under the control of the presiding justice of the Appellate Division, and abolishing borough collection of licensing fees. Fosdick's initiatives led to the creation of New York City's first consumer protection unit, which investigated private businesses licensed or regulated by the city. He ordered investigations of the courts, the Departments of Fire, Police, Health, and Parks, the Municipal Reference Library, Bellevue Hospital, and a host of other agencies and organizations, and he eliminated the County Coroner's office.[14]

In addition, Fosdick bolstered the OCA's quasi–law enforcement role; his investigations produced bribery convictions of the Queens borough president and numerous city employees and officials. Fosdick, however, always maintained that the OCA's most important role was "to prevent errors and defalcations by suggesting and installing proper methods of control, [rather] than to detect inaccuracies and losses after they have occurred."[15]

If anything, the OCA achieved even more prominence in 1914, when former OCA commissioner John Purroy Mitchel became mayor (1914–1917). (It was during Mitchel's incumbency that Lincoln Steffins wrote his classic book, *Shame of the Cities,* in which he cited New York City as an outstanding example of honest government.) The OCA was assigned expanded responsibilities by the 1916 charter and by mayoral executive orders. A new Bureau of Efficiency was established within the OCA with the mandate to apply "scientific management principles" to city agencies.

The OCA's fortunes waxed and waned with various mayors. In 1918, the election of Tammany's mayoral candidate, John Hylan (1918–25), ended a decade of Progressive reform. Tammany's passion was patronage, not efficient administration, and certainly not corruption control. Mayor Hylan abolished the Bureau of Efficiency and left the OCA to atrophy. (In 1924, the name of the agency was changed to the Department of Investigation and Accounts;[16] a few years later it was shortened to the Department of Investigation.)

The next Tammany mayor, the notoriously corrupt "Gentleman" Jimmy Walker (1926–32), had even less use for the DOI. Walker's DOI Commissioner of Investigation, Joseph Warren, relegated the DOI to simple accounting functions. Warren lamented that in the past twenty years, the department's most important work (accounting and auditing) had "been largely neglected, while the activities of the Department were being devoted to extraneous and immaterial matters."[17] During Warren's first year as commissioner, he produced 281 financial reports and conducted only six investigations of non-financial matters.[18]

Mayor Walker frequently used the department as a "burial ground" for scandal. When media outrage over a corrupt pier-leasing scheme reached the boiling point, Mayor Walker announced that a DOI investigation was under way. Nothing was ever done.[19] Critics complained that

> because the Mayor is the Mayor, he is given a newspaper headline every time he announces that an "investigation" will be made of some scandal in his administration. The public indignation dies down pending the outcome of the investigation, and months later everyone has forgotten that no result of the investigation was ever announced.[20]

A severe blow was dealt to Mayor Walker and Tammany Hall when the state legislature created a commission (headed by Judge Samuel Seabury) to investigate corruption in New York City government. The work of the Seabury Commission, as it came to be known, has been characterized as the "biggest investigation in the history of an American municipality."[21] The thoroughness of Judge Seabury's three-year inquisition has not been surpassed in the history of municipal investigations. Seabury and his staff exposed bribery, bid-rigging, extortion, kickbacks, and fraud in many city agencies, including the Sheriff's Department, the Police Department, the Magistrate's Court, relief agencies, public transport companies, public sewer and road construction bureaus, and the Board of Standards and Appeals.[22] Further, the Seabury Commission revealed that Mayor Walker ignored or suppressed the DOI's few corruption investigations and reports. Governor Franklin Roosevelt summoned Mayor Walker to Albany and forced his resignation, causing Walker to flee to Europe.

The widespread corruption of Mayor Walker's administration swept the Republican and Fusion candidate, Fiorello LaGuardia, into the mayoralty.[23] Not surprisingly, during LaGuardia's three-term reign (1934–45), the DOI was predominantly corruption-oriented. One plank in LaGuardia's campaign platform was the establishment of a Bureau of Complaints within the DOI, to which citizens could bring information and allegations about corruption.[24] In 1933, the year before the Bureau of Complaints was installed, only 113 complaints were filed with the DOI. In 1934, the new bureau processed six thousand citizen complaints.

In 1938, LaGuardia appointed William Herlands to be commissioner of investigation. Herlands, continuing the trend started by Commissioners Mitchel and Fosdick, focused on dishonesty, waste, inefficiency, and neglect of duty. One investigation led to the conviction of the secretary of the Department of Finance for embezzling $80,000. Another revealed that the city had been defrauded out of hundreds of thousands of dollars by corruption in the award of printing contracts.

The transformation of the DOI into an organ of intragovernmental anticorruption investigation and enforcement had begun, although Herlands also supported the DOI's role as an instrument of administrative reform. He appointed two deputies, one for field investigations and the other for preparing reports and studies. He also established a Division of Coordination and Research, which hired college students to conduct studies of agencies, programs, and problems. The 1938 Annual Report noted as follows:

> In making investigations, the Department does not limit itself to the particular abuse uncovered or the specific complaint. It treats the individual irregu-

larities complained of as symptomatic of broader underlying deficiencies in municipal government and administration. The suggestions and recommendations contained in these reports are designed to remove the deficiencies.[25]

Three years later, Harold Seidman, a member of Herlands' staff, in his book on the history of the DOI, observed,

> Although the courts have ruled that the Department is not a part of the police system or legal department of the City, a superficial examination of its work has probably engendered the mistaken belief that it is nothing more than a highly specialized police force assigned exclusively to detecting and prosecuting the crimes of City employees. . . .
>
> A crime is not considered as an isolated case but as a single factor in a complex situation. It is the Department's function to draft plans designed to prevent similar crimes in the future.
>
> The Department is a major force for honest government. Its mere existence tends to discourage City officials who would violate their trust. More important and more permanent, however, are the contributions of both the Department of Investigation and the Office of the Commissioners of Accounts to progressive administrative reform. Perhaps no other office has done so much to improve the government of New York City.[26]

After the LaGuardia mayoralty, clubhouse politics regained its ascendancy, and the DOI's investigations primarily involved corruption by low-level employees, particularly building inspectors.[27] LaGuardia's successor, William O'Dwyer (1946–50), resigned as a result of alleged graft involving the fire and police commissioners, poor administration, and alleged ties to organized crime. Independent DOI commissioners like Fosdick and Herlands were succeeded by commissioners more concerned with pleasing the mayor than ferreting out corruption. Indeed, Mayor O'Dwyer's DOI commissioner, John Murtagh, viewed the DOI as "the bromo-seltzer for the Mayor." Murtagh was later charged with misdemeanor "neglect of duty" based on his actions (or inactions) while serving as commissioner. He allegedly failed to report the results of seventeen police corruption investigations and ignored complaints of payoffs and bribes to police officers.[28]

In 1961, a state commission came close to branding the DOI corrupt. The commission, chaired by the highly respected Whitney North Seymour, Jr., issued a blistering report on widespread corruption in New York City. The report bluntly alleged that Mayor Robert Wagner (1954–65), his agency heads, and the commissioner of investigation had attempted to stonewall the commission's investigation:

Whenever new disclosures have been made through investigations by the [commission], the City embarked upon a program of harassing the witnesses, issuing loud and irresponsible charges against the investigators, and doing its utmost to sweep all evidence of wrongdoing under the rug. Officials on every level of City government have participated in efforts to divert public attention from the facts they are unwilling to face or correct. This complete vacuum in moral leadership is probably the most serious defect in present-day City government disclosed by our investigation.[29]

The commission's harshest criticism was leveled at the DOI:

[The DOI's] brazen interference continued throughout our various investigations. The City Department of Investigation constantly blocked access to City files, dogged the trail of our witnesses, and cross-examined City employees to find out what they had told our staff. At every turn the efforts of the [commission] were met with a stubborn and vindictive rear guard action by the man whose sworn obligation it was to root out corruption. The Commissioner's conduct clearly suggested that he was much more interested in hiding the City's dirty linen than in cleaning it.[30]

The Modern Department of Investigation as a Law-Enforcement Agency

Beginning in the mid-1950s, the DOI evolved inexorably into a law-enforcement agency whose primary goal was to investigate possible cases of corruption with an eye toward prosecution. A significant step in the DOI's evolution came with the Abraham Beame administration (1974–77) and the appointment of Nicholas Scopetta as DOI Commissioner. Scopetta, a former prosecutor and commissioner of the Waterfront Commission, spent his first months in office identifying areas of city government likely to be affected by corruption. He placed the inspectional agencies, particularly the Department of Buildings, at the top of the list. Scopetta and Deputy DOI Commissioner Stanley Lupkin launched an intensive investigation that utilized undercover agents, witnesses, and informants. Wearing "wires," the informants recorded over six hundred hours of incriminating conversations between inspectors and contractors. In its sophistication, duration, comprehensiveness, and coordination with other agencies, this investigation marked a milestone in the DOI's history and its emergence as a modern law-enforcement agency (see tables 1 and 2). According to the DOI's report to Mayor Beame,

We found that the highest ranking employees of the Buildings Department enforcement section are not immune from corruption. Of the 95 employees

Table 1   DOI Arrests and Referrals

Arrests/Referrals	1966–77[a]	1978–89[b]	Total
Arrests			
City employees (crimes related to city business)	373	579	952
Nonemployees	229	573	802
City employees (crimes not related to city business)	10	22	32
Nonemployees (crimes unrelated to city business)	19	68	87
Unknown employment status (crimes related to city business)	128	84	212
Unknown employment status (crimes unrelated to city business)	15	0	15
Unknown employment status and unknown crime category	85	208	293
Referrals[c]			
City employees referred for serious crimes related to city business	157	408	565
Unknown employment status, referred for alleged crimes related to city business	9	8	17
Totals	1,025	1,950	2,975

Source: New York City Department of Investigation

[a]Information on referrals available only for 1973–77

[b]Information on arrests and referrals available only up to 2/89

[c]Referrals to prosecuting authorities are for alleged serious offenses related to city business by city employees or others where there is no indication of arrests

against whom we obtained evidence of criminal conduct, 9 are executives who shoulder top management responsibilities, 15 are supervisors, and 43 are inspectors. The other 28 include plans examiners and employees in the office support categories, such as clerks and typists.[31]

The days of studious OCA reports on administrative, operational, and organizational issues were gone. From this point on, DOI commissioners would be drawn from the law-enforcement community and would view their agency as an integral part of that community.

Commissioner Stanley Lupkin, who succeeded Scopetta, argued that prosecutorial experience was necessary for inspectors general because, "in virtually every case where the target was a city employee, there was the possibility of criminal prosecution."[32] His 1982 summary of major cases for the previous three years shows how the DOI's priorities had evolved:

Table 2 Annual Budget and Staff Increases and Decreases (percentage above or below previous year)

FY	Budget	Full-Time Employees	Change from Previous Year
1978–79	−0.63%	86	+6.97%
1979–1980	+5.39%	92	−3.26
1980–81	+13.91%	89	−2.25
1981–82	+13.39%	87	+5.75
1982–83	+9.33%	92	−2.17
1983–84	+11.57%	90	+3.33
1984–85	+50.84%	93	+20.43
1985–86	+4.61%	112	+8.04
1986–87	+142.17%	121	+142.98
1987–88	+88.09%	294	+119.05
1988–89	+8.42%	644	+1.71
1989–90	+2.8%	655	−13.44
1990–91	−15.76%	501	−21.87

Source: Annual New York City Mayor's Management Report

- Sixteen felony convictions of city employees and contractors involving more than $100,000 in kickbacks for maintenance and repair contracts in city-owned residential buildings.

- Six convictions of employees of a private security firm for systematically stealing millions of dollars during daily collections from parking meters.

- Three convictions of principals of fuel oil companies which billed the city nearly $4 million for heating oil that was never delivered to city-owned residential buildings.

- Fifteen arrests of Taxi and Limousine Commission inspectors, Department of Environmental Protection inspectors, and garage owners and mechanics for payoffs in exchange for waiving cab-safety emission inspections.

- More than 125 arrests and indictments for bribes of Consumer Affairs inspectors, by supermarket employees, food company agents, and corporations, for ignoring consumer protection violations.

- A year-long study of the Transit Authority that led to a series of arrests and penalties involving senior officials for conflicts of interest, negligence, and waste.

The DOI's 1983 "Operation Ampscam" is another excellent illustration of the DOI's evolution as a law-enforcement agency specializing in official corruption. The DOI created two undercover electrical contracting companies and had them apply for permission to turn on power at twenty-five derelict buildings supposedly under renovation. None of the buildings met electrical code standards. Nevertheless, electrical inspectors approved turn-on permits for all twenty-five buildings. Of the fifteen inspectors involved, thirteen accepted bribes.[33]

Operation Ampscam also revealed a "pad" in the inspectional division: inspectors had to turn over half their bribe money to their supervisors. Sometimes, supervisors received payoffs directly from contractors. Ultimately, twelve inspectors and two borough supervisors were indicted on federal charges. All but one of the defendants pleaded guilty. As a result of the sting, the Department of General Service's Bureau of Electrical Control was transferred to the Department of Buildings.

Mayor Edward I. Koch (1978–89) appointed strong DOI commissioners, kept budgets high, and in the wake of the 1986 Parking Violations Bureau (PVB) scandals, supported the merger of the inspectors-general system into the DOI. As a result of media attacks and allegations that his administration was mired in corruption, the mayor could not afford to drag his heels or take half-hearted remedial measures in response to fraud and corruption. Mayor Koch appointed Kenneth Conboy, former special counsel to the police commissioner and the former New York City criminal justice coordinator, as commissioner of investigation. A highly respected figure in law-enforcement circles, Conboy moved swiftly to reestablish the DOI's credibility. He recruited individuals with law-enforcement experience to fill the top positions of first deputy commissioner, deputy commissioner for management, assistant commissioner for corruption prevention, background investigation, fingerprinting, and Complaints Bureau, and assistant commissioner in charge of the inspector-general system. Conboy convinced the U.S. attorneys for the Southern and Eastern Districts of New York, the five county prosecutors, and the New York State Organized Crime Task Force to "cross-designate" DOI lawyers as special deputies on cases they jointly investigated. Thereafter, it became customary for DOI personnel to participate in joint law-enforcement task forces utilizing police and other city employees as operatives in the creation of dummy businesses (stings) to infiltrate criminal relationships and enterprises. Conboy also inaugurated "field associate" programs whereby recruits in some agencies secretly functioned as DOI informers.[34]

Inspectors-General System

One of the most important developments for the DOI was the establishment, under its aegis, of the inspectors-general (IG) system.[35] The IG system can be traced to Mayor Lindsay's August 1970 executive order requiring each agency to "establish a procedure to receive complaints by the general public."[36] The executive order also required each agency head to designate one or more subordinates to investigate these complaints. This marked the first time in New York City history that executive agency heads were assigned responsibility for preventing corruption. The DOI supervised the agencies' efforts.

The first executive order of Lindsay's successor, Abraham Beame, required each agency head to appoint a "liaison officer" to the DOI and, if the number of corruption complaints warranted, to establish an "independent investigative unit."[37] By the end of the Beame administration, about half of the twenty-four city agencies had established what were essentially inspectors-general offices. The 1977 Charter, following the federal inspector-general law, mandated that the DOI "promulgate standards of conduct and . . . monitor and evaluate the activity of Inspectors General in the agencies to assure uniformity of activity by them." When Ed Koch became mayor in 1978, he issued Executive Order 16, which expanded on the 1977 Charter provisions:

All agencies shall have an inspector general who shall report directly to the respective agency head and to the [DOI] Commissioner and be responsible for maintaining standards of conduct that may be established in such agency under this Order. Inspectors General shall be responsible for the investigation and elimination of corrupt or other criminal activity, conflict of interest, unethical conduct, misconduct, and incompetence within their respective agencies.[38]

The evolving consensus within the DOI during the 1970s and 1980s was that the IG system needed professional law-enforcement direction, and that such direction was not possible as long as the IGs owed their appointment and career advancement to agency heads. The IGs themselves bristled at being assigned to "Mickey Mouse" matters like employee abuse of sick leave and sleeping on the job rather than to "real" corruption investigations; some charged that the agency heads did not want such investigations in their agencies.

In 1978, Mayor Koch made the IGs responsible to both the agency heads and the DOI. This change constituted a significant step toward integrating the IGs into the DOI. However, while making the IG system more professional from a law-enforcement perspective, it also created tension between agency heads and "their" IGs. Were the IGs working for them to ferret out fraud, waste, and abuse, or were the IGs working for an external law-enforcement agency interested in "making cases" against personnel in their agencies and against agency heads themselves?

In the agency administrators' eyes, the IGs had become the functional equivalent of spies out "to get something" on the agency and its employees. Rather than being players on the agency team, the IGs increasingly distanced themselves and their staffs from the agencies in order to monitor operations. In some cases, in close coordination with central DOI headquarters and other law-enforcement agencies, the IGs mounted proactive investigations to test the integrity of systems and personnel. For example, when the DOI decided that the number of corruption cases emanating from the Sanitation Department was too low, the DOI and the Sanitation Department IG, without notifying the Sanitation Department commissioner, conducted a series of stings and undercover operations. After the press conference announcing the arrest of Sanitation Department employees for a number of minor offenses, the commissioner strenuously objected to this investigation of his department that had taken place without his knowledge.

There were drawbacks to having the IGs work for two masters. IGs were in the awkward position of being dependent for career advancement on the commissioner whose agency they were charged with investigating. Moreover, their values and priorities were rooted in law enforcement. Some IGs charged that agency heads purposely assigned them disciplinary and other tasks in order to limit their investigative capacity.

The corruption scandals that engulfed Mayor Koch's third term (1985–89) inevitably focused attention on the DOI: Why had it not prevented the scandals? A report authored by former U.S. Attorney John S. Martin, Jr. concluded that there had been a great deal of DOI foot-dragging, if not incompetence, in failing to investigate the Parking Violations Bureau despite credible complaints and inside information about corruption within that agency.[39] Commissioner Conboy's December 1986 review of the IG system criticized it for being bogged down with disciplinary cases (unauthorized absences, misuse of phones, insubordination) and recommended that the IGs be relieved of responsibility for "personnel matters." Thereafter, the IGs increasingly focused on corruption control.

Given the criticism of his administration for not preventing corruption, Mayor Koch had little choice but to follow Conboy's recommendations. Thus, despite vigorous protest by the agency heads, the mayor placed the IG system under the sole authority of the commissioner of investigation. The IGs were completely absorbed by the DOI. Agency "disciplinary investigators" assumed responsibility for disciplinary functions. Henceforth, the IGs would function as the DOI's field officers. Personnel matters would be investigated by each agency's disciplinary officer. Cases of serious discipline would be "tried" before an administrative tribunal (Office of Administrative Tribunals and Hearings). Koch's Executive Order instituting this reorganization also provided that

> The Inspector General for each agency shall be notified of all complaints received within an agency involving corrupt or other criminal activity, conflicts of interest, unethical conduct, misconduct and incompetence by (i) city agencies, (ii) by city officers and employees, and (iii) by persons dealing with the city, and has jurisdiction to investigate any such complaint.
>
> *In furtherance of these objectives, the Inspectors General shall be informed of and have unrestricted access to all regular meetings of agency executives and managerial staff, and to all records and documents maintained by each agency* (emphasis added).[40]

Assigning agents of a specialized law-enforcement agency to city agencies and vesting them with wide-ranging authority to look, listen, and rummage as they please marks an extraordinary development in public administration.

Nevertheless, the executive order establishing this system contained provisions acknowledging agency heads' authority. For example: (1) in developing policy and strategy for the IGs, the DOI commissioner was instructed to consult and collaborate with the agency heads; (2) all agency heads were reminded that they remained principally responsible for maintaining corruption-free agencies through collaborative arrangement by developing procedures and systems to protect against corrupt and other criminal activity; and (3) the IGs were required on a regular basis to inform the commissioner of the progress of the anticorruption program and of all pending investigative studies and investigations *except those which the DOI commissioner determined should not be disclosed.* That it was necessary to add these face-saving provisions indicates just how much authority the agency heads had lost.

The inspectors general have changed the way that major agencies operate and make decisions. Many managers in city government do not make decisions without first clearing them with their IGs for fear of becoming the target of a DOI inquiry; nor do they want to be in the position, in the event of a corruption scandal, of having to explain why the IG's advice was not sought or not heeded.

Corruption Prevention and Management Review Bureau

The DOI's administrative reform role, which had such an impressive history early in the century, has atrophied. In 1975, the DOI obtained a grant from the Law Enforcement Assistance Administration (LEAA) to establish a Corruption Prevention Bureau (CPB) whose purpose would be to address the following questions: "What was done and who did it? . . . What controls were absent or weak; where should responsibility and accountability be placed; and what new or improved controls should be installed?"[41] The CPB's primary emphasis would be on "identifying systemic and management failures and correcting these, concentrating on corruption prevention, rather than on efficiency and effectiveness for their own sakes."[42]

The CPB's duties increased in 1986, when Mayor Koch issued an executive order requiring each agency head, in consultation with the DOI, "to formulate a comprehensive anticorruption program . . . to identify, evaluate, and eliminate corruption hazards and to identify significant areas warranting investigation."[43] Once such self-examination for vulnerability to corruption became an institutionalized practice, the DOI commissioner would be required "to provide the Mayor with an assessment of the progress made in the annual anticorruption program for each agency." These duties quite logically fell to the CPB, which consisted of only a handful of personnel.

Since 1988, the agency corruption assessments have been compiled by the CPB and reported to the mayor as the annual "Report on the City-Wide Anticorruption Program." These reports provide an excellent example of the panoptic vision of corruption control; in effect, they depict city government as a breeding ground for corrupt opportunities. The reports inevitably find "corruption hazards" in virtually every major component and operation of New York City government. In 1989, for example, the CPB identified *175 corruption hazards.* The 1991 Report found major corruption hazards in "contracting for goods and services . . . inventory control and management . . . purchasing . . . contracting for capital construction work . . . monitoring of and payment for construction work . . . control over fees, rents, and concessions . . . and inspections."[44] One wonders how many operations would have had to be sacrificed in order to address all 175 corruption hazards.

The DOI's Effects on Public Administration

The DOI has a number of important direct and indirect effects on city government. Some of the direct effects are obvious. For example, the annual corruption vulnerability assessments and recommendations consume time and resources. The assessments may save money in the long run, but that proposition has not been examined, much less proven.

An incident during the Koch administration illustrates how the prerogatives of investigations trump agency operations. In 1982, the DOI set up a sting operation using a phony corporation to nail Herb Ryan, one of the city's taxi and limousine commissioners and an intimate associate of Queens Borough President Donald Manes. The DOI undercover operative agreed to pay Ryan $700 per month until Ryan was able to secure enough votes for a taxi license for the phony company. While the DOI had enough evidence for an arrest and indictment of Ryan, it was reluctant to act immediately. The DOI wanted to continue watching Ryan in the hope of catching a bigger fish—Donald Manes. When Mayor Koch found out that Ryan had accepted bribes, he demanded Ryan's immediate arrest and refused to follow the DOI's suggestion that Ryan, who was up for reappointment, be reappointed so that the investigation could continue. Knowing that Koch's decision to fire Ryan would destroy the investigation, the DOI arrested Ryan. Mayor Koch was blasted for terminating the Ryan investigation, which was "a way to open a wide-ranging probe of the Queens democratic machine."[45] While the desire to make a bigger case was a sound idea from a law-enforcement perspective, it failed to consider the impact on efficient governing. Not only would morale suffer and the mayor's decision-making abilities be compromised, but retaining a corrupt public servant would jeopardize public confidence as well as public money.

The presence of IGs and undercover field associates in various agencies has created a system of city government that some people describe as "Big Brother" and "like the Soviet Union." No one knows whether a city employee is actually working for the DOI as a field associate or whether an apparent member of the public is actually an undercover DOI investigator conducting a sting or an integrity test. While line personnel might grudgingly admit the need for something like the DOI, they claim that the DOI's operations seem to assume that agency personnel are untrustworthy. Sting operations and integrity tests reinforce the atmosphere of suspicion and paranoia. An official supervising the repaving of 14th Street, a project bogged down for years in contracting difficulties, explained that every time the supervisor received a poor batch of concrete he suspected that it had been sent by the DOI as an integrity test. The supervisor feared that if he failed to report the bad shipment immediately he would be accused of taking bribes and was therefore constantly anxious.

A commissioner in the Koch Administration, reflecting on her experiences, commented that the worst part of the job was the fear that the DOI would one day summon her for questioning about a matter that, on a busy day, had escaped her attention. "It's like living with the sword of Damocles perpetually threatening to drop." At one point, she found herself using pay phones because she worried that the DOI might be wiretapping. "It seems funny now, but at the time it was frightening." Another former administrator explained that "you cannot assume that innocence will protect you."

The DOI has authority to require all city employees "to answer questions concerning any matter related to the performance of his or her official duties." Failure to cooperate constitutes cause for removal from office. Employees who are summoned to answer questions need not be told who is the investigation's target or its subject matter. While any information they provide cannot be used against them in a future criminal prosecution,[46] such information can be used against them in future administrative disciplinary proceedings, which mete out sanctions ranging from reprimand to termination.

City employees describe a DOI investigation as a Kafkaesque experience. The DOI does not initially screen its cases; therefore, if a complaint is made, an investigative file is opened. Any agency employee may get the dreaded call to report to the DOI headquarters to be "interviewed." The questioned employee may hear nothing more for months. Even though the investigation may have been suspended because of lack of evidence or lack of resources, the file will not be closed. Many investigations remain "open" for years. The targeted employee does not know if she has been exonerated (assuming she had ever been under suspicion) or whether she is still being investigated. Not knowing whether and for what an employee is under suspicion or whether she has been cleared generates anxiety and undermines morale.

K. P. (not real initials), a former top-level administrator in a city agency, related his experience. One Monday afternoon, K. P., then director of the agency's training program, received a call ordering him to report the next morning to the DOI central headquarters. He was given no indication of the reason for the meeting, whether he was a witness or a potential target, or which persons, events, and issues were the subject of the questioning. The DOI "interview" turned out to be a full-fledged interrogation, involving charges by several female agency trainees who claimed to have been told that if they became pregnant during their training, they would have to choose between resigning or terminating the pregnancy. K. P. told the interrogators that he knew of no such policy, did not subscribe to it, and had no knowledge of its being communicated to recruits. He inferred from the "interview" that another top administrator in the agency was the target of the investigation.

After several such interviews, K. P. began to suspect that he himself was the target. He feared that someone might have falsely accused him in order to divert suspicion, but this was only conjecture. There was no opportunity to learn whether there were any accusations against him, much less the opportunity to rebut them. After the fourth interview, K. P. was told that he could consider the matter closed.

A short time later, K. P. was informed that the DOI's report to the agency head had concluded that he was the highest-level official responsible for promulgating a "forced abortion" policy. Without being shown a copy of the report, or being briefed on the evidence against him, K. P. was given five days to provide the commissioner with a response to the report, and he was ordered not to talk to the press. The agency head rejected K. P.'s response and presented him with three alternatives: (1) termination; (2) resignation; or (3) demotion and a $10,000 fine, to be collected by withholding his next two paychecks in full. The agency head strongly urged resignation. However, K. P. chose the third option, hired an attorney, and filed an administrative appeal, once again to the agency head. Not surprisingly, the agency head rejected this appeal too.

When the original complainants filed a multimillion-dollar civil suit against K. P., other agency officials, and the city, the corporation counsel's office became involved. Suddenly, it was against the city's interest to maintain K. P.'s "guilt." Ultimately, the corporation counsel "cleared" K. P. and reimbursed him for the $10,000 fine. However, he was not restored to his previous rank in the agency, nor was he reimbursed for his private legal fees or compensated for a year of torment. He subsequently resigned and moved to another city.

It is little wonder that government employees respond with trepidation to news of a DOI investigation. As one high-level official told us, "[i]t simply is not true that if you are innocent you have nothing to fear; in fact, there is a kind of paranoia in some of the agencies." Whether or not this overstates the case, it seems reasonable to conclude that the DOI's existence and operations definitely affect how decision makers and supervisors exercise their authority.

Conclusion

Progressive Era reformers considered administrative efficiency and law enforcement to be integral elements of investigation. According to theorists like Leonard White and Woodrow Wilson, efficiency could not be ensured without aggressive pursuit of corruption; moreover, corruption would wither away under efficient administration. Thus, administrative reform and criminal investigation were seen as mutually reinforcing. If anything, the Office of the Commissioners of Accounts emphasized the perfection of administration over ferreting out wrongdoers.

Today the DOI's mandate is to investigate corruption by and against city government and to carry out other investigations as the mayor requires. The City Charter requires that the DOI have a commissioner with at least five years law-enforcement experience, and a staff of lawyers/prosecutors and investigators, some of whom must be former New York City police officers. In fiscal year 1990, the DOI completed nearly 2,000 investigations, approximately one investigation for every 150 city employees. In addition, every city agency is obliged to submit an annual corruption vulnerability assessment to the DOI's Corruption Prevention Bureau, which also conducts corruption vulnerability audits. With respect to the DOI's impact on government administration, the whole is greater than the sum of its parts. Commissioners, lower-level managers, and line personnel perceive the DOI to be a brooding omnipresence that operates through inspectors general, undercover field associates, stings, and law-enforcement-type investigations.

After corruption scandals rocked city government in the late 1980s, city politics required an aggressive DOI response. As a result, the DOI was transformed into what is essentially a specialized police force. The IGs were firmly established as DOI field officers, and smooth working relationships were forged with federal, state, and local police and prosecutorial agencies. The DOI now pursues the goals of the anticorruption project more vigorously than ever before.

Recently, the Association of the Bar of the City of New York proposed giving the DOI more power and independence by removing mayoral control over the DOI and transforming it into a completely independent law-enforcement agency.[47] The transformation of the DOI into a bona fide law-enforcement agency has important implications for public administration. Agency heads operate by constantly looking over their shoulders trying to anticipate how their decisions will be perceived by DOI investigators and wondering which of their operations may be surreptitiously monitored. All public employees are aware that the DOI may be watching, and so they must conduct themselves accordingly. It would be surprising if all this suspicion, monitoring, and investigation did not, at least at times, affect morale.

SEVEN

State and Federal Prosecutors: Putting Public Officials on Ice

> I see, as one of the main responsibilities, the task of creating a climate
> which makes it impossible for the corrupter and the corruptible to survive.
> A thorough, careful, painstaking, tenacious, and unrelenting pursuit of
> corrupters is what I promise you.
>
> John F. Keenan upon accepting the position of Special State Prosecutor
> of Corruption, 30 June 1976

The law-enforcement establishment, especially the prosecutorial agencies, is the ultimate external controller. They have the power to compel testimony before the grand jury, search files, plant bugs and wiretaps, create stings, and turn subordinates into informants. Their very existence threatens wrong-doers, including corrupt officials, with jail and prison, in addition to disgrace and ignominy. It is difficult to imagine the anticorruption project being successful without the commitment and active participation of prosecutors. Yet, for most of this century, New York City's five district attorneys have played only a minimal role in combatting official corruption.

There are several reasons why, at least until recently, prosecutorial power has been ineffective when it comes to official corruption. First, normal reactive police methods, whereby the police respond to citizen complaints, do not normally yield corruption cases. Citizens do not complain because they are unaware of corruption or, if they are aware, they may be participants in a corrupt exchange.[1] Second, even if there is a complaint, corruption is hard to investigate and prove. High-level officials use sophisticated methods (e.g., via intermediaries and indirect payments) to organize their corrupt activities.[2] Moreover, they can resist subpoenas on the ground (if they are legislators) that their activities and papers are protected under the speech and debate clause or other doctrines protecting robust political activity. Third, the law of bribery has been rather arcane, traditionally requiring proof that the official performed or promised a quid pro quo in exchange for some illicit remuneration. Fourth, there are professional, political, and personal disincentives for police and prosecutors to investigate and prosecute political corruption.[3] Public officials, especially those at the higher levels, have the power to punish aggressive law-enforcement agencies (and agents) by cutting their funding, firing their personnel, or circumscribing their jurisdiction.[4] Fifth, prosecutors are frequently politically allied to the same party as the local legislators and executive branch personnel; these officials can withhold political support which the district attorney needs to win the party's nomination and even the general election.[5] Indeed, during certain periods of New York City's history, the prosecutors have been part of the very political machine that was the font of political corruption. Sixth, appellate courts have been notoriously hostile to corruption cases, perhaps because judges (in New York State) are dependent for their jobs on the political party's endorsement.[6] For all these reasons, corruption has traditionally been underprosecuted. Those cases which have been prosecuted have overwhelmingly involved low-level employees, and convictions of both high-level and low-level employees have been followed by lenient sentences.[7] Thus, to some extent, the growth of the anticorruption project in public administration is a search for alternatives to traditional law enforcement. Consequently, it is reasonable to ask whether, if law-enforcement made corruption control a higher priority, some of the other more burdensome anticorruption controls could be relaxed.

There are indications that law-enforcement agencies are becoming more significant participants in the anticorruption project. In part, this is an inevitable consequence of the DOI's increased capacity for conducting sustained and sophisticated investigations and its mandate to refer all possible criminal cases to the district attorney.[8] Even more important is the willingness of the U.S. Department of Justice to assert jurisdiction over state and local corruption.

Background

Despite rampant corruption in the late nineteenth and early twentieth centuries, few New York City politicians and employees were actually prosecuted and sent to prison. While Tammany boss William Marcy Tweed was eventually convicted and jailed, this was the exception that proves the rule. Moreover, even Tweed's experience in the criminal justice system illustrates the special treatment received by corrupt public officials and the difficulty of convicting them.

Tweed was arrested in October 1871, and re-elected Alderman in November. After a second trial, he was found guilty on 204 counts and sentenced to 12 years in prison. He was released on appeal, after a year. Jailed again on civil fraud charges, while awaiting trial, he was allowed home each day for lunch. In December 1875, he escaped to Cuba and later to Spain. Deported in November 1876, he was returned to a common jail, having been tried in absentia. He died of a heart attack in prison in 1878, unable to pay a $6,000,000 civil judgment.[9]

For the most part, the district attorney's office ignored corruption by political machine officials. This is hardly surprising since the political machine supported the district attorneys.[10] The historian Alan Block summed up the state of affairs in New York County's criminal justice system in 1935 as follows:

> New York's criminal justice bureaucracies were politicized; the various positions, such as judge, court officer, assistant district attorney, district attorney, etc., were the rewards of successful politics. Most offices in the criminal justice bureaucracies were part of the patronage of municipal politicians and their patrons and clients who included organized criminals.[11]

Only infrequently, when citizens became aroused by corruption and voted for reformers, did the politicians lose their de facto immunity from prosecution.[12] Once public outrage subsided and calls for reform died down, the Tammany machine would resurface. According to a turn-of-the-century gangster who profited from Tammany power, "These reform movements are like queen hornets. They sting you once and then they die."[13]

The legislative hearings in the early 1930s, over which Judge Samuel Seabury presided, exposed rampant corruption throughout city government, especially in the magistrate's court.[14] Seabury found that the magistrate's court was riddled with job buying, "fixes," and favors for the party bosses. There was good reason to believe that blatant corruption reached into the district attorney's office as well.[15]

Although the Seabury Commission's incredible revelations led to resignations by numerous magistrates, city officials, and Mayor Jimmy Walker,[16] relatively few criminal prosecutions were brought to trial.[17] One explanation for the lack of prosecutions is that Manhattan District Attorney and loyal Tammany man Thomas C. T. Crain was hardly anxious to assist Seabury, since he was himself one of Seabury's investigatory targets. Additionally, the Seabury Commission did not have the full support of the local judiciary. The Appellate Division for the Second Department, with jurisdiction over Brooklyn, Queens, and Staten Island, opposed the extension of the commission's investigation into its jurisdiction.[18] Another reason may be that while Governor Franklin Roosevelt was (reluctantly) willing to support the Seabury Commission's investigations of Tammany Hall, his support was partial and cautious because he needed Tammany's support for his presidential bid.

As early as 1931, leaders of the City Club, a bastion of good government reformers, petitioned Governor Roosevelt to appoint a special prosecutor to investigate District Attorney Crain's failure to deal with corruption. Specifically, they cited Crain's failure to pursue cases involving the magistrate's courts, gangster Arnold Rothstein's murder, stock fraud, graft in city government, and racketeering.[19] Roosevelt expanded Seabury's jurisdiction to include an investigation of Crain. The Seabury Commission found Crain to be ineffective and incompetent; however, the commission recommended that charges calling for Crain's dismissal be dropped:

> The fact that the people of the County do not elect the best man for the position, or one who acts in the most efficient manner, is not ground for his removal. In such cases, the people must suffer the consequences of their conduct. . . . Where . . . there is no suggestion of dishonesty or willful wrong-doing on the part of an elected official, he should not be lightly removed from office.[20]

In 1935, a grand jury impaneled to investigate gambling and racketeering rebelled against William Copeland Dodge, the Tammany district attorney, and transformed itself into the most famous "runaway grand jury" in American history. Instead of presenting evidence to the grand jury, Dodge talked about Communism's threat to New York. The grand jurors, joined by reformers, the bar association, and the media, successfully lobbied the governor for a special prosecutor. Governor Herbert Lehman chose Thomas E. Dewey.[21] Unhampered by politics or civil service, Dewey handpicked his own assistants.[22] As special prosecutor from 1935 to 1937, Dewey and his staff mounted an unprecedented attack on corruption and racketeering in New York City. Later, as Manhattan District Attorney, Dewey turned his attention to the link between Tammany and organized crime; his most notable corruption prosecutions were those involving Tammany boss Jimmy Hines, City Clerk Albert Marinelli, and the presiding judge of the federal circuit court of appeals, Martin Manton.[23] Meanwhile, Mayor Fiorello LaGuardia took a number of housecleaning steps, including the appointment of a reform police commissioner, Lewis Valentine.

Frank Hogan, one of Dewey's young assistants, succeeded him as Manhattan district attorney and held that office for more than thirty years (1941–

73).[24] Hogan followed Dewey's example in keeping the district attorney's office relatively apolitical and recruiting graduates of the nation's leading law schools as assistants. In the other boroughs, however, the district attorneys' offices remained heavily politicized well into the 1970s and beyond.[25]

While Hogan's office pioneered many important law-enforcement initiatives, attacking corruption was not one of them. To be fair, there were periodic prosecutions of inspectors and rank-and-file police officers, and even the occasional "big case" like the prosecutions of tax assessors in the late 1940s, but these were exceptional cases, and they did not lead to prosecutions of higher-level officials.[26] In the early 1970s, it was not the district attorney's office that investigated and revealed massive corruption in the police department, but a special commission (the Knapp Commission).

The Special State Prosecutor

In 1970, in response to *The New York Times'* exposé of extensive corruption in the New York City Police Department, Mayor John Lindsay established the Commission to Investigate Allegations of Corruption in the City of New York, popularly known as the Knapp Commission. The commission held sensational public hearings which exposed pervasive police corruption, primarily bribery and extortion.[27] Ultimately, the commission issued dozens of recommendations, including one for a special anticorruption prosecutor for the police department and other criminal justice agencies. The commission reasoned that an independent prosecutor was necessary because the district attorneys were such "close allies" of the police and judges that they could not be trusted to vigorously ferret out corruption.[28] Accordingly, in 1972, Governor Nelson Rockefeller issued a series of executive orders authorizing the New York State attorney general to create the Office of the Special Prosecutor of Corruption (OSPC), with jurisdiction over any corrupt act "arising out of, relating to, or in any way connected with the enforcement of law or administration of criminal justice in the City of New York."[29] The governor said,

> I have taken this action in recognition of a fundamental reality: that under the present circumstances, only an independent agency with city-wide authority, assigned a clear and specific mission and armed with full prosecutorial power and independent investigative capacity, can break through the natural resistance of government agencies to investigate themselves or their close allies, can overcome the force of inertia, and can finally deal a decisive blow to narcotics, crime and corruption in New York City.[30]

State Attorney General Louis Lefkowitz appointed Maurice H. Nadjari, a career prosecutor who once had served as an assistant in Frank Hogan's office, to head the OSPC. Nadjari's goals included (1) cracking down on police corruption; (2) investigating the courts where, according to rumors which had persisted for decades, judgeships were available for purchase from political bosses, and reduced sentences could be obtained through bribery; and (3) monitoring the district attorneys who had been accused of indifference and apathy towards corruption.

Nadjari utilized undercover operations and integrity testing to investigate prosecutors and judges. As he explained, "When you are involved with drug sellers, you have to go out and buy the drugs . . . when judges are selling fixes you have to go out and buy the fix."[31] In one case, Nadjari set up a sting operation designed to nab judges who accepted bribes in exchange for fixing criminal cases. Nadjari arranged for an undercover agent to pose as a defendant accused of robbery. Neither the grand jury that indicted the phony defendant nor the Brooklyn district attorney's office was aware that the robbery charge was fictitious.[32] A second undercover agent, carrying a recording device, approached Judge Paul Rao, who was presiding over the case, to ask what could be done for his friend, the indicted "robber." Following Judge Rao's suggestion, the robber hired Rao's son as defense counsel. Ultimately, Judge Rao, his son, and his son's law partner were charged with conspiracy to bribe a judicial officer. The conspiracy charge did not stick, but they were indicted and convicted for perjury in connection with statements made before the grand jury.[33] Like so many of Nadjari's corruption cases, however, the convictions of Judge Rao, his son, and his son's law partner ran into trouble on appeal.[34] In reversing Judge Rao's conviction, the appellate court criticized Nadjari's tactics: "Such a perversion of the criminal justice system by an overzealous prosecutor is illegal, outrageous and intolerable and we condemn it."[35] The court blasted Nadjari's "misuse" of the grand jury and the district attorney's office to secure an indictment for a phony crime.[36]

Nadjari obtained indictments against eleven judges; none of these prosecutions survived both trial and appeal.[37] His prosecutions of public officials fared no better on appeal. Nadjari brought Queens District Attorney Thomas J. Mackell to trial for blocking the prosecution of Joseph Ferdinando, who had set up a phony company which defrauded investors; Mackell was the first New York City district attorney indicted while in office. On appeal, the indictment was dismissed because of insufficient evidence. The court criticized Nadjari for his "constant and patent disregard of the basic rules of evidence,"[38] and for attempting to "introduce irrelevant evidence having a severely prejudicial effect."[39]

Nadjari prosecuted Irving Goldman, New York City cultural affairs commissioner and president of the Shubert Foundation, for bribery, grand larceny, and perjury arising out of a scheme that defrauded the New York City Transit Authority of more than $500,000. Judge Murtagh, who presided over special grand juries impaneled to hear evidence presented by the special prosecutor, dismissed Goldman's indictment for insufficient evidence.[40] That same week, Judge Murtagh also dismissed a five-count perjury indictment against Alvin Geller, former chief of the Manhattan district attorney's Narcotics Bureau, stating that Geller's indictment was "completely unsupported by any evidence."[41]

Nadjari's aggressive initiatives prompted charges that he was abusing his office. Bronx District Attorney Mario Merola balked when Nadjari's investigations moved into the Bronx. Merola questioned the good faith of Nadjari's inquiries and claimed that once Nadjari's investigations began in his district, Merola's prosecutorial power would go up in smoke—the only cases Merola would be permitted to prosecute "would be rape and homicide, as long as they don't occur in a public building."[42] Merola also complained about Nadjari's ability to destroy reputations: "What the hell do you think we've got after 25 years of public office? All we've got is our name, and our reputation, and he can just do it like that to you, even if you've done nothing wrong. . . . You couldn't be called to the grand jury by Nadjari without being smeared."[43] Governor Hugh Carey fired Nadjari on 23 December 1975 on the ground that his prosecutions were ineffective and of dubious propriety. Nadjari fought back, claiming that the political establishment was circling the wagons to protect itself. He claimed that the criticism of his methods began "the moment that [his staff] utilize[d] against judges investigative procedures that ha[d] been used against drug sellers, and against others suspected of committing crime."[44]

Nadjari charged that Governor Carey's real motivation was to abort his investigation of the Bronx Democratic Party Chairman (and Carey ally) Patrick J. Cunningham for selling judgeships. He maintained that his investigative and prosecutorial methods, which were criticized as "pernicious" and "absolutely intolerable,"[45] including undercover operations, wiretaps, surveillance, and decoys, were routinely used by other prosecutors. Nadjari declared that "from the outset I have experienced difficulty probing the upper reaches of the justice system. . . . The closer I get to those remaining—the hard core—the greater the abuse to which I am subjected."[46] New York

State Attorney General Louis Lefkowitz, who formally had the authority to dismiss Nadjari, decided that he should remain in office for another six months so he could complete ongoing investigations.

Nadjari continued to obtain indictments. State Supreme Court Justice Irving H. Saypol was charged with bribery and perjury, Manhattan Surrogate Samuel DiFalco with conspiracy and official misconduct, and former Tammany Hall leader Carmine DeSapio with perjury. The courts dismissed every one of these cases.[47] Nadjari ultimately obtained indictments charging Cunningham with official misconduct and violations of the state election law. Both charges were dismissed.[48]

On 4 June 1976, New York's highest court, the Court of Appeals, curtailed Nadjari's jurisdiction in a case involving bribery of a police officer. The court held that since "the Special Prosecutor's power is to be confined strictly to the criminal justice process or system [as the executive order decreed], then obviously the Special Prosecutor's jurisdiction does not embrace the judicial system in general or the civil justice process in particular."[49]

The final blow to Nadjari was delivered by Special New York State Deputy Attorney General Jacob B. Grumet, whom Attorney General Lefkowitz had appointed to determine whether Governor Carey dismissed Nadjari solely because he was investigating high-level Democrats. Grumet concluded that Carey's decision was "based upon his 'individual judgment' and not [as Nadjari charged] on his being influenced by 'self-motivated' or 'politically motivated' people."[50] Following this report, Lefkowitz abandoned his efforts to work out a compromise and dismissed Nadjari as special prosecutor. John Keenan, a highly respected prosecutor, succeeded Nadjari. A subsequent 1976 report by the Temporary Commission of Investigation accused Nadjari and his former chief assistant of deliberately disclosing and leaking information to the press and of tarnishing the reputations of numerous officials.[51]

During his almost four years in office (September 1972 to June 1976), Nadjari obtained 343 indictments, 188 guilty pleas and 73 convictions at trial. Most of these defendants were low-ranking police officers and other rank-and-file criminal justice system personnel. More than 80 percent of these convictions were affirmed by higher courts.[52]

After the Nadjari rampage, the Office of the Special Prosecutor of Corruption continued to attack corruption, albeit with reduced staff and budget. The OSPC placed undercover agents in the various criminal justice agencies. The office also regularly conducted grand jury investigations of systemic criminal justice problems, like corruption in the bail system and the need for legislation authorizing pension forfeiture for public officials convicted of corruption.

The OSPC reached its peak strength in 1975 with a staff of 160. By 1980, however, the staff had shrunk to 112, by 1982 to less than 80, and by 1985 to 50.[53] Indictments and convictions declined commensurately. Perhaps more importantly, nearly all its cases involved corruption by the rank and file, mostly police and correctional officers. In 1984, the OSPC indicted only fifty-one defendants, twenty-five of whom were police officers accused of accepting bribes from drug dealers.

The OSPC was almost abolished in 1985 due to a dispute between Governor Mario Cuomo and Attorney General Robert Abrams, who had appointed his aide, William F. Dowling, as special prosecutor. Cuomo claimed he should have been consulted before the appointment, refused to pay Dowling, and threatened to abolish the post. Dowling finally resigned, and Charles J. Hynes, Cuomo's choice, was appointed.[54] Hynes served from 1985 until June 1989, when he was replaced by Helman R. Brook. In 1989, the final year of the OSPC's existence, the office operated on a budget of $3.7 million with a staff of 43. Its last major case involved thirteen police officers accused of burglaries and extorting drugs and money from narcotics dealers. In March 1990, Governor Mario Cuomo abolished the office.[55] According to Governor Cuomo, "The compelling need that once justified superseding local prosecutorial authority [had] abated."[56] Cuomo explained that each of the five New York City district attorneys had pledged to establish a bureau to investigate and prosecute official corruption.

The dismantling of the OSPC is a rare example of scaling back the anticorruption project, but this diminution may turn out to be temporary. As we shall see in chapter 10, since the 1994 Mollen Commission hearings on police corruption, there has been significant pressure to revive the OSPC as an external monitor for the police. Perhaps the lesson to be learned from the rise and fall of the OSPC is that it is perilous for the anticorruption project to take on wrongdoing in high places. Intensifying the law-enforcement presence in the lives and operations of low-level public employees, on the other hand, poses no such risks.

The District Attorneys

With the demise of the OSPC, New York City's five independently elected district attorneys once again were responsible for prosecuting all official corruption cases. The aggressive federal law-enforcement response to the mid-1980s corruption scandals embarrassed the district attorneys and led to a surge of anticorruption activity. The Manhattan district attorney's office in particular felt upstaged. Indeed, its famous rackets bureau, which had achieved so many successes under Dewey and Hogan, had been allowed to wither. District Attorney Robert Morgenthau strengthened the rackets bureau and began to compete with the federal prosecutors in prosecuting corrupt city officials.

After United States Attorney Rudolph Giuliani obtained a racketeering indictment against Bronx Democratic party boss Stanley Friedman for his role in the Parking Violations Bureau scandals, the Manhattan district attorney's office indicted Friedman for bribery and conspiracy. While Morgenthau ultimately deferred to the federal prosecutor on Friedman,[57] he moved ahead with prosecutions of Transportation Commissioner Anthony Ameruso for perjury[58] and of the former president of the Health and Hospitals Corporation, John McLaughlin, for stealing money from clients, lying on financial disclosure forms, and bribery.[59]

Corruption cases in the Manhattan district attorney's office are dealt with by two units: the special prosecutions unit handles low-level corruption, mostly based upon referrals from the DOI, and the rackets bureau handles "big cases," either those against top officials or those brought against whole units of low-level employees. Since the late 1980s, the special prosecutions unit has become deeply involved in investigating and prosecuting government employees. The office, for the first time, is even prosecuting misconduct that used to be considered suitable only for administrative disciplinary action like sick leave fraud and abuse (employees taking sick leave and drawing pay when they are not really sick). The office takes the view that public officials ought to be held to a higher standard of integrity than private-sector workers. Consequently, it seeks to indict low-level officials who take small bribes or engage in the petty theft of, for example, boxes of office paper or, in one case, ten door locks. In short, the state prosecutorial component of the anticorruption project is slowly expanding its investigative eye to more forms of conduct, increasing its resources and activities, and seeking more severe punishments.

Notwithstanding the enhanced attention being paid to corruption cases, appendix 1, which lists corruption prosecutions by the Manhattan district attorney's office from 1992 to 1994, shows that the actual number of prosecutions is still rather modest. Over the course of three years, it brought only forty-nine corruption cases, most of which involved low-level employees.

Federal Law Enforcement and Local Corruption

The biggest change in the law-enforcement component of the anticorruption project is the aggressive role of the federal law-enforcement agencies in investigating and prosecuting corruption by high-level state and local officials, including governors and mayors. According to Stephen S. Trott, the assistant attorney general for criminal cases at the Department of Justice (DOJ), "We've got a full-court press on this stuff. It's absolutely clear to me that there have been increased efforts to find public corruption."[60] Until the mid-1970s, the federal government played practically no role in investigating state and local corruption.[61] In 1975, President Gerald Ford and Attorney General Edward Levi announced that the DOJ would make official corruption in state and local government a high priority. At DOJ headquarters in Washington, D.C., Richard Thornburgh (later attorney general) was appointed first head of the new Public Integrity Section.

The expansion of criminal law, especially regarding federal mail and wire fraud[62] has made it possible for the FBI to investigate and for the Department of Justice to prosecute just about any significant local corruption. Federal law-enforcement officials may be more willing and able to prosecute local corruption than their state and local counterparts. The federal prosecutors have more resources and are not as involved in local politics as local prosecutors.[63] Conversely, federal officials may be unfamiliar with the nuances of local politics and, as a result, have to rely on and work with local law enforcement.[64] Since the mid-1970s a number of governors, dozens of mayors, and hundreds of local public officials have been indicted and convicted for official corruption in federal courts.[65]

To understand what difference it makes to have the federal law-enforcement establishment focusing on state and local corruption, consider the major scandal involving the New York City Parking Violations Bureau (PVB). In early 1986, a large-scale FBI investigation (Operation Greylord) of corruption in the Chicago court system turned up a company which, when it agreed to cooperate with the government, divulged that it had paid off New York City officials to obtain contracts to collect parking fines.[66] The federal investigation led to PVB Commissioner Lester Shafran, Deputy Commissioner Geoffrey Lindenauer, and ultimately to Queens Borough President and party boss Donald Manes and Bronx Democratic Party Chairman Stanley Friedman. Manes allegedly took bribes in exchange for contracts to collect parking fines, and Friedman, in addition to taking bribes, used his influence to obtain a multimillion dollar contract for a company in which he was the majority shareholder. Ultimately, the U.S. attorneys for the southern and eastern districts of New York targeted for investigation, among others, Manes, Friedman, Bronx Borough President Stanley Simon, and some of their closest political associates. Rudolph Giuliani's racketeering indictment of Michael Lazar, a lawyer, developer, former city councilman, Taxi Commission chairman, and transportation administrator, charged that he and others (including Manes, who escaped indictment by committing suicide) used patronage to run the PVB as a money-making machine for their personal benefit. The indictment charged that Lazar installed his long-time friend Lester Shafran as PVB director and that Manes installed his protégé, Geoffrey Lindenauer, as deputy director. Shafran and Lindenauer were later convicted for taking bribes and splitting the proceeds with Manes and Lazar.[67] Lazar's indictment further alleged that as a result of this influence peddling, Friedman and Manes were able to make considerable personal profits. Ultimately, Lazar was sentenced to three years in prison and a $200,000 fine for racketeering, conspiracy, and mail fraud.[68] Friedman received a twelve-year sentence for racketeering, conspiracy, and mail fraud.[69]

The investigation of Queens Borough President Donald Manes continued even after he committed suicide. Manes' bagman, Michael Nussbaum, was convicted for helping Manes to solicit a $250,000 bribe from a cable television company that was seeking a franchise in Queens. Nussbaum's conviction was reversed on appeal on grounds of insufficient evidence.[70]

During the height of the New York City corruption scandals, from 1986 to 1987, the U.S. attorney's office for the southern district of New York prosecuted only thirty-two individuals (see appendix 2). The U.S. attorney's office, unlike the Manhattan district attorney's office, appears more successful at investigating and prosecuting large pockets of corruption in city agencies, rather than prosecuting isolated corrupt employees. For example, in 1984, 14 electrical inspectors and supervisors, nabbed in Operation Ampscam, 10 water and sewer inspectors, nabbed in Operation Norton, and 14 Housing Authority employees were prosecuted. The following year, 18 more Housing Authority employees were convicted. In 1987, Operation Double Steel resulted in the prosecution of 39 employees and supervisors from various cities' purchasing, public works, and highway departments. In 1990, 34 Division of Motor Vehicles employees were prosecuted for bribery.

The Wedtech Scandal

In March 1986, U.S. Attorney General Edwin Meese told a New York audience, "We intend to go on knocking such corrupt heads—that's our business; that's our duty."[71] Similarly, the FBI's special agent in charge of the New York City office said, "We're just not going to quit until we can identify, successfully investigate, and prosecute every corrupt politician in our territory."[72] This rhetoric was at least partially fulfilled by the extraordinary investigation that came to be known as Wedtech.

In 1965, John Mariotta, a tool and die maker of Puerto Rican descent, founded a small machine shop, the Welbit Electronic Tool & Die Corporation, later known as Wedtech. Five years later, Mariotta took on Fred Neurberger as partner. Mariotta and Neurberger then hired David Schaffer Epstein, a Manhattan public relations adviser, to help them shape an image for their small enterprise. Located in an impoverished Bronx neighborhood, the company hired former prisoners and drug abusers. These efforts caught the attention of President Ronald Reagan, who was stressing private-sector remedies for urban decay.[73] What better proof than the success of this small company in the south Bronx?

Promoting itself as a minority business enterprise, and with the help of several well-connected consultants, former government officials, and relatives of politicians, Wedtech successfully procured more than $400 million in federal contracts for armored cars, small gasoline engines for the Army, portable pontoons for the Navy, and mail containers for the Postal Service.[74] In 1984, President Reagan called John Mariotta one of the "heroes of the 80s."

In late 1986, FBI investigators discovered widespread bribery in Wedtech's operations. For years its executives had been making illegal campaign contributions, hiring politicians' relatives and aides, bribing politically connected consultants to arrange new contracts and auditors to overlook bookkeeping irregularities, and paying off inspectors to evaluate Wedtech's contract work favorably.[75] The investigation revealed that an array of politicians and government officials at the local and national levels, both Democrats and Republicans, were on Wedtech's "payroll," including Bronx Congressman Mario Biaggi. Biaggi's involvement with Wedtech began in 1978, when Wedtech hired Biaggi & Ehrlich, Mario Biaggi's law firm. The firm received Wedtech stock worth about $3.6 million. In return, Biaggi used his influence to obtain federal contracts for Wedtech. Although Biaggi formally withdrew from the law firm in 1979, part of the firm's fees were channeled to him through his son and his partner, Bernard G. Ehrlich. Wedtech also benefited from the services of attorney E. Robert Wallach and former White House assistant Lyn Nofziger. On several occasions, Wallach contacted Ed Meese, then White House chief of staff, on Wedtech's behalf.[76]

In the late 1970s, Wedtech began making campaign contributions to

Bronx Borough President Stanley Simon. In 1984, Wedtech sought Simon's help in obtaining a Bronx waterside property. Simon arranged for Wedtech officials to meet with Susan Frank, the New York City commissioner of ports and terminals. A few days later, Wedtech secured a $50,000-a-year, three-year lease on a property for which the city had originally sought $150,000. Simon, who was also a member of the Board of Estimate, received $50,000 from Wedtech for his assistance in obtaining the Board of Estimate's final approval of the lease.[77]

Federal prosecutors obtained convictions of Mario Biaggi for extorting Wedtech stock worth $1.8 million, filing false tax returns, racketeering, and perjury.[78] Stanley Simon was convicted of extorting $50,000 in campaign contributions and cash, racketeering, lying to the grand jury, and income tax invasion.[79] More than a dozen other individuals, both government officials and Wedtech personnel, were also convicted.

Implications for Public Administration

Prosecutors are a greater presence in the daily lives of public administrators than they were a generation ago. Federal and large local prosecution offices are likely to have specialized public corruption units, professionally committed to making cases. Prosecutors now expect public administrators to share their commitment to integrity in government and to fighting corruption and racketeering generally.

The best example of the "prosecutorialization" of city government is the recent effort to blacklist morally tainted contractors from doing business with the city. As we will see in the next chapter, prosecutors and the law-enforcement community have taken the position that no public contracts should be awarded to mob-influenced companies. From their perspective, all government agencies should be committed to busting the mob, even if this impedes city operations.

Some commissioners complain that efficiency is being sacrificed to law-enforcement goals of making criminal cases. If the commissioner or one of his top staff identify a corrupt employee, he cannot expeditiously get rid of him. He must defer to the DOI and the prosecutors who take control of the case. If the employee does not know that he has been found out, the DOI may decide to keep him on the job in order to see if anyone else is involved and to continue building its criminal case. Administrators understandably chafe at the idea that a corrupt employee is being left in place; among other things, they worry that if the newspapers find out, they will be excoriated as incompetent or corrupt. However, if they fire the employee, they may be charged with cutting off an investigation before it reached high-level officials. As we saw in chapter 6, Mayor Koch's decision to terminate an investigation of Taxi and Limousine Commissioner Herb Ryan by firing him, against the advice of the DOI commissioner, prompted a great deal of criticism.[80]

Even when the corrupt employee has been arrested, administrative discipline must be placed on hold pending the resolution of the criminal case, which can take months or even longer. During this time, a corrupt employee sometimes remains on the job, thereby undermining agency morale. Furthermore, if the criminal case is ultimately dismissed or results in an acquittal, the administrative case may be too stale to pursue successfully. In short, public administration must now adapt to the realities of the panoptic vision of anticorruption control.

Conclusion

Historically, corruption prosecutions were infrequent and episodic. Even the remarkable Seabury investigations generated few prosecutions. "Mr. District Attorney," Frank Hogan, also failed to prosecute many corrupt public officials. In the 1980s and 1990s, however, local, state, and especially federal prosecutors have become much more involved in dealing with corruption in New York City government. It remains to be seen, of course, whether these developments are simply a short-lived blip on the screen, or whether they mark the beginning of a new long-term trend.

On the one hand, with the power of Tammany Hall and the old political machine apparently gone forever, New York City's county prosecutors are likely to be much more independent for the foreseeable future. Indeed, they may evolve from allies into opponents and rivals of the mayor and his administration. If so, it will be in their interest to expose corruption. On the other hand, there are deeply entrenched political reasons for official corruption to remain a low- or possibly mid-level prosecutorial priority. Corruption cases are expensive and resource-intense. They are difficult to win at trial and on appeal.[81] Moreover, the public is more concerned about violent crime, organized crime, and drug trafficking than corruption. This means that there are limits to prosecutors' commitment to the anticorruption project.

Appendix 1 Public Employee Prosecutions, 1992–1994

Inv #	Title	Charges	Disposition	Facts of Case
19/92	Director, Permits Unit, Department of Transportation	§200.10 Bribe Receiving 3	PG: §200.25 (EF) Receiving Reward Official Misconduct 2 Sent: Conditional discharge	Kickback scheme—illegally sold city permits for the operatio of overweight trucks to the highest bidder and received $100,00 in kickbacks.
19/92	Employee, Permits Unit, Department of Transportation	§200.10 Bribe Receiving 3	PG: §200.30 (AM) Unlawful Gratuities Sent: Fine	Kickback scheme—illegally sold overweight permits.
32/92	Cashier	§155.30 Grand Larceny 4	PG: §155.25 (AM) Petit Larceny Sent: 3 yrs probation	Cashier at Triborough Bridge & Tunnel Authority processing center stole cash.
63/92	Secretary	§155.25 Petit Larceny	Dismissed (ACD), restitution, counseling	Secretary at New York County District Attorney's Office stole checks and attempted to cash them.
64/92	Health Department Employee	§155.35 Grand Larceny 3	PG: §155.25 (AM) Petit Larceny Sent: 3 yrs probation	Employee of New York State Department of Health stole $10,000 via checks and credit cards after AIDS patient's death.
111/92	Postal Worker	§155.30 Grand Larceny 4	PG: §155.25 (AM) Petit Larceny Sent: Conditional discharge	Postal worker collected $10,000 from coworkers for a cruise and kept the money.
134/92	Corrections Officer	§155.30 Grand Larceny 4	Dismissed	Used Corrections Department credit card without permission.

Inv #	Title	Charge (PG)	Disposition	Description
135/92	School Custodian	§200.10 Bribe Receiving 3	PG: 195.00 (AM) Official Misconduct Sent: Conditional discharge	School custodian pocketed $500 from a community group to use school space for free (Board of Education should have received rent).
169/92	School Board Member	Conflict of Interest (Misdemeanor violation of NYC Charter)	PG: to charge Sent: Dismissed—death of defendant	Election fraud—false filing and used influence to raise funds.
169/92	School Principal	§200.00 Bribery 3	PG: §200.00 (DF) Sent: 5 yrs probation, $2000 fine	Bribed School Board member Cain to obtain appointment as principal.
175/92	Police Officer	§175.35 Offering False Instrument for Filing 1	Open indictment	Submitted fraudulent summonses to precinct to make "daily quota."
199/92	Sanitation Enforcement Agents (12 arrested)	§200.10 Bribe Receiving 3 §460.20 Organized Crime Control Act (Enterprise Corruption)	10, PG §200.10 (DF) 1, PG Sale Controlled Substance (AF) 1, Awaiting trial Sent: 5, state prison 2, 5 yrs probation 4, awaiting sentence	Organized scheme where agents extorted bribes form merchants in Chinatown and Lower Manhattan in exchange for not writing summonses.
205/92	Fiscal Unit Clerk	§155.25 Petit Larceny	PG: §155.25 (AM) Sent: Conditional discharge, restitution	Fiscal Unit employee stole $2,200 from cash box.
212/92	Traffic Enforcement Agent	§155.40 Grand Larceny 2 (Extortion by Public Official)	Convicted after jury trial: — 155.40 (CF) Sent: 5 yrs probation	Department of Transportation traffic agent told victims to pay him $15 or pay a $50 ticket.
217/92	Accountant	§155.35 Grand Larceny 3	PG: §155.35 (DF) Sent: 5 yrs probation	School District accountant had 103 checks issued to fictitious payees ($24,000 stolen).

Note: This table lists public employee prosecutions in New York City for a two-year period. Each case is identified by an investigation number (Inv #). The disposition indicates whether the accused pled guilty (PG) and what sentence, if any, was imposed.

Appendix 1 *(continued)*

Inv #	Title	Charges	Disposition	Facts of Case
230/92	Office Aide	§175.25 Tampering with Public Records 1	PG: §200.10 Bribe Receiving 3 (DF) Sent: 5 yrs probation	Parking Violations Bureau employee took $47,934 to illegally dismiss 966 parking tickets.
11/93	Store Clerk	§170.10 Forgery 2	PG: §170.05 Forgery 3 (AM) Sent: 3 yrs probation	Police Department civilian employee stole $1400 cash and submitted phony refund claims.
19/93	Court Aide	§200.10 Bribe Receiving 3	PG: Public Officers Law §73 (5)—Gifts Prohibited (AM) Sent: Conditional discharge	Solicited $150 to accept and file retainer agreements from law firm Jacoby and Meyers by messenger rather than by mail.
45/93	HRA Employee (not specific)	§155.35 Grand Larceny 3	PG: 110/155.30 Attempted Grand Larceny 4 (AM) Sent: 3 yrs probation	Stole $9975 by being paid salary after he left job, by paying off HRA timekeeper.
56/93	Traffic Enforcement Agent	§200.10 Bribe Receiving 3	PG: §200.10 Sent: 5 yrs probation	Solicited $20 bribe to alter a ticket he had written and stated he knew someone at the Parking Violations Bureau who could fix the ticket.
60/93	City Marshal	§165.52 Criminal Poss. Stolen Property 2	PG: §155.35 Grand Larceny 3 (DF) Sent: 5 yrs probation	Stole creditors' funds being held in his trust account.
68/93	Corrections Officer	§155.30 Grand Larceny 4	Acquitted after jury trial	While on paid sick leave, held unauthorized job at crafts store.
69/93	Corrections Officer	§155.30 Grand Larceny 4	PG: §195.20 Defrauding Government (EF) Sent: 5 yrs probation	While on paid sick leave for 11 months, employed as driver at Regency Vans, Inc.

75/93	Finance Office Employee	§155.25 Petit Larceny	Dismissed—§30.30 granted	Department of Consumer Affairs employee took $236 from the Consumer Refund Account to buy a postal money order that he endorsed to himself.
77/93	Paraprofessional (teacher's assistant)	§155.25 Petit Larceny	Dismissed—§30.30 granted	Submitted forged vouchers for subway tokens and received $2,800.
99/93	City Employee (not specified)	§220.39 Criminal Poss. Controlled Substance 3	PG: §220.03 CPCS7 (AM) Sent: Conditional discharge	Sold cocaine to an undercover detective for $30.
112/93	Transit Police Officer	§120.00 Assault 3	Mistrial, 10/94 Adjourned to 2/95 for new trial	Off-duty officer assaulted a woman on the street, pointed a loaded gun at her, and threatened to kill her.
126/93	Offtrack Betting Employee	§155.35 Grand Larceny 3	PG: 170.20 Criminal Poss. Forged Instrument 3 (AM) Sent: 3 yrs probation	Authorized a $12,400 cash withdrawal from a client's OTB account. Another person (also arrested) pretended to be the client and withdrew the money from an OTB branch.
140/93	Employee, TBTA (Triborough Bridge & Tunnel Authority)	§155.35 Grand Larceny 3	PG: §240.20 Disorderly Conduct (violation) Sent: Conditional discharge	TBTA Officer defrauded the TBTA by calling in sick or injured for four years while he was employed by the New York State Office of Mental Health.
141/93	Employee, TBTA	§170.10 Forgery 2	PG: §170.05 Forgery 3 (AM) Sent: Conditional discharge	Employee said he was on jury duty, forged all the court slips, and was paid for two months when he did not serve on jury duty at all.
177/93	Department of Health Employee (not specific)	§170.10 Forgery 2	PG: §155.25 Petit Larceny (AM) Sent: 6 months jail	City employee stole the checkbook of another employee and forged four checks.

(continued)

Appendix 1 *(continued)*

Inv #	Title	Charges	Disposition	Facts of Case
181/93	Traffic Enforcement Agent	§200.10 Bribe Receiving 3	PG: §195.00 Official Misconduct (AM) Sent: 3 yrs probation	Traffic enforcement agents who were partners solicited a bribe from a motorist in exchange for the release of his vehicle from a Dept. of Transportation tow truck.
182/93	Traffic Enforcement Agent	§200.10 Bribe Receiving 3	PG: §200.10 (DF) Sent: 5 yrs probation	Same as 181/93.
184/93	NYC Housing Authority Employee	§155.35 Grand Larceny 3	PG: §175.05 Falsifying Business Records 2 (AM) Sent: 4 yrs probation	Submitted fraudulent overtime records; didn't get any money but attempted to collect over $3,000.
194/93	Computer Operator at HRA	§170.25 Criminal Poss. Forged Instrument 2	Dismissed—$30.30 granted	Accepted money to open fraudulent Medicaid cases.
237/93	Mailroom Employee	§155.40 Grand Larceny 2	PG: §155.35 Grand Larceny 3 (DF) Not sentenced yet	Mailroom employee at Borough of Manhattan Community College stole approximately 20 checks worth over $50,000.
240/93	NYC Law Dept Administrative Assistant	§155.30 Grand Larceny 4	PG: §155.25 Petit Larceny (AM) Sent: Conditional discharge	Employee whose responsibilities included picking up payroll checks for other employees stole several checks, which were cashed by a third party (also arrested).
6/94	Supervisor, Bureau of Health Services, Fire Dept	§155.40 Grand Larceny 2	PG: §155.40 (CF) Sent: 18 months to 54 months prison	Created phoney medical bills and authorized payment on them. Eleven others arrested for cashing the checks generated to pay the claims.
13/94	Data Entry Employee, Lab Division, NYC Dept. of Health	§156.25 Computer Tampering 3	Open case	Changed HIV test results from positive to negative for one patient without permission or authority.
21/94	Clerk, Housing Preservation and Development	§170.10 Forgery 2	PG: §110/155.30 (AM) Attempted GL 4 Sent: Conditional discharge	Took three checks totaling $2,900 made out to HPD employees on leave and cashed them, using fake HPD identification cards.

Case	Position	Charge / Disposition	Description
28/94	Temp. Tolltaker Henry Hudson Bridge, TBTA	§155.35 Grand Larceny 3 PG: §155.25 Petit Larceny (AM) Sent: 3 yrs probation	Pocketed $4,631.80 in tolls during his 90-day work period.
117/94	Employee, NYC Dept. of Health	$200.10 Bribe Receiving 3 PG: §200.35 Receiving Unlawful Gratuities (AM) Sent: 3 yrs probation	Accepted money to expedite the issuance or correction of death certificates.
126/94	Temp. Tolltaker Henry Hudson Bridge, TBTA	§155.35 Grand Larceny 3 PG: §155.25 Petit Larceny (AM) Sent: 3 yrs probation	Stole $4386 in tolls collected in 12 days.
148/94	Supervisor of Collections, Parking Violations Bureau	§155.35 Grand Larceny 3 PG: §155.35 (DF) Sent: Conditional discharge	Altered and negotiatied 18 money orders worth $5,392 intended for the Parking Violation Bureau.
200/94	Temp. Tolltaker, Triborough Bridge, TBTA	§155.30 Grand Larceny 4 Open case	Stole $2716 in tolls collected.
216/94	Tow Truck Operator, Dept. of Transportation	$200.10 Bribe Receiving 3 Open case	Solicited and accepted a $100 bribe to release a car from being towed.
223/94 and 269/94	Traffic Enforcement Agents	$200.10 Bribe Receiving 3 Open cases	Solicited and received bribes in lieu of issuing moving violation summonses.
232/94	Brooklyn Deputy City Collector	$175.35 Offering False Instrument Open case	Submitted falsified documents hiding the fact that he was a city employee to apply for and win contracts with HPD to manage and rehabilitate city-owned buildings.
249/94	Mechanic, Bus Depot	§155.25 Petit Larceny 11/94, Adjourned contemplating dismissal	Stole diesel fuel from bus depot at 146 Street and Lenox Avenue.

Appendix 2   1984–1991 Federal Prosecutions of State/Local Officials

Position	Offense	Disposition
1984		
Joseph Pisani State Senator	Mail fraud; tax evasion; filing false tax returns	Convicted
14 NYC electrical inspectors and supervisors	Operation Ampscam bribery	13 convicted 1 acquittal
John Cassiliano Former NYC Dept. of Sanitation Supervisor	Racketeering; conspiracy; extortion; tax evasion	Convicted
10 NYC Water and Sewer Inspectors	Operation Norton extortion; mail fraud; racketeering; bribery	10 convicted
14 NYC Housing Authority Employees	Bribery; extortion; kickbacks	14 convicted
Leonard S. Caruso NYC Police Officer	Extortion	Indicted
Augustus C. Julbes NYC Police Officer	Extortion	Indicted
1985 No State Officials		
Dewanda Howard NYC DOT, Traffic Enforcement Lieutenant	Extortion; conspiracy to commit bribery	Convicted
Charles Underwood DOT, Traffic Enforcement Agent	Extortion; conspiracy to commit bribery	Convicted
Eric Prescott DOT, Traffic Enforcement Agent	Extortion; conspiracy to commit bribery	Convicted
John Cooper DOT, Security Guard Supervisor	Extortion; conspiracy to commit bribery	Convicted
Ronald Coppedgo DOT, Security Guard	Extortion; conspiracy to commit bribery	Convicted
Joseph Savino, Jr. Former NYC Councilman	Poss. of automatic machine gun with silencer, 3 pistols with silencers; tax evasion	Convicted
Robin Thomas Manhattan DA Clerical Employee	Conspiracy to arrange sham marriages for aliens; false filings to INS	Complaint filed
Patricia Clay Manhattan DA Clerical Employee	Conspiracy to arrange sham marriages for aliens; false filings to INS	Complaint filed
Robert N. Sternberg Former Chief Accountant NYC Human Resources Administration	Conspiracy and embezzlement of Medicaid funds	Convicted

Appendix 2   *(continued)*

Position	Offense	Disposition
Howard Scheiner Social Worker, NYC Human Resources Administration	Conspiracy and embezzlement of Medicaid funds	Convicted
Brian Ingber Supervisor, Town of Fallsburg and Chair of County Board Supervisors	RICO; mail fraud; obstruction of justice re: Sewer Waste Project	Convicted
Wayne Pirnos Town Officials, Fallsburg	RICO; mail fraud; obstruction of justice re: Sewer Waste Project	Convicted
Theodore Marsden, Town Councilman, New Windsor	Extortion; obstruction of justice	Convicted
Charles Rispoli Dept of Sanitation	Conspiracy; tax fraud	Convicted
Ernest Green NYC Commissioner of Public Works	Conspiracy	Convicted
18 Housing Authority Superintendents and Employees	Extortion; bribery; kickbacks	Convicted
1986 Fernando Bragaglia Retired NYS Building Inspector	Extortion; tax evasion	Convicted
Stanley Friedman Bronx Democratic Chair	RICO; mail fraud	Convicted
Michael Lazar Real Estate Developer, Former Chair of NYC Taxi & Limousine Commission	RICO; mail fraud	Convicted
Lester Shafman Director, NYC Parking Violations Bureau	RICO; mail fraud	Convicted
6 Housing Authority Superintendents	Mail fraud; extortion; bribery; kickbacks	Convicted
Krishan Taneja Civil Engineer, Manhattan Borough President's Office	Insider trading	Convicted
Robert Chislom Employee, NYC Human Resources Administration	False statements to VA	Indicted
Leroy Elvitt Employee, NYC Dept. of General Services	False statements to VA	Indicted
Mary Ann Ricetti Employee, NYC Board of Education	False statements to VA	Indicted

continued

Appendix 2   (*continued*)

Position	Offense	Disposition
Milagros Rivera Employee, NYC Board of Education		Indicted
Joseph Spagnoli Employee, NYC Dept. of Parks	False statements to VA	Indicted
Geoffrey Lindenauer Deputy Director, NYC Parking Violations Bureau	RICO; mail fraud	Convicted
Roy Norman Slusher Rockville Centre Police Officer	Conspiracy; credit card fraud	Convicted
1987 Hortense Gabel NYS Supreme Court Justice	Abuse of position	Indicted
Cheryl Lee NYS Corrections Officer	Tipped off drug dealer to DEA investigation	Indicted
James F. Tansey NYS Police Officer	Conspiracy; aiding and abetting false statements in passport application; poss. of false identification documents	Complaint filed
David Allen Clerk, NYC Bureau of Vital Records	Issuing false birth certificates	Indicted
Jerome Clemmons Clerk, NYC Bureau of Vital Records	Issuing false birth certificates	Indicted
Charles Cino NYC Housing Authority Superintendent	Kickbacks	Convicted
Gregory Pagoulatog NYC Housing Authority Superintendent	Kickbacks	Convicted
Louis Cosentino NYC Housing Authority Superintendent	Kickbacks	Convicted
Joseph Eisenberg Section Head, Operating Services, NYC Office of Management and Budget	Kickbacks; filing false tax returns	Convicted
Frank Feaster Section Head, Operating Services, NYC Office of Management and Budget	Same	Convicted
Trevor Thomas Clerk, NYC Bureau of Vital Records	Issuing false birth certificates	Indicted

Appendix 2   (*continued*)

Position	Offense	Disposition
39 employees from various cities, Directors of Purchasing, Commissioners of Public Works, and Highway Superintendents	Operation Double Steel kickback schemes	32 convicted 7 indicted
Bess Myerson Commissioner, NYC Dept of Cultural Affairs	Scheme to defraud in hiring of Hortence Gabel's daughter; obstruction of justice	Indicted
Stanley Simon Bronx Borough President	Wedtech scandal; extortion; racketeering; perjury; tax evasion	Convicted
1988		
Israel Ruiz, Jr. State Senator	Perjury; submitting false financial statements to a bank	Indicted
Audrey Booker Inspector, NYC Housing Authority	Extortion	Convicted
George Robinson Former Lieutenant, Edison, NJ Police	Conspiracy to deal in counterfeit currency; interstate transportation of stolen property	Indicted
Nicholas Sorrentino Former Deputy Director, NYC Dept of Environmental Protection	Bribery; extortion	Convicted
Salvatore Ascione Former Deputy Director, NYC Dept. of Environmental Protection	Bribery; extortion	Convicted
Frank Bianco Former Director, Motor Equipment Maintenance, NYC Dept of Sanitation	Conspiracy to steal property	Convicted
Philip Episcopo Former Supervisor, Triborough Bridge and Tunnel Authority	Bribery	Convicted
Arthur Kindred Deputy Director, Minority Business Development Office	Extortion	Convicted
Sal Ascione Director of Motor Vehicles, NYC Dept. of Environmental Protection	Conspiracy to accept bribes; mail fraud; tax evasion	Convicted
1989		
Richard E. Schermerhorn State Senator	Tax evasion; obstruction of justice; making false statements to a bank	Convicted
Peter Nacarato Highway Superintendent	Bribery	Acquitted

continued

Appendix 2   (*continued*)

Position	Offense	Disposition
George Moncayo Clerk, Dept. of Motor Vehicles	Bribery	Convicted
William T. Martin NYS Supreme Court Justice	Tax evasion; conspiracy	Convicted
Bruno Nagler NYC Bureau of Water Supply	Extortion	Convicted
John Perykasz NYC Bureau of Water Supply	Extortion	Convicted
Vincent Petino Guard, Corrections Dept.	Illegal sale of firearms	Indicted
William Sheffel Laborer	Bribery	Resigned and paid restitution. Charges dropped.
1990		
Peter Albertini Road Test Examiner, Dept. of Motor Vehicles	Bribery	Convicted
Andrew Jenkins New York State Senator	Use of wires to launder money	Indicted
Dominick Valente NYC Building Inspector	Extortion	Indicted
Thomas Verderosa NYC Building Inspector	Extortion	Indicted
Sylvester Smith NYC Building Inspector	Extortion	Indicted
Ted Weber Olive, New York, Highway Supervisor	Kickbacks	Indicted
Thomas Bogert NYC Police Officer	Distribution of narcotics	Convicted
Bernie Cawley NYC Police Officer	Sale of illegal firearms	Convicted
34 Licensing Examiners and Clerks NYS Dept. of Motor Vehicles	Bribery; issuance of false drivers licenses, vehicle registrations, and other documents	Complaint filed
4 Data Processors, NYC Office of Child Support Enforcement	Theft of child support funds	Convicted
Vincent J. Catalfo Court-Appointed Guardian (held 80 guardianships)	Tax evasion; mail fraud; money laundering	Convicted

Appendix 2 (*continued*)

Position	Offense	Disposition
Leona Nicholas Administrative Aide, NYC Public Administrator	Theft of public assistance checks made out to deceased individuals	Complaint filed
Frank Ling Aide to Mayor Dinkins	Counterfeited immigration documents; made false statements during security clearance	Complaint filed
James Gribben NYC Police Officer	Conspiracy to commit perjury	Indicted
Carlos Maldonado NYC Police Officer	Conspiracy to commit perjury	Indicted
Krishnanan Hiralal Employee, NYC Housing Authority	Bribery	Indicted

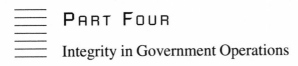

PART FOUR

Integrity in Government Operations

Eight

Purging Corruption from Public Contracting: Blacklists,
Debarments, and the Paralysis of Procurement

> We're trying to streamline our extensive procurement system, but each time
> we take a step forward PPB [Policy Procurement Board] adopts a new and
> more complex set of procurement rules that creates more paperwork and
> slows things down. The new rules do not permit the city to purchase fast or
> efficiently. We sacrifice speed and efficiency in order to prevent corruption. I
> just don't believe corruption can be prevented by rulemaking.
>
> Interview with a New York City Department of
> Transportation Official, June 1992

New York City is one of the biggest contracting entities in the world. Each
year city agencies enter into approximately 40,000 contracts worth almost
$8 billion, approximately one-fourth of the total city budget. These con-
tracts cover everything from pencils to legal services for indigent criminal
defendants, from methadone treatment for heroin addicts to architectural
consultants, from external auditing to billion-dollar construction.[1] Awarding and supervising contracts with private firms is one of city government's
most important responsibilities. In this chapter we will see how, over the
years, anticorruption mechanisms, including scrupulous "neutrality" in
choosing contractors and conformity to multiple layers of investigation and
accountability, have transformed the public contracting process into a laby-
rinth which jeopardizes governmental efficiency.

Competitive Bidding in New York City

Perhaps the most notorious scandal in nineteenth-century New York City
involved the awarding and administering of contracts for the construction
of the Manhattan courthouse. In 1858, the County Board of Supervisors
allocated $250,000 for this project. Four years later, Tammany Hall boss
William Marcy Tweed and his supporters gained control of the board. Boss

Tweed steered lucrative contracts to firms which gave him kickbacks or in which he and his cronies had personal financial interests. They brazenly allowed contractors to pad their bills in exchange for a percentage of their fraudulent overcharges. By the time the courthouse was completed, over a decade later, its cost had escalated to over $13 million. It has been estimated that from the courthouse alone, Tweed and his friends siphoned $9 million.[2]

In one of the bursts of reform fervor that have punctuated New York City history, reformers in the 1870s threw out the Tweed ring and sent Tweed himself to prison. The new administration created the Office of the Commissioner of Accounts (OCA), the precursor of today's Department of Investigation, and redesigned the contracting system so that city officials did not have unrestrained discretion in awarding contracts. The reformers fought for the adoption of competitive bidding, an anticorruption strategy dating back to the Revolutionary War.[3]

The essentials of competitive bidding require the government agency that wishes to purchase goods or services to publicize its specifications and invite bids. An interested individual or firm submits a sealed bid, offering to perform the contract for a specified price. The bids are opened at a public meeting, and the contract is awarded to the lowest "responsible" bidder. In theory, a city using a competitive lowest-responsible-bidder system reaps the benefits of (1) lowest price, (2) prevention of official corruption, and (3) providing equal opportunities to all would-be contractors. One of the drum beats of the anticorruption project has been the demand that a higher percentage of contracts be awarded by competitive bidding.

The 1986 New York City Parking Violations Bureau (PVB) scandals reinforced distrust of and opposition to contracts that were not competitively bid. Corrupt PVB officials had used the "sole-source" exception to competitive bidding to award "sweetheart" contracts for collecting parking fines to companies with connections to top PVB officials and the Democratic party bosses, Donald Manes and Stanley Friedman. Even when competitive bids were sought by the PVB, the process was corruptly manipulated. The city's contract for hand-held computers with Citisource, the firm in which Stanley Friedman was the controlling shareholder, was "fixed." Citisource played a hidden role in writing the city's specifications. Geoffrey Lindenauer, deputy director of the PVB and a Citisource shareholder, drafted the contract specifications in such a way that Citisource had an enormous advantage. Despite criticism of Citisource by the PVB's technical unit head, Lindenauer pushed the contract through. He even went so far as to fire the technical unit head and then lied to PVB's contract selection committee, telling them he had visited the Citisource plant and had seen the hand-held computers. In reality, Citisource was a shell company created by Manes, Lindenauer, and Friedman; it had no assets, no employees, no history of operations, and no hand-held computers.[4]

The media and reformers blasted the contracting process that permitted officials to bypass or manipulate the competitive bidding system. The state comptroller testified before the Charter Revision Commission that

> [t]wo billion dollars, or 40 percent [of all City contracts], are awarded on a no-bid basis, without reliance on competitive bidding, the basic safeguard of our public contracting. This amounts to 10 percent of the entire City budget. But it is an activity—as our audits and reports have shown—which has been so loosely managed and so little controlled that it has been an open invitation to steal.[5]

In the wake of the PVB scandals, aversion to noncompetitive contracting was so strong that several public officials were fired for failing to use competitive bidding to award a barge contract (to house jail inmates) to a company with which the agency had a good long-term relationship. When the corruption scandals erupted in 1986, the New York City Charter Revision Commission, which was appointed several years earlier to redesign city government, was already well into its deliberations about the future structure of city government. According to one of the principle draftsmen, the charter's new "procurement system was primarily shaped in reaction to the corruption scandals." The 1989 Charter restricts the types of contracts (principally "emergency") that can be awarded without competitive bids. In an "emergency," defined as "an unforeseen danger to life, safety, property, or a necessary service," contracts may be let without competitive bids. The charter also excuses an agency from competitive bidding where it is "not practicable or not advantageous." The agency head must submit a written explanation to the Procurement Policy Board for approval. Where there is only one source for the goods or services or where the contract is for $500 or less, competitive bidding is also not required.[6]

In all other circumstances, contracts must be awarded to the lowest responsible bidder. In order to be deemed responsible, contractors must satisfy vague integrity standards. The charter permits the comptroller to object to the award of a contract and an agency's designation of a particular contractor as responsible, "if in the comptroller's judgment there is sufficient reason to believe that there is possible corruption . . . or that the proposed contractor is involved in corrupt activity."

The 1989 Charter established a Procurement Policy Board (PPB) which, for the first time in New York City history, sets citywide contracting policy.

Within a year, the PPB issued several hundred pages of regulations covering every aspect of contracting. The preamble to this comprehensive procurement code states that one of the underlying purposes of the rules is "to safeguard the integrity of the procurement system and protect against corruption, waste, fraud, and abuse."[7] In a "Statement of Ethics Policy," the rules explain that

> City contracting personnel work under the constant scrutiny of their superiors, their peers, contractors and prospective contractors, the press and the public. As public employees responsible for the expenditure of billions of taxpayer dollars, City contracting personnel have a responsibility to ensure that their conduct will not violate the public trust placed in them. They must make certain that their conduct does not raise suspicion or give the appearance that they are in violation of their public trust. It is not too much to say that City contracting personnel must be above reproach. Their actions must be governed at all times by the highest standards of honesty, integrity, and impartiality. Rules cannot address specifically every incident or situation which may arise.[8]

The "Statement of Ethics Policy" sets forth golden rules to guide the conduct of public officials involved in procurement, including: (1) always encourage competition, prevent and avoid favoritism, and get the best value for the city; (2) accept no gifts, favors, or entertainment from contractors or prospective contractors, and place the public interest above self-interest; (3) do not use confidential information obtained in the performance of city duties; and (4) "[r]eport corruption and unethical practices, wherever and whenever discovered, to the appropriate official."[9]

The procurement code requires each agency's chief contracting officer and chief administrator to determine whether a contractor or vendor is financially, operationally, and *morally* responsible.[10] The burden of proof on the issue of responsibility falls on the contractor. In order to be deemed responsible, a vendor must demonstrate a satisfactory record of business activity.[11] City officials have established a computerized data bank, the Vendor Information Exchange System (VENDEX), to assist officials in determining whether the contractor is morally qualified to do business with the city. Firms and their principals must complete a twenty-six-page VENDEX questionnaire which calls for extensive background information about the business, its principals, its tax returns, and its history of government contracting.[12] Former Executive Director of the PPB Constance Cushman stated that "the burden in filling out these forms is so great it can discourage small or minority-owned contractors from bidding."[13] The questionnaire contains questions such as the following:

Has this business or any subsidiary of this business, or any current or former directors, principals, officers, or managerial employees of this business, either before or during their employment:

- been formally debarred from being awarded a contract or been informed that it could not bid on a contract by any government agency?
- been a respondent before a City Board of Responsibility?
- been denied a contract despite being a low bidder or as a result of an administrative action by any administrative agency?
- been suspended or otherwise declared ineligible by any government agency?

Has this business or any subsidiary of this business, or any current or former directors, principals, officers, or managerial employees of this business, either before or during their employment:

- [had] any felony charges pending?
- [had] any misdemeanor charges pending?
- been convicted, after trial or plea, of a felony in the past 10 years?
- been convicted, after trial or plea, of a misdemeanor in the past 3 years?

An affirmative answer to any of these questions is likely to be disqualifying.

VENDEX also maintains a computerized database that, by law, must include all convictions, indictments, debarments, and findings of nonresponsibility that have been entered against public contractors, their owners, and their high-level employees.[14] The original idea was to include data bearing on the future performance and integrity of contractors (e.g., those contractors who had defaulted on a previous public contract). However, the only information consistently entered into the database is whether a company has been either debarred from all city contracts or found "not responsible" by one or more agencies for fraud (in bidding, performance, or certification as a minority business enterprise), or declared a "poor performer," and even on these matters there are many omissions and some mistaken inclusions.[15]

New York City Local Law 5 mandates that VENDEX contain "cautions" for any firm or person who has been debarred by "any other government entity" and for firms alleged to be involved in criminal activity as shown by "reports of . . . the New York State Organized Crime Task Force."[16] Under Comptroller Elizabeth Holtzman (1989–93), the comptroller's staff pushed aggressively to expand the criteria and sources for cautions, so that a wider variety of allegations, investigations, and suspicious business relationships are entered into VENDEX.[17]

Before formally awarding a contract to a low bidder, an agency must check the VENDEX computer system for cautions. The bidder's questionnaire responses are also checked for false or misleading statements. The agency can make further inquiries to the Department of Investigation (DOI). While the DOI may have information about past wrongdoing, it does not and claims it cannot divulge information about pending investigations. Ultimately, the decision whether to let the contract to a particular contractor rests with the agency head.

If the agency's chief contracting officer believes the would-be contractor is "corrupt," the contract *must* be denied. The contractor can appeal to the agency head and, if unsuccessful, to the mayor. Even if the agency head judges the contractor morally qualified to do business with the city, the comptroller may object to and temporarily delay the registration of the contract. The mayor may override the comptroller's objection, but this must be done in writing and will invariably attract criticism.

Ultimately, the officials who decide whether a contractor's integrity meets the responsibility standard must be sensitive to the political risks of giving the would-be contractor the benefit of the doubt. It is understandable that agency officials believe that the safer course is to disqualify a contractor against whom there is *any negative entry* in VENDEX or the DOI files. One contractor, who had done satisfactory work for the Department of Housing Preservation and Development in the past, left unanswered a portion of a VENDEX questionnaire regarding subcontractor performance, because the contractor had not used any subcontractors on the project. As a result of this omission, the contractor received a "U" or "unsatisfactory" designation on VENDEX, and subsequently lost out on a $500,000 city contract. The contractor's lawyer stated,

> Now my client is branded. The nightmare becomes Kafkaesque. He goes to another agency where he's worked for years and always got glowing reviews. He's the low bidder on a Department of General Services job. But then the "U" comes up again on the computer. One black mark, and it's all over . . . VENDEX is like a virus, and now he's infected forever.[18]

Blacklisting Contractors

The law-enforcement community has sought to enlist the assistance of city agencies in the war against organized crime by denying public contracts to firms that are owned or strongly influenced by Cosa Nostra.[19] The School Construction Authority's (SCA) inspector general and vice president has been at the vanguard of this effort. The SCA's organization and operation indicate the direction in which the anticorruption project is evolving. The SCA Board of Directors was determined not to have the multi-billion-dollar school construction effort derailed by the kind of corruption scandals that previously afflicted the Board of Education's building program.[20] Therefore, the board established a state-of-the-art internal inspector general's office with a sixty-person staff and appointed Thomas Thacher II, formerly head of the Organized Crime Task Force's initiative against corruption and racketeering in the New York City construction industry, to be inspector general as well as an SCA vice-president (symbolically indicating the agency's commitment to preventing corruption).

Thacher moved aggressively to protect the SCA's $6-billion construction program from the taint of corruption by implementing, among other strategies, a prequalification procedure for contractors. The first step for would-be contractors was to answer a thirty-page questionnaire which, among other things, asked the following:

> In the past ten years has the applicant firm, or any of its current or past key people or affiliate firms . . . taken the Fifth Amendment in testimony regarding a business related crime? . . . given or offered to give money or any other benefit to a labor official or public servant with intent to influence that labor official or public servant with respect to any of his or her official acts, duties or decisions as a labor official . . . [or] agreed with another to bid below the market rate?[21]

False answers disqualify the contractor from SCA contracts and may result in criminal prosecution.

In August 1991, Thacher announced that the SCA was debarring, for up to five years, more than fifty construction firms. Nearly half of these debarments were based on suspected mob ties or criminality, not on poor contract performance.[22] Even more novel, the SCA required some firms of questionable integrity to hire independent investigative auditing firms as a condition for getting SCA work. The consulting firm's task is to implement an in-house corruption prevention program, including a code of business ethics for the contractor, and to monitor the contractor's compliance with both the program and the code. The SCA requires the consulting firm to report to both the contractor's top management and to the SCA's inspector general.[23] This anticorruption strategy, in effect, projects the anticorruption project into the private sector.

The Comptroller's Purge of Dishonest Contractors

In 1989, after the voters approved the new City Charter, the New York City Comptroller's Office quickly formed a special Contract Audit Unit to carry out its responsibility for determining whether city contractors met standards of integrity. The Audit Unit has taken this responsibility very seriously, seeking information on city contractors from VENDEX, the SCA, and a range of federal, state, and local law-enforcement agencies. The comptroller objected to scores of city contracts, mostly because of the contractor's alleged organized crime ties, but in some cases because of other "character defects" such as bad debts or obtaining a performance bond from a broker or sham bonding company, a common fraud in the construction industry.

In one high-visibility case, Comptroller Holtzman persuaded the city to rescind a contract to remove abandoned cars from Brooklyn streets held by a company run by Carmine Agnello, mob-boss John Gotti's son-in-law. According to Holtzman, the C & M Agnello Company and its owner "had been implicated in a 'chop shop' (stripping down stolen cars) in Queens and [Carmine Agnello] was under investigation for possible jury tampering in an organized-crime trial in Brooklyn involving Mr. Gotti's brother, Gene."[24] Agnello employees, in protests widely covered by the media, argued that they were engaged in a legitimate business, that Mr. Agnello was on the job every day, and that the company's employees were, in effect, being convicted and punished without trial and for alleged offenses unrelated to the public contract they had been performing. Certainly Agnello and his employees were pleading from self-interest. Nevertheless, this and similar stories point out that in a panoptic regime, even an unproven ethics allegation will trump evidence of competent contract performance.

During the summer and fall of 1991, the Comptroller sparred with the Department of Correction (DOC) in another high-visibility case concerning a jail construction contract. The DOC asserted that the contract it intended to sign with the DeMatteis Construction Company did not need to be let by competitive bidding because of an overcrowding emergency at the jail complex on Rikers Island.[25] The comptroller disagreed, criticizing the DOC for having entered into a contract with a company whose president owned a majority interest in a concrete company that was operated by the son-in-law of former Gambino (Cosa Nostra) crime family boss Paul Castellano. The DOC countered that the comptroller was risking a public safety crisis by attacking the integrity of a legitimate and competent contractor which had even passed the SCA's scrutiny. After the contract became an issue in the press, Mayor David Dinkins canceled it and debarred the company from all city work.[26] DeMatteis sued the city, claiming that the comptroller's and mayor's determination of nonresponsibility was unfounded. The state supreme court agreed and held that "[o]ther than innuendo, speculation, and guilt by association, particularly by one with an Italian surname, there is simply no evidence of a probative value to show a link between [DeMatteis] and underworld figures or a link between [Dematteis] and corrupt activity."[27] The appellate court, in affirming the lower court decision, characterized the city's debarment as "arbitrary and capricious."[28]

The city has occasionally sought, in effect, to cancel a contract even *after* it has been satisfactorily performed. According to New York law, the city may bring suit for return of all money paid to a contractor who has completed work if the contractor has been *subsequently* convicted of a criminal offense. In *S.T. Grand, Inc. v. City of New York*,[29] the city awarded an emergency contract to S.T. Grand for the cleanup of the Jerome Park Reservoir. After completing the project, S.T. Grand sued the city for the unpaid balance. The city counterclaimed that the contract was "illegal" because after completing the project, S.T. Grand was convicted of bribing a city official in exchange for awarding the contract. The court held that where work is done under an "illegal" contract, the contractor is not entitled to any payment and must return any money that has been paid.

The city has applied the reasoning of *S.T. Grand* to instances where a contractor's criminal conviction was unrelated to the award or performance of the contract. In 1992, the Housing Authority (HA) awarded a contract for plumbing repairs at a Bronx public housing project to Hi-Tech Mechanical, Inc. The media criticized the award because four months earlier the SCA debarred Hi-Tech from school construction projects. Allegedly, Hi-Tech was the alter ego of ARC Plumbing, a company that for many years employed as a salesman John Gotti, head of the Gambino crime family. There was, however, no question that Hi-Tech's previous work for the HA, as well as for other city agencies, had been satisfactory. Nevertheless, Councilwoman Carolyn Maloney, chair of the city council's Subcommittee on Contracts, urged the HA to rescind its award.

After a federal grand jury indicted three Hi-Tech officials on federal money-laundering charges, the HA moved to terminate all Hi-Tech contracts. The HA took the position that all money owed to Hi-Tech for services rendered should be withheld and that $9.6 million previously paid to the firm should be returned.[30]

The current trend is unmistakable. The character and integrity of private contractors wishing to do business with New York City are now relevant. Would-be city contractors must submit full disclosures about company and personal finances. The VENDEX data base is expanding. Dozens of city agencies and independent authorities are making independent judgments about whether contractors are honest enough to do business with the city. A negative determination by any government agency may eliminate opportunities to obtain city contracts because other agency heads will want to avoid criticism for doing business with "racketeers." A single agency's favorable finding, however, will not qualify a firm to do business with every city agency, because each agency (and the comptroller) is responsible for making its own responsibility determination every time a contract is awarded.

Impacts of Anticorruption Contracting Controls on Public Administration

The negative impacts on public administration of competitive bidding, the principal anticorruption strategy in contracting, although much written about, are hard to exaggerate.[31] By removing the public official's discretion over choice of contractor, competitive bidding eliminates the official's ability to obtain superior goods and services, especially for construction projects. In effect, the city does not choose its contractors; they choose themselves. Not surprisingly, the quality of goods and services suffers.

Contracts are awarded according to lowest cost, not according to performance record. Even a contractor that does a shoddy job must be awarded future contracts if it is the lowest bidder, unless it is found nonresponsible. Consequently, many firms with terrible performance records continue to be awarded city contracts. As one city official told us,

> The feeling is that under current rules disqualification of a contractor for bad performance is too heavy a penalty. Contract officials think, Who will defend me in court when contractors sue when they're called poor performers? The charter revision fought the last war—the PVB scandal. It doesn't address the problem of performance.

The comptroller's 1990 investigative report on Diversified Products of New York, Ltd. illustrates how an incompetent and unscrupulous contractor can continue to obtain city contracts despite an appalling performance record. The report documents how, over a seven-year period, Diversified and other companies owned by the same principals repeatedly failed to perform adequately, and in some cases failed to perform at all. Despite having been cajoled, threatened, and even declared nonresponsible by one city agency, Diversified and its predecessor company continued to receive numerous contracts. As the report observes,

> This is a case study of official indifference and the costs of that indifference to New York City taxpayers. This interim report reveals that several apparently unscrupulous contractors have obtained millions of dollars from the City's

treasury over a seven-and-one-half-year period despite a contemporaneously documented pattern of their poor performance, their failure of performance, and their persistent misrepresentations.[32]

The secondary and tertiary effects of the competitive bidding system are also calamitous; indeed, they go a long way toward explaining New York City's difficulty in completing public works. First, many quality contractors refuse to bid on public projects because they cannot compete with unscrupulous contractors who know how to manipulate the system by bidding low and then piling on costs through fraudulent change orders. Second, many contractors refuse to subject themselves to the red tape and onerous VENDEX questionnaires. Third, those contractors who do bid on city jobs have become cynical and rationalize shoddy work and dishonest practices by pointing to the city's incompetence, inefficiency, and unreasonableness. Thus, competitive bidding may have reduced favoritism and sweetheart contracts only to increase fraud in contract performance.

The Kings County Hospital construction fiasco is a good example. In 1984, the city embarked on a $1-billion project to build a new public hospital in an impoverished Brooklyn neighborhood. Ten years and $119 million later, the New York City Health and Hospitals Corporation (HHC) had an administrative building, a food service building, a couple of holes in the ground, and a few parking spots.[33] This debacle led to a fusillade of accusations, criticism from the community's political leaders and the mayor, and an estimated cost of $100,000 for each day the project was delayed.[34] The chairman of the HHC Board of Directors acknowledged that his agency (but not his administration) had "completely screwed up."[35] Notwithstanding this confession, he blamed the general contractor, Santa Fe, for not properly discharging its responsibilities.

Santa Fe, chosen in 1987 to jointly manage the huge project with Turner Construction Company, encountered continuous problems, including faulty architectural plans and difficulties in hiring qualified minority subcontractors. A former project supervisor for Turner Construction stated, "We did everything we could. Seven days a week, 14-hour days. It was a never-ending battle. The problem is the system and the system doesn't work."[36] In April 1992, for instance, Turner/Santa Fe awarded an excavation subcontract to the second lowest bidder because the lowest bidder did not properly complete necessary paperwork. The lowest bidder then sued the city and was awarded the contract, only to be fired ten months later when the agency discovered that this subcontractor had failed to report its past criminal record. After a nineteen-month delay, the subcontract was finally awarded to the third lowest bidder.[37] Despite repeated warnings from Coopers & Lybrand, an independent auditing firm, that Turner/Santa Fe was mismanaging the project, the HHC approved a $16-million supplement to the management company's original $19-million bid.

Meanwhile, conflict-of-interest allegations arose concerning three contracts worth $2.5 million awarded by HHC to Darryl E. Greene & Associates, the third awarded without competitive bidding. Then it was revealed that Greene was a law partner of Assemblyman Clarence Norman Jr., a supporter of the Kings County Hospital project.[38]

Even the Feerick Commission, usually eager to recommend more anticorruption rules and monitoring strategies, recognized that the corruption controls imposed on city procurement were crippling the contracting process. Its scathing report, *A Ship without a Captain: The Contracting Process in New York City,* began with this blunt assessment:

> The problems facing New York City's contracting system have reached a state of crisis, no less and no less serious than the more conspicuous problems facing the City. A 12-month review has convinced the Commission that the City's labyrinthine contracting system wastes millions of taxpayer dollars—dollars which otherwise could be spent fighting crime, drug abuse, and homelessness. It is mired in red tape, scares away vendors, and remains vulnerable to corruption.[39]

The commission examined 798 competitively bid service contracts (comprising 75 percent of the dollar value of all Human Resources Administration [HRA] contracts) awarded by the HRA and found that 49 percent were awarded with *fewer than a bare minimum of three bids.* "HRA was unable to attract more than two bids for a wide range of services. For instance, only two vendors stepped forward to bid on a $5.2-million contract to provide cooked meals for the homeless, although 30 companies had been invited to bid."[40] The same pattern appears throughout city government. "All too often, the City is faced with a small number of 'niche' bidders, firms whose expertise lies in threading their way through the City contracting maze and who have adapted themselves to its peculiar and confounding logic."[41] The commission stressed the overall negative impact of layer upon layer of checks, balances, and anticorruption reforms and summarized the bleak state of the city contracting process as follows:

> The problems of the City's contracting system have been compounded by the City's reaction to municipal corruption scandals which began to unfold in late 1985 and early 1986. As a result, the contracting process has been saddled

with an ever-increasing burden of paperwork requiring review and approval by many different oversight agencies.

To be sure, each added layer of oversight originates in a well-intentioned response to a particular scandal or crisis. Together, however, they add up to a blueprint for paralysis. Instead of a clear vision of what constitutes good contracting practice, the City has pieced together a patchwork of checkpoints and barriers. The cumulative effect is to slow the City's business to a crawl and to deter vendors from bidding on City business.[42]

The commission made five recommendations for improving the city contracting system. First, the city should place increased emphasis on attracting more contractors, rather than identifying bad contractors. Second, the mayor should appoint a temporary deputy mayor whose sole responsibility would be to oversee and reform city contracting. Third, each agency should appoint a chief contracting officer with a professional procurement background. Fourth, the city must train contracting personnel so that they have "the skills and the tools necessary to get the best possible deal for the City." Finally, in order to cut down on delay, the city should review contracts on "a selective post-audit basis" after they are awarded, rather than before, to make sure city contracting rules are followed.[43]

The negative effects flowing from the competitive bidding system snowball. The perception that greedy, dishonest contractors are poised to exploit any opportunity to defraud the city has lead to more monitoring, double-checks, stringent contract terms, slow payments, and lately the screening of contractors for integrity. In turn, this leads to increased cynicism among contractors who feel that they are treated like quasi-criminals, and it provides them with a rationalization for further dubious practices. This, in turn is likely to spawn more safeguards and greater suspicion. One city council staffer told us that in her opinion "all contractors are crooks." It is hard to see how the city could successfully carry out desperately needed capital construction and service contracts with that operating assumption.

In such a grim situation, one of the only ways that necessary public works can proceed is by turning them over to public authorities (e.g., the Port Authority, Dormitory Authority, Urban Development Corporation, School Construction Authority), which are not constrained to the same extent by the rules that govern city contracting. Again the irony—reformed and sanitized so that it is corruption-proof, fair, and equitable, public administration has become unworkable. Essential responsibilities have to be farmed out to public authorities. These authorities, however, are not immune from pressures to fight corruption. Therefore, they are also vulnerable to the same administrative disease.

Impact of Contracting Reforms on Racketeering

It is at least difficult and probably impossible to know whether the recent efforts of the SCA, comptroller, and some city agencies to exclude corrupt and mob-connected contractors from business dealings with New York City will reduce racketeering in contracting, but there is reason to be skeptical. The effort to exclude mob-tainted firms from city contracts assumes that contractors will sever ties with racketeers. However, this assumption must be carefully examined.

It is not easy to eliminate mobbed-up or otherwise nonresponsible companies from government contracting. The New York City construction industry is a tough industry. More genteel firms have long ago been driven away or voluntarily departed. Those who now bid regularly on city contracts have learned how to make money in dealing with the city and its Byzantine contracting rules. They also have learned how to deal with corrupt building inspectors, incompetent site supervisors, mob-dominated labor unions, and in some cases dangerous, crime-ridden neighborhoods. Whether these firms can be purged from the field and, if so, whether ethically responsible firms will emerge to replace them remains to be seen. The organized crime ties or influence of many construction contractors makes the situation that much more intractable. Historically, mob-dominated construction unions have established and enforced employer cartels which can allocate contracts and determine prices. A company which challenges the system finds itself without workers or threatened with sabotage.

Debarred companies can continue and have continued to bid on government contracts under a different corporate identity and through different officers, fronts without criminal records, or as subcontractors. It is extremely difficult to prove that a new firm is the alter ego of a previously excluded firm.

Any chance of success in excluding mobbed-up firms would require extensive, expensive, and time-consuming investigation and monitoring. While there are no systematic cost figures on the exclusion process, the SCA has rough estimates based on administering questionnaires and investigating approximately two thousand contractors a year. Investigating a typical applicant costs approximately $2,000; a complex case can cost $10,000.[44] If the same kind of effort were to be implemented across all city agencies (and there is reason to believe that nothing less would be adequate), the costs would be prohibitive, and the process would exacerbate the already crippling delays that plague the contracting process.

Even if policy makers determined that these costs are worth shouldering in order to weaken organized crime, protect the city from fraud, and maintain "purity" in contractual relations, it is hardly clear that they will succeed. The hypothesis that legitimate businessmen will be deterred from involvement with racketeers if their public contracts are at risk assumes that they are substantially free to enter and exit from relationships with racketeers and that, if properly motivated, they can resist the pressures of racketeers. In many cases—and the New York City construction market is a good example—contractors have had no real option to refuse to deal with mobsters and racketeers. Failure to cooperate has meant being put out of business by mobbed-up labor unions that can bring a contractor to his knees.[45]

Conclusion

Each fiscal year, New York City expends about one-fourth of its budget on contracts with private-sector firms to supply goods and services. Such a vast amount of money dispersed in thousands of ad hoc transactions presents innumerable opportunities for corruption. The city's main defense against fraud is competitive bidding, which was originally aimed at preventing officials from accepting or extorting kickbacks in exchange for sweetheart contracts. This system has not altogether stopped the payoffs and kickbacks, but it has broken down any ongoing working relationship between agencies and their contractors. The fear of official corruption and the appearance of corruption makes it impossible to vest city officials with the discretionary authority to choose to work with those contractors in whom they have most faith and confidence, as a private person would do in building a private house or office. The competitive bidding system has contributed to a contracting system that makes it difficult to accomplish the most basic contracting goals and that continues to be abused by corrupt officials and contractors.

Ironically, the competitive bidding system does not necessarily get the job done for the lowest cost. One reason is that the system fails to generate competition. Construction and most human services contractors usually work for public- *or* private-sector owners, not both. The lowest-responsible-bidder system, poor contract specifications, dilatory decision making on change orders, massive red tape, and extremely slow payments make city contracting a venture that only a minority of contractors are willing to undertake.

In the corruption-sensitive political environment that has dominated New York City since the corruption scandals of the mid-1980s, the charter's new contracting provisions direct city officials to give more attention than ever before to the integrity of their contractors. Consequently, city officials have designed comprehensive disclosure forms for contractors to fill out on pain of perjury and disqualification for false statements. Furthermore, city officials are busy entering all sorts of information about contractors into the VENDEX database, which is supposed to warn agency officials about contractors' possible lack of integrity. Even the nonmayoral agencies and authorities are competing to appear the most holy in their contractual relationships. As one official in the city comptroller's office told us, in the rush to ferret out "bad actors," lack of evidence does not stand in the way:

> It's appropriate to not do business with a shady contractor even if there is not enough evidence to prove a violation of law and prosecute. New York City should be able to make market choices about who it does business with like its exclusion of contracts with South Africa and Northern Ireland.

The drive to rid New York City contracting of corrupt influences is similar to other contemporary social control movements such as the war on drugs. The overreach of various drug-war strategies is said to be the price that must be paid for a drug-free society. Likewise, the goal of a corruption-free city would require a war on corruption, the costly investigation and monitoring of thousands of contractors, subcontractors and vendors, and the exclusion of an indeterminable number, depending upon the breadth of the eligibility criteria and the vigor of the government's investigative effort. The whole enterprise bristles with questions of practicality and fairness. Perhaps even more important, when the drive to prevent corruption, and even the appearance of corruption, in public contracting is not carefully thought through, it makes the implementation of public works more difficult and more costly.

An entire system of norms, rules, and procedures, not to mention a large bureaucracy, will ultimately be necessary to implement a fair and comprehensive system to assess the integrity of government contractors. Ironically, the higher the moral position that government takes, the higher the standard that it will be held to, and the greater the criticism to which it will be subjected when it becomes known, as it will inevitably, that a particular contract is being performed by a firm "associated" with this or that "gangster."[46] That kind of exaggerated ambition will ultimately reinforce the cycle of scandals and reforms.

NINE

Auditing and Accounting Controls: Beyond Bean Counting

The requirement for accountability has caused a demand for more information about government programs and services. Public officials, legislators, and private citizens want and need to know not only whether government funds are handled properly and in compliance with laws and regulations but also whether government organizations, programs, and services are achieving the purposes for which they were authorized and funded and whether they are doing so economically and efficiently.

> Comptroller General of the United States,
> "Government Auditing Standards"

It's like branding cattle. . . . Get 'em in the pen where the only way out is toward you—and you're standing there ready to poke 'em.

> Joseph T. Wells, Chairman of the National Association of Certified Fraud
> Examiners, on how to interview employees suspected of fraud.

In the last twenty years, all levels of governments have enhanced internal and external accounting and auditing controls. The auditing process has become more intensive and comprehensive. Financial controls are an increasingly important component of the anticorruption project, with significant implications for the organization and operation of public administration. Public-sector auditing is now a specialty of practitioners who have better training, more sophisticated tools, and more formal authority then they did a generation ago. They are empowered by laws, rules, and professional standards that expand their responsibility for preventing and detecting "fraud, waste, and abuse," a phrase which signals the widening domain of the anticorruption project. Auditors have become more influential actors because of their numerous mandates and responsibilities and because negative audits, particularly those charging or intimating corruption, have the potential to undermine or destroy administrators. Scandal-sensitive politicians and bureaucrats implement financial controls, preaudits, and postaudits to protect themselves against the possibility of future charges that they ignored fraud and corruption.

The Evolution of Financial Controls
in Public Administration

Some early twentieth-century reformers, glimpsing the panoptic vision that would come much more clearly into focus at the end of the century, demanded comprehensive accounting and auditing to combat corruption and assure accountability. In a 1909 pamphlet entitled "What Should New York's Next Comptroller Do?" the reform-oriented Bureau of Municipal Research criticized the incumbent comptroller and articulated a vision of an aggressive and omniscient "chief audit officer" that would satisfy the aspirations of contemporary anticorruption reformers. "He will be incompetent if he does not know day by day, month by month, how every dollar is being spent, or if he fails to keep the public informed as to the acts of public trustees, including himself."[1]

The bureau proposed a two-part "test" for "control over the details of public business:

> Each contract presented for certification and each open market order issued can and should be known by the comptroller or persons responsible to him *to be expressed in such terms and subject to such conditions as will leave no doubt with respect to the quality and quantity of goods to be delivered and service to be rendered.*
>
> Invoices can and should be checked and initialed and the fact of delivery so certified as to make the persons checking, initialing and certifying responsible for knowledge of the fact certified to and *criminally liable for false certification as to the quality and quantity of goods delivered or services rendered.* [Emphasis in original][2]

The bureau saw accounting and auditing as key tools for management, as well as for preventing corruption. Ideally, the financial control system would create a "paper trail" that would enable a postaudit to determine who, at each step of a complicated procurement process, was responsible for certifying that the city obtained what it paid for.

The bureau's model of an aggressive, omniscient auditor of public accounts was not adopted. In a 1917 report, the bureau charged that practically all of New York City's accounts were in shambles. The comptroller had not even been successful in installing expense accounts, inventory accounts, and cost accounts.[3] Each agency was responsible for accounting for its own appropriations and expenditures. This system provided corrupt politicians in the Democratic party machine with ample opportunities for graft with little risk of detection. Moreover, as long as the party machine also chose the comptroller, that potential fiscal watchdog did not function as an objective, effective, external monitor of governmental operations.[4]

Anticorruption reformers in the late 1930s and 1940s advocated corruption prevention through scientific administration. The federal Budget and Accounting Act of 1921 established the General Accounting Office, headed by the comptroller general, who was responsible for reviewing agency expenditures.

> The Budget and Accounting Act strengthened the auditing function in several respects. Certification of both revenues and expenditures was vested in the General Accounting Office, as well as broad powers of investigation, a system of allotments was inaugurated, steps were taken to introduce a uniform system of accounting, pre-audit was introduced in some cases and the interpretation of appropriation acts was assumed by the Comptroller General, subject only to the over-riding authority of the Supreme Court.[5]

State and local governments gradually adopted these innovations, which included expanding accounting and auditing authority, requiring more record keeping, and centralizing accounts in the Comptroller's Office.[6] New York City significantly strengthened its financial controls by the designation of a professional budget director in 1924 and the adoption of accounting and purchasing procedures in Mayor Fiorello LaGuardia's second term (1938–41).

Nevertheless, financial controls lagged far behind the aspirations of good government reformers. In 1961, a state commission decried the absence of financial controls to strengthen management and prevent corruption:

> The accounts now kept by the Comptroller are of little use to the City departments. . . . The Comptroller's power over the departmental accounts is seldom exercised, although his postaudit reports often suggest changes in procedures. The installation of departmental systems was once a major activity of the Comptroller, but now remains practically dormant.[7]

Thus, as late as the mid-1960s and perhaps the mid-1970s, the comptroller's ability to ensure conformity to rules and accountability to the taxpayers was still inadequate.

In the 1970s, a confluence of forces combined to fulfill, and in some cases surpass, the anticorruption reformers' agendas of the first half-century. Watergate, Abscam, Operation Greylord, and a string of other scandals and investigations focused national attention on corruption and corruption control.[8] In addition, the 1975 New York City fiscal crisis generated a surge of demands for better accounting and auditing.[9] The Municipal Assistance Corporation, created in June 1975 and empowered to monitor the city budget, thoroughly criticized the city's entire financial control system, including the comptroller's office.[10]

The development of new accounting and auditing standards, and the aspirations of the federal government and the accounting profession itself, contributed to the rapid evolution of financial controls. The use of auditing as a management tool gained significant momentum as the number of accountants in the public sector increased.[11] The American Institute of Certified Public Accountants promulgated three volumes of comprehensive accounting and auditing standards: *Governmental Accounting, Auditing, and Financial Reporting* (1968), *Audits of State and Local Governmental Units* (1974), and *Consideration of the Internal Control Structure in a Financial Statement Audit* (1990). Furthermore, the profession spawned a new specialty in fraud auditing and a new professional organization, the National Association of Certified Fraud Auditors. Financial control systems of all types proliferated, including increasingly sophisticated record-keeping requirements, accounting and reporting standards and procedures, and powerful auditing methods.

Agencies were required to incorporate financial controls in their basic operations to facilitate subsequent auditing and evaluation. In some agencies, electronic data processing (EDP) empowered auditors to monitor operations unobtrusively, like the controllers in Bentham's tower.[12] Audit programs monitor agency business to determine whether rules are being followed. If not, an investigation is initiated.[13]

Big city governments now function in an environment thick with financial controls, especially internal and external audits designed to detect inconsistencies, procedural irregularities, and corruption. In New York City, the key agency is the Office of the Comptroller. However, auditing is also carried out by the United States General Accounting Office, the New York State Deputy State Comptroller for New York City, the Mayor's Office of Operations, the New York City Department of Investigation, and other city, state, and federal agencies. A description of these agencies and what they do provides a picture of the contemporary financial control component of the anticorruption project.

The New York City Comptroller

With the defeat of Carmine DeSapio and the demise of Tammany Hall in the early 1960s,[14] the political independence of the comptroller became possible. Indeed, the comptroller with an independent political base has become a potential political rival to the mayor. The main way that the comptroller can garner headlines is by exposing fraud, waste, and abuse in the mayor's administration.

The 1989 City Charter, drafted in the wake of the Parking Violations Bureau corruption scandals, relieved the comptroller of some routine responsibilities (e.g., voucher clearance) and invested the office with greater authority to monitor and evaluate agencies' organization, management, and operations:

> The comptroller shall have power to audit all City agencies . . . and all agencies, the majority of whose members are appointed by city officials. The comptroller shall be entitled to obtain access to agency records required by law to be kept confidential, other than records which are protected by the privileges for attorney-client communications. . . . The comptroller shall establish a regular auditing cycle to ensure that one or more of the programs or activities of each city agency, or one or more aspects of each agency's operations, is audited at least once every four years.
>
> The comptroller shall investigate the processing of vouchers and the payment of bills by city agencies and shall audit agency compliance with applicable procedures in procuring goods, services and construction.[15]

If not yet the "controller" in Bentham's panopticon, the New York City comptroller's office is a much more significant investigator and monitor than it was a generation ago. Like the Internal Revenue Service, the office audits some agencies and programs at random, and others because of their potential for corruption and mismanagement. Its auditors often invade an operating agency and occupy it for months.

In order to identify agency programs at risk of corruption, comptroller's directive #1 "requires agency heads to conduct [an annual] review of the adequacy of internal controls . . . and to file an 'Agency Financial Integrity Compliance Statement.'"[16] Directive #1 explains as follows:

> Internal controls are designed to encourage adherence to managerial policies. To evaluate controls, managers should ask, "What can go wrong with my operation?" and "What can I do to prevent it?" . . .
>
> Agency heads are responsible for maintaining adequate internal control systems and should perform reviews to assure compliance with various procedures, policies, laws and directives. Implementation plans for recommendations made in audit reports issued by the City Comptroller's Office and other groups should be closely monitored.[17]
>
> . . . Controls consist of all the procedures an agency used to safeguard re-

sources, provide accurate information, and assure adherence to applicable laws, regulations and policies.

Control systems include both administrative and internal accounting controls. Administrative controls encompass all agency activities. Their purpose is to insure that agency objectives are met economically, efficiently, and effectively. Internal accounting controls are those related to authorizing and reporting transactions. They deal with the reliability of accounting reports and the safeguarding of assets.[18]

According to the directive, the "control environment" covers every aspect of an agency's operations, including senior managers' attitudes toward and commitment to fighting corruption.

In the early 1990s, the Comptroller's Office established the special investigations unit (SPIN) to look into allegations of corruption brought to its attention either through tips and accusations or through the comptroller's own corruption-vulnerability assessments. SPIN's investigations are practically indistinguishable from those of a law-enforcement agency.[19] For example, in May 1990, after an arsonist burned down the Happy Land Social Club in the Bronx, killing 87 people, SPIN launched an investigation of the Mayor's Social Club Task Force, comprised of police investigators and Department of Buildings inspectors. SPIN's report declared that "the City's efforts at enforcement of the social club safety laws were inconsistent and at times seemingly at cross purposes with the administration's stated objectives. With respect to the universe of clubs studied here, those efforts appear to have left the public at substantial risk."[20] SPIN concluded that more and better inspection and enforcement was needed and that "[t]he Mayor's Office of Operations *should randomly and covertly monitor* [emphasis added] the Task Force to verify the accuracy of the relevant inspection reports, and to assess the propriety of the actions taken in relation thereto."[21] These recommendations were substantially implemented.

A comptroller's audit of the Department of Buildings provides another example of how auditing shapes the operations and priorities of city agencies. The comptroller recommended that supervisors spend a specified number of hours per day in the field monitoring line inspectors. Whether bribes and other corrupt conduct have declined is not known, but it is undisputed that supervisors have less time to meet other responsibilities. Another comptroller's recommendation led the Department of Buildings to require inspectors to report back to headquarters at the end of the work day rather than to leave for home from the field. While this reform may prevent some shirkers from going home early, it also results in nearly 30 percent fewer inspections.

General Accounting Office

The United States government General Accounting Office (GAO) is the comptroller for the federal government. Because of its size, resources, and expertise, it sets standards and provides a model for financial controls at the state and local level. The 1972 GAO "Standards for Audit of Governmental Organizations, Programs, Activities, and Functions" states that government audits should encompass both traditional financial audits and performance and program audits.[22] The goals of the performance audit include determining whether the entity is acquiring, protecting, and using its resources (such as personnel, property, and space) economically and efficiently; the causes of inefficiencies or uneconomical practices; and whether the entity has complied with laws and regulations concerning matters of economy and efficiency. The program audit is meant to be intensive and comprehensive. It seeks to determine the effectiveness of organizations, programs, activities, or functions, and whether the agency has complied with laws and regulations applicable to the program.[23] In effect, program audits provide a basis for future monitoring of the audited agency.

The GAO's 1988 *Generally Accepted Government Auditing Standards* (GAGAS) makes government auditors responsible for designing procedures to detect fraud, waste, and abuse. The comptroller general, as well as the professional auditing and accounting associations, have promoted new techniques of "investigative auditing," further eroding the distinction between investigation and auditing.

The GAO itself has authority to audit New York City agencies and federally funded programs,[24] including many programs in the areas of welfare, education, and public works. A recent statutory change authorizes the GAO to expand an audit of one federally funded program to all the programs and private contractors associated with that program.[25] For example, an audit of the Department of Environmental Protection's wastewater treatment plant project could include audits of other agencies involved in the project, such as the Department of Transportation, the Department of Buildings, the Department of General Services, and the Department of Personnel.

An example of how GAO auditors influence local governmental operations can be gleaned from the GAO's audit of the New York City Transit Authority's and the Long Island Railroad's management of federal grants. The GAO found that the two agencies did not have adequate financial control systems to ensure compliance with federal requirements and thereby left federal transit funds "vulnerable to fraud, waste, and mismanagement." The 1992 report concluded that "more than $90 million has been wasted, misused, or mismanaged since October, 1987,"[26] and recommended wide-ranging changes in the way that the agencies calculate and allocate overhead charges on grants. The effect was to cede control over a portion of the local agency budgets to federal auditors.

Deputy State Comptroller

The state constitution and statutes give the New York State Comptroller authority to audit New York City agencies that receive state funds.[27] As the audit arm of the Municipal Assistance Corporation (MAC), a state-funded bonding authority that backs the city's credit, the Deputy State Comptroller (DSC) has independent authority to audit any city agency. The DSC's forty auditors carry out hundreds of audits (95 percent program audits and 5 percent EDP audits) of New York City agencies each year.

A dramatic example of the DSC's impact on city government is its *ten* audits of the Parking Violations Bureau from September 1988 to February 1991. Among other administrative reforms, DSC recommended registering all contracts, creating a citywide contracts budget, creating a citywide office of contracts, and hiring professional contract officers at the agency level. The 1989 charter revision embodied all four recommendations, an excellent example of how auditing now influences the organization and operation of city government.[28]

Mayor's Office of Operations

The Mayor's Office of Operations includes two agencies which conduct audits of executive agencies. The Office of Management and Budget (OMB) monitors all city agencies on a quarterly basis; moreover, it has authority to analyze, audit, and investigate agency operations. In effect, the OMB's mandate is to continuously search out fraud, waste, and abuse. However, because of the size of this assignment, the OMB often looks for easily measurable indicators of agency performance. The creation and use of such indicators has a profound impact on agency operations. As one city official explained,

> [The] OMB has an enormous job and cannot cover the nuances of agency operations. Its tendency is to emphasize those things that can be counted. . . . *Meeting OMB production and anti-fraud and waste targets distorts the whole agency management process.* [Emphasis added]

The Office of Contract Audits (OCA), the other agency under the umbrella of the Mayor's Office of Operations, has similar auditing authority.

The OCA monitors agencies' compliance with procurement rules and regulations; its goal is a paperless, continuously auditable contracting system. Toward that end, it has implemented an integrated, computerized procurement information system (ICPINS) which aims to integrate four contract information networks. The planners believe that when procurement rules are incorporated into the ICPINS software, it will be virtually impossible to execute a contract in violation of the complex rules.

The New York City Department of Investigation

The New York City Department of Investigation (DOI) is directly responsible for investigating official corruption. Each year, every city agency must submit an *anticorruption audit* to the DOI. In addition, the DOI's Corruption Prevention and Management Review Bureau audits selected agencies for "corruption vulnerability."

The DOI's audit report on the Department of General Services' office-leasing procedures illustrates the reach of its anticorruption controls. The report criticized practically every aspect of leasing procedures, record keeping, and financial controls. For example:

- Documentation pertinent to important steps in the leasing process is either not maintained or is inadequate. [Rather], [t]he type and amount of documentation created and filed is determined by each employee.

- There are no written policies and procedures, resulting in employees having excessive discretion in carrying out their duties that deprives management of a standard against which actions and decisions of staff can be reviewed and monitored.[29]

The DOI's strategy for creating and bolstering internal controls within operating agencies is also illustrated by its recommendations concerning the supervision of Department of Buildings inspectors:

- Require that management better monitor the work of supervisors.

- Develop, distribute, and require the routine use by managers and supervisors of management reports that reflect the flow, progress, and processing exceptions of work performed in the various units. . . .

- Establish an independent, professionally competent double-check capability of sufficient size to provide timely, adequate coverage, and deterrence.[30]

In addition to agency-specific recommendations, the DOI has formulated general principles for making agency operations and structures corruption-proof. Segregation of money collection and fund accounting is of primary importance. In other words, those who receive funds, such as bail payments and fines, should not be responsible for certifying their receipt. A separate person or unit should be responsible for checking amounts and recording receipts.

The DOI has also merged auditing and investigation in the inspectors-general (IG) system. Until recently, each IG operated under the joint authority of the Commissioner of Investigation (the DOI commissioner) and the commissioner of the agency which she or he monitored.[31] After the corruption scandals in the mid-1980s, the IGs were made solely responsible to the DOI Commissioner, but they remained physically located in the line agencies. Accountants and auditors are key personnel in all significant IG initiatives,[32] and auditing and financial controls are key weapons in their anticorruption armory.

Implications for Public Administration

Public administration reformers throughout the century have advocated the use of financial controls in order to achieve corruption-free government. They have understood implicitly what Bentham and Foucault understood explicitly, that conformity can be produced by surveillance, monitoring, and control of information. Toward that end they have constantly lobbied for more intensive and comprehensive financial controls, promising that such controls would contribute to governmental efficiency as well as honesty.

Despite the persistence of the reformers' lobbying, comprehensive and effective accounting and auditing controls remained an aspiration rather than a reality in New York City until the mid-1970s. Then a fiscal crisis, evolutionary developments within the accounting profession, GAO leadership, and heightened concern about corruption led to the implementation of new financial controls, particularly in key auditing/oversight agencies like the comptroller's office. The personnel in these agencies, their authority and prerogatives greatly enhanced, sought ways to monitor projects and operations, indeed to redesign government, in order to reduce corruption vulnerabilities.

The profound organizational and operational implications of these developments are only now becoming apparent. As accounting professors Keith Hoskin and Richard H. Macve observe,

> [M]odern societies cannot now envisage how they could organize themselves
> without these [accounting and auditing] techniques, and it is impossible for
> us, even while recognizing their implications for power-relations, to stand

outside the regimes of knowledge they produce. Having invented them we cannot either avoid or simply transcend them: we are bound at best it seems to trying to improve them, either by reducing their inadequacies and arbitrary effects as far as possible, or by extending their number and scope.[33]

Our study of the anticorruption project in New York City leads us to hypothesize that the expansion of financial controls contributes to a steady shift in power from executive and legislative officials to the comptroller and other auditing agencies. These information-gathering and monitoring agencies are becoming more important units of government. Their wide-ranging audits generate recommendations aimed at practically every aspect of agency organization, operations, and personnel policies. Because of the politics of corruption and reform, administrators ignore such recommendations at their peril. Administrators fear the consequences of rejecting a recommendation that is directed at preventing corruption. The auditing agencies have become key shapers and determiners of public administration.

The auditing environment has led to a proliferation of internal rules, reporting forms, and bookkeeping requirements—in short, to more controls.[34] Auditing requires the audited entity to keep its books and records of transactions and operations in a manner that makes it possible to determine how and why money has been spent and with what results. All transactions and operations have to be documented and must meticulously conform to rules, regulations, and protocols. As new scandals and audits reveal gaps in control, managers must institute more regulations, which "reflects the ritual application of theory and convention, while ignoring or suppressing behavior which does not fit these preconceptions."[35] Thus, more intensive auditing generates a continuous demand for more and better accounting, reporting, and standardized procedures—that is, more bureaucracy.[36]

In the event of a corruption scandal, managers know that they will be excoriated in the media for failure to follow written audit recommendations on internal control. Top managers feel more accountable for the integrity of their organizations than for their agency's overall effectiveness. As one former commissioner told us, "It's more important to look honest than to get anything done."

Conclusion

From the beginning of the twentieth century, it was obvious to anticorruption crusaders and reformers that accounting and auditing could play a potentially crucial role in preventing corruption by constantly monitoring conduct and transactions. However, only in the last two decades has it become politically, organizationally, and technologically possible to begin instituting such controls. It seems a worthy hypothesis that expansion of financial controls and the anticorruption project are having significant effects on public administration, not all of them positive. Financial controls are essential for good management; when they also deter wrongdoing and promote integrity, so much the better. But too much (or the wrong kind of) corruption control can create a panopticon-like environment that reinforces all the pathologies of bureaucracy. One scholar warns that "[t]he orientation toward short-run fraud has led public sector accountants to overlook serious long-run problems, such as valuing public assets and debts, and managing public pensions. . . . [A] preoccupation with corruption can be costly—not only in terms of the funds spent to control corruption, but in the deflection of attention and organizational competence away from other important matters."[37] This chapter cautions against reconceptualizing the main goal of financial controls as preventing corruption, thereby permitting the anticorruption tail to wag the public administration dog. The National Academy of Public Administration said it well in its 1983 call for reforming federal management:

> Checks and balances are essential in our form of government, and there have been enough examples of abuse of power to make this clear. The question, therefore, is not whether they are needed, but how much of such protection is required and how it can be brought to bear without impairing effectiveness. The panel believes that the accumulation of such protections has, in total, become excessive and has often been represented as the answer to poor management in situations where the emphasis should more realistically have been placed on strengthening management.[38]

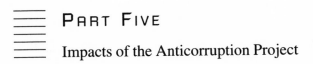

PART FIVE

Impacts of the Anticorruption Project

TEN

Waging War Against the Inevitable

> [Corruption] is an unquantified phenomenon; it is impossible to say whether the multiplication of laws and prosecutions is reducing it, keeping even with it, or falling behind. In the absence of a quantitative basis for evaluating the efficacy of criminal laws in this area, the success of the law is measured in terms of its symbolic impact.
>
> John T. Noonan, "Bribery," in *Encyclopedia of Crime and Justice*

Previous chapters have emphasized the costs that the anticorruption project imposes on public administration. These costs might be a good investment if the anticorruption project significantly reduced corruption. It is precisely this question that ought to inform policymaking and the more sophisticated discourse on corruption control that we call for in chapter 12.

Evaluating any crime control initiative is difficult, but evaluating the crime control impact of the anticorruption project is especially challenging because, as we explained in chapter 1, there are no measures or estimates of the corruption rate. By contrast, neither the Uniform Crime Report (FBI tabulation of crimes reported to the police) nor the National Crime Survey (tabulation of victimizations reported by random sample of respondents) attempts to collect data on the incidence of corruption. We therefore remain totally in the dark as to whether corruption is increasing, decreasing, or holding constant. How, then, could we determine whether the anticorruption project as a whole, much less any particular anticorruption initiative, has reduced corruption?

It should not be assumed that the ever-expanding anticorruption project has been successful in suppressing the corruption rate. If the anticorruption project has had an impact on the extent of corruption, it should be evident in the agencies and operations which have been the targets of the most comprehensive anticorruption measures. In fact, in the New York City Department of Buildings and in the Police Department, where the most intensive anticorruption efforts have been implemented, it is arguable that corruption has not been reduced. In the area of public contracting where, as we saw in chapter 8, so many anticorruption controls have been applied, corruption also flourishes.

Corruption in the Department of Buildings

As we have already seen, New York City's regulation of building permits and standards has been a target of anticorruption controls since the beginning of the century. Yet, despite the implementation of one reform after another, the following incidents, drawn primarily from the *New York Times,* reveal the remarkable persistence of bribery and extortion over the course of fifty years.

> *November 1940:* Mayor Fiorello LaGuardia suspended twenty-six elevator inspectors for extorting payoffs from contractors.[1]
>
> *March 1942:* Mayor LaGuardia suspended thirty-two plumbing inspectors for extorting payoffs in return for prompt inspection of newly constructed buildings.[2]
>
> *June 1947:* Department of Housing and Building clerks were indicted by the Brooklyn district attorney for destroying records and issuing certificates of occupancy for at least twelve buildings which had never been inspected.[3]
>
> *October 1950–January 1951:* Several building inspectors were convicted of perjury after lying about the source of large amounts of money in their bank accounts. What turned out to be bribes amounted to several times an inspector's annual salary.[4]
>
> *November 1957:* Manhattan District Attorney Frank Hogan announced an investigation into the sale of condemnation permits by inspectors to realtors. After condemnation, realtors would buy the buildings for development at greatly reduced prices. The State Assembly's Committee on Government Operations also launched an investigation of the Department of Buildings.[5]
>
> *March 1958:* A Special Mayoral Commission on Inspectional Services reported allegations that realtors maintained special accounts for payoffs to Department of Buildings personnel. The commission recommended daily, random assignment of inspectors in order to avoid the formation of corrupt relationships among the inspectors, contractors, and realtors.[6]

January 1959: The chief inspector in the Manhattan Department of Buildings was arrested for taking bribes in exchange for ignoring building code violations.[7]

February 1959: Kings County Judge Hyman Barshay ordered a grand jury investigation of the Brooklyn office of the Department of Buildings after the indictment of an inspector for "mutilating and destroying official records." A New York County grand jury was, at the same time, investigating the Department's Manhattan office, and the Department of Investigation was conducting a citywide investigation.[8]

March 1959: A New York County grand jury criticized the Department of Buildings as being run so poorly that "essential services were administered in a completely disorganized, if not chaotic manner." The grand jury found that mismanagement resulted in "improper and corrupt practices."[9]

January 1961: Buildings Commissioner Peter Reidy announced new anticorruption efforts, including higher pay for inspectors, increased engineering staff, better liaison with the construction industry, and reduced time for application processing. Subsequently, the State Commission of Investigation, chaired by Jacob Grumet, released a report based on the anonymous testimony of architects, charging that corruption existed "at every stage of operations in the plan-examining division of the city buildings department."[10]

February 1962: Mayor Robert Wagner suspended construction of residential developments in Canarsie and Mill Basin following revelations by a Brooklyn grand jury of fraudulent inspections and police shakedowns. A week later, the Board of Estimate created the position of special assistant to the buildings commissioner, responsible for "strengthen[ing] the control of the inspectional activities of the Buildings Department."[11]

May 1966: Buildings Commissioner Charles Moerdler transferred eighteen Staten Island construction inspectors suspected of "acts of impropriety and loose practices" as part of an effort to clean up the Department of Buildings' reputation. The city council rejected Moerdler's proposal that inspectors wear pocketless uniforms in order to deter them from accepting bribes.[12]

June 1972: *New York Times* investigative reporter David Shipler described extensive corruption in the construction industry, including payoffs to organized crime and public officials. He found graft at every level, especially in the Department of Buildings' inspectional services. Builders, architects, and union officials interviewed during the

Times investigation estimated that $25 million per year was paid out in bribes, an average of $10,000 per year for each corrupt inspector.[13]

1974: Following a two-year investigation, the DOI issued a highly critical report of the Department of Buildings. Using undercover techniques, DOI agents found the inspection system riddled with graft. Subsequently, 95 Department of Buildings employees were indicted, including 9 managers, 15 supervisors, 43 inspectors, and 23 plan examiners and clerical employees.[14]

February 1978–December 1981: DOI Commissioner Stanley Lupkin reported that between February 1978 and December 1981, the DOI was responsible for sixteen felony convictions of public officials and contractors for kickbacks given in exchange for awarding maintenance and repair contracts.[15]

August 1986: Two building inspectors pleaded guilty to extorting more than $40,000 in bribes and kickbacks from contractors engaged in a $2-million masonry job at the Co-Op City housing project in the Bronx. One inspector was sentenced to five years in prison and a $10,000 fine; the other received a three-year sentence and a $10,000 fine. Eventually, twenty people were indicted, and sixteen convicted for corruption, including bribery, kickbacks, and extortion.[16]

June 1989: The Construction Industry Strike Force obtained an indictment charging a Department of Buildings supervising inspector with extortion and bribery arising out of a $4,000 payoff from a Manhattan contractor to expedite two temporary and four final certificates of occupancy. In March 1990, the defendant pleaded guilty to bribe receiving in the third degree and was sentenced to five years probation, a $3,000 fine, and 280 hours of community service.[17]

1990: A joint investigation by the DOI and the FBI revealed that over a three-year period, thirty Department of Buildings Construction Unit inspectors and supervisors extorted over $150,000 from building owners, contractors, and architects to expedite inspections.[18]

March 1992: Twenty-three Department of Buildings inspectors were indicted on 124 counts of bribery and extortion for granting certificates of occupancy in exchange for cash.[19]

September 1993: Twenty-five current and former Department of Buildings inspectors were arrested for extortion.[20]

On the basis of this record, one could hardly accept on faith the claim that the anticorruption project has successfully suppressed corruption in the Department of Buildings. Corruption seems to persist and even flourish despite threats, scores of arrests, administrative sanctions, prosecutions, organizational reshuffling, stings, undercover operations, intensive monitoring, and operational initiatives to strengthen central authority and the chain of command.[21]

The New York City Police Department

Every twenty years, New Yorkers have been treated to a police scandal involving corrupt relationships between criminals and individual police officers or sometimes whole police units. Since the 1890s, six special commissions have investigated corruption in the New York City Police Department (NYPD): 1895, The Lexow Commission; 1913, The Curran Committee; 1932, The Seabury Commission; 1954, The Gross Committee; 1973, The Knapp Commission; and 1994, The Mollen Commission.[22] During the "quiescent" periods between major scandals there have also been many instances of police corruption, although they have not been treated as serious problems or scandals.

In 1895, the Lexow Commission found that police engaged in a variety of corrupt practices, including intimidating and preventing individuals opposed to the political machine from voting, taking monthly payoffs from gamblers and prostitutes, extorting money from legitimate businesses, and assaulting and harassing immigrants.[23] The commission revealed the existence of an extortion scheme among police, criminals, and bail bondsmen by which citizens were threatened with arrest and imprisonment unless they paid off.

> Men whose poverty has prevented them [from paying off the police] . . . yielded when torn away from wife and children, and have borrowed from friends and pawned their personal effects to raise the required moneys, and have then been released [from jail]. One man who could not raise the required amount of money was advised to pawn his wife.[24]

Seventeen years later, in 1912, police corruption again commanded public attention. The New York City Board of Aldermen created the Curran Committee after the murder of Herman Rosenthal, a professional gambler who was scheduled to testify for the prosecution in a case against police officers accused of conspiring with criminals and sharing the profits from their crimes. A few hours before Rosenthal was scheduled to testify, four assassins killed him. The Curran Committee found that despite the presence of several police officers, "the murderers made their escape in an automobile without interference."[25] A police officer against whom Rosenthal would have testified was convicted of instigating the assassination and sentenced to death.[26] The Curran Committee reported that corruption and graft flourished in the Police Department and that an extensive system of extortion and blackmail thrived. It branded Police Commissioner Rhineland Waldo "incompetent and unfit," and concluded that "[m]any of the existing evils of the Department [were] traced directly to his inefficiency and administrative blunders."[27] Waldo did nothing to stop the widespread police extortion. In fact, the committee found that Waldo permitted officers accused of corruption to investigate themselves, and he approved the removal of identification numbers from lieutenants' badges, making it difficult for citizens to lodge complaints.[28] The committee recommended a reorganization of the Police Department, salary increases for all police officers from patrolmen to the commissioner, more thorough record keeping for reporting crimes, tracking case progress, and improved training and recruitment.

In 1932, a commission headed by Judge Samuel Seabury (the Seabury Commission) uncovered widespread corruption in the magistrate's courts involving judges, prosecutors, defense attorneys, bail bondsmen, clerks, and police. Seabury found that police extorted money from innocent citizens by threatening arrest and imprisonment. One woman, framed by police and falsely arrested for prostitution, testified before the commission that a bail bondsman advised her to come up with the money demanded by the police because "they are not the cops for nothing."[29] The bondsman told her,

> We fix these cases up all the time. No matter how innocent you are, you are going to get yourself in a jam and they might jail you because they all work hand in hand and they [the magistrates] will take their [the police] word.[30]

The Seabury Commission's recommendations focused primarily on reforming the magistrate's courts, not the Police Department. However, Seabury's investigation led to the appointment of Special Prosecutor Thomas Dewey, who sought to destroy corruption by attacking the link between law-enforcement officials and organized crime. Dewey successfully prosecuted Tammany Hall boss Jimmy Hines, federal judge Martin Manton, numerous gangsters, such as Charles "Lucky" Luciano, and many corrupt police officers.[31]

Reports of police accepting bribes and shaking down gamblers, bootleggers, and legitimate businesses led Mayor Fiorello LaGuardia to appoint a reform police commissioner, Lewis Valentine.[32] LaGuardia ordered Valentine to bear down hard on organized crime and racketeers who exerted substantial control over the Police Department. The commissioner vowed to "[m]ake the thugs learn that this town is not a place for muscle men or racketeers,"[33] and to investigate civilian complaints of police corruption. Invariably, the officers in charge of the investigation would report back that the complaint was unfounded.[34] The following memo from LaGuardia to the commissioner illustrates the mayor's frustration at being unable to end the corruption:

> Fortunately the report [on a citizen complaint of police collusion with the mob] is on the letterhead of the Police Department, written in great big black letters. Otherwise I would be at a loss to know whether such a report came from the boy scouts or from some student of a correspondence school on How To Be A Detective. It is the most idiotic, incomplete, stupid investigation that I have seen and I have seen a great many along the same line. . . . . It is this kind of conduct that brings scorn upon the whole department. A known crook is pointed out to the police and he is called in and says he is a good man and that is all there is to it. . . . . Hereafter you will be good enough to read the reports before submitting any such drivel and rot to the Mayor. I am too busy to read such stupid writings, but I am not too busy to go over to headquarters and take hold of the department if that is necessary.[35]

Lucky Luciano, a Cosa Nostra godfather who made millions selling liquor during Prohibition and whom LaGuardia nicknamed "whoremaster of Gotham,"[36] mocked LaGuardia's and Valentine's reform agenda: "[W]hat the hell, let him keep City Hall, we got all the rest—the D.A., the cops, everythin'."[37]

Despite LaGuardia's and Valentine's efforts, collusion between cops and criminals continued. In 1950, another police scandal rocked the city when Harry Gross, head of a mammoth New York City gambling syndicate, agreed to testify before a grand jury about extensive police extortion and bribery related to gambling operations. Gross testified that he had been paying off police officers since the early 1940s.

> On the first and fifteenth of each month Gross paid the plainclothes squad in every division in which he had a gambling spot. In addition, he paid a set fee for each telephone he used in a given division. There were extra payments to precinct plainclothesmen and precinct commanders. . . . . Inspectors in charge of divisions received regular payments, as did lieutenants in charge of plainclothes squads.[38]

Gross's grand jury testimony led to the indictment of twenty-one police officers.[39]

The Gross scandal led the mayor's Committee on Management to direct the Institute of Public Administration to make recommendations for improving the efficiency of the Police Department. The institute's report reflects the scientific administration vision of corruption control which was dominant in the 1950s:

> Despite the detonation of explosive issues in recent months, we therefore address ourselves to those abiding questions of police control and administration that underlie a systematic program of police improvement. The effectiveness of police efforts is profoundly influenced by the management patterns that are employed, and even the irregular and criminal practices can be brought under control by them. This survey is intended to serve as a blueprint to that end.[40]

The changes put in place, including improved training, reorganization into functional divisions, and centralization of command, further centralized and bureaucratized the department. Corruption investigation units were established in the Police Department to deal with allegations of police corruption.[41]

Despite these reforms, history repeated itself with an extraordinary police corruption scandal in 1970. Since 1967, Patrolman Frank Serpico and Sergeant David Durk had tried without success to bring widespread police graft to the attention of department officials and then to the mayor's office. When Serpico complained about the rampant corruption to Captain Philip J. Foran, Captain Foran told him, "Well, we do one of two things. I'll take you into the Commissioner and he'll drag you in front of a grand jury and by the time this thing is through you'll be found floating in the East River, face down. Or you can just forget the whole thing." According to journalists Jack Newfield and Paul DuBrul, Mayor John Lindsay, believing that a police corruption scandal would spark riots in the ghettos and hurt his chances for reelection, informed Serpico and Durk that an investigation would begin after the 1969 election.[42] Serpico and Durk then went to DOI Commissioner Arnold Fraiman, who declined to conduct an investigation because Serpico struck him as a "psycho."[43]

In desperation, Serpico and Durk contacted the *New York Times* in 1970. The *Times* stories detailed a highly organized system of payoffs from gamblers to police officers of all ranks. One police officer interviewed by the *Times* stated that his colleagues harassed him because he arrested every gambler he could catch, instead of only those who failed to pay off the police. The officer said that "[i]t seemed like our real purpose was to beat down the competition of the gamblers who paid, to help them maintain their monopoly."[44] The *Times* stories also revealed that corrupt officers were rarely disciplined by the department: of 137 cases of police misconduct referred to the department from 1967 to 1970, only 7 resulted in dismissal.[45]

The sensational *Times* stories set off the scandal. Police Commissioner Howard Leary resigned. Mayor Lindsay appointed an independent investigatory commission chaired by Wall Street lawyer Whitman Knapp to determine the extent and nature of police corruption in the city, examine existing anticorruption controls, and recommend new and improved controls.[46] Ultimately, the Knapp Commission blasted both the mayor's office and the DOI for failing to take seriously Serpico's and Durk's allegations:

> No effective actions were taken [by the mayor's office] to find out why the [Police Department] had delayed investigating the charges, or to explore the broader significance of a situation which indicated widespread corruption among the police.
>
> Similarly, the Commissioner of Investigation failed to take the action that was clearly called for in a situation which seemed to involve one of the most serious kinds of corruption ever to come to the attention of his office, and which seemed to be precisely the sort of case his office was set up to handle.[47]

The Knapp Commission conducted an extensive investigation. Its investigators interviewed countless business people, criminals, and police officers, conducted surveillance, gathered information from paid informants, and went undercover, posing as business people or criminals who paid off the police.[48] Five corrupt police officers were recruited to wear wires to collect incontrovertible evidence of corruption in the department.[49]

The Knapp Commission held dramatic public hearings in October and December 1971, at which Patrolman William Phillips, two other corrupt officers, gamblers, and legitimate business people testified about various types of corruption, including payoffs from gamblers, extortion and shakedowns of criminals and legitimate businesses, and payoffs to destroy evidence or to keep quiet about crimes. Testimony showed that not much had changed since Mayor LaGuardia's days.

> [P]lainclothesmen collected regular biweekly or monthly payoffs [called a "pad"] from gamblers on the first and fifteenth of each month. . . . The proceeds [or "nut"] were then pooled and divided up among all or virtually all of the division's plainclothesmen, with each plainclothes patrolman receiving an equal share. Supervisory lieutenants who were on the pad customarily received a share and a half. (P. 74)

According to the commission, corruption in the narcotics bureau was one of "the most serious problems facing the Department" (p. 91). The investigations and hearings revealed rampant corruption, including police officers keeping money or narcotics taken during raids, obtaining drugs for informants, and using the fruits of illegal wiretaps for blackmail. In one instance, police raided the hotel room of a federal undercover agent posing as a dealer. Twelve thousand dollars was found in the room, and the police demanded $10,000 in exchange for letting the dealer go.

In its official report, released in December 1972, the commission characterized corrupt police officers as falling into one of two categories—"meat-eaters" and "grass-eaters." Meat-eaters, such as Patrolman Phillips (who earned $30,000–$40,000 in payoffs annually and was later sentenced to twenty-five years to life for the double murder of a pimp and prostitute) "aggressively misuse their police powers for personal gain. The grass-eaters simply accept the payoffs that the happenstance of police work throw[s] their way" (p. 4). While meat-eaters' behavior is generally more egregious and makes headlines, the commission found that grass-eaters are at the heart of police corruption. Because the majority of corrupt officers are grass-eaters, their large numbers lend an aura of respectability to their behavior. Further, grass-eaters encourage and enforce the "code of silence" that demands absolute loyalty to fellow officers. Any officer who violates the code and exposes corruption does so at great personal risk and is labeled a traitor.

Significant responsibility for police corruption was laid at the Police Department's door. The commission blasted the department for its hostile attitude toward any outside inquiry into its workings and for its refusal to acknowledge that a serious problem existed. Department officials, when confronted with corruption, typically characterized the corrupt officer as "a rotten apple in an otherwise clean barrel" (p. 6). The commission found that the rotten apple theory "bordered on official Department doctrine," reinforced the code of silence, and made reform nearly impossible.

> [The rotten apple theory coupled with the code of silence] inhibited any officer who wished to disclose corruption and justified any who preferred to remain silent. . . . A high command unwilling to acknowledge that the problem of corruption is extensive cannot very well argue that drastic changes are necessary to deal with the problem. (P. 7)

In its final report, the Knapp Commission noted that the Police Department had publicly repudiated the rotten apple theory, and the public hearings brought about a drastic change in the way police officials discussed and viewed corruption. According to one police official, "Not very long ago we talked about corruption with all the enthusiasm of a group of little old ladies talking about venereal disease. Now there is a little more open discussion about combatting graft as if it were a public health problem" (p. 11).

As a result of the scandal, investigation, and hearings, the Police Department instituted numerous internal reforms, beginning with the appointment of a new police commissioner, Patrick Murphy. Murphy, a former police commissioner in Detroit, Syracuse, and Washington, vowed to clean up the department. Murphy undertook a comprehensive corruption-vulnerability study that resulted in a decision to restructure and enlarge the Internal Affairs Division (IAD), the centerpiece of the new anticorruption effort. He doubled the number of officers assigned to internal investigations, from 150 to 300. In addition to the central IAD, which had department-wide authority, the IAD created subunits for each police command, consisting of several precincts. In addition, an IAD field unit was assigned to investigate allegations of corruption in each bureau or special unit (patrol, detective, narcotics, etc.). Under this system, both the local commander and the central IAD could initiate an integrity investigation. A special IAD team followed up and double-checked local command investigations.

Further, Commissioner Murphy required commanders to submit yearly reports detailing corruption hazards in their precincts and suggesting plans to reduce the hazards. As Murphy described it, "[E]very field commander, once or twice a year, submitted a report which was his estimate of integrity in his command. Even if there wasn't a hint of anything wrong, he was expected to take the temperature every now and then."[50]

Murphy also instituted the "accountability principle," which held commanders responsible for corruption in their precincts. Under this principle, commanders would be transferred or passed over for promotions if corruption occurred in their precincts. This created contradictory incentives: to try to prevent corruption, but to cover it up if it occurred. According to Murphy, "We won't assume you are automatically guilty if something happens under your command. But we will thoroughly investigate the methods you used to prevent it, and make a judgment as to whether you were careless, or not using your resources effectively."[51] Local commanders protested, arguing that, "[w]e can't follow every police officer eight hours a day when he's working, or the 16 hours when he's off, when he could be into corruption in his own command or another command. That's impossible for us to do."[52] The Knapp Commission applauded Murphy's reforms as "another step toward holding them [commanders] to account for the conditions in their command" (p. 236).

The second part of the department's reforms involved peppering each precinct with "field associates," internal informers who would report instances of corruption to the IAD. Rookies, fresh from the police academy, would be called to police headquarters, where they would sit outside the office of Murphy's anticorruption coordinator, William McCarthy. "[S]ome would sit quietly the whole day long, and others would be summoned inside and signed up as field associates. Those not so honored would then be sent back to their precincts, where their colleagues would immediately assume, notwithstanding any denials, that they were now under official surveillance

and had better watch their steps."[53] Murphy also instituted "integrity testing," where, for example, an officer would be given a wallet to see if he
turned it in to lost property.[54] If he did not, the IAD would take disciplinary
action.

The department's own reforms were no doubt meant to preempt those that
would be recommended by the Knapp Commission and which might be
more onerous to implement and enforce. The Knapp Commission applauded the department's efforts, but nevertheless issued recommendations
that did go beyond the department's reforms. The commission proposed a
new system for receiving and processing citizen complaints of corruption, a
special prosecutor for the New York City criminal justice system, a system
of centralized police personnel records, more disciplinary options for the
police commissioner, pension forfeiture for officers found guilty of corruption, full background investigations of recruits, and a number of changes in
training curricula and patrol assignment procedures.

The politics of the police scandal made it practically incumbent upon
the politicians and the police commissioner to be responsive to the Knapp
Commission. Over the district attorneys' opposition, Governor Nelson
Rockefeller issued a series of executive orders authorizing the state attorney
general to create the Office of the Special Prosecutor of Corruption with jurisdiction over corruption that was "in any way connected with the enforcement of law or administration of criminal justice in New York City."[55] The
governor appointed Maurice Nadjari as special prosecutor. As we saw in
chapter 7, Nadjari and his successors uncovered and prosecuted corruption
by law-enforcement officials, including judges, bail bondsmen, politicians,
and police officers throughout the 1970s and 1980s, but the salience of the
issue remained relatively low until the early 1990s.

In 1992, as the Knapp Commission members held their twenty-year reunion at the Merchant Club near City Hall, the next great police corruption
scandal was beginning to unfold.[56] The scandal began in May when Officer
Michael Dowd of the 94th precinct was arrested by Suffolk County Police
for running a cocaine ring out of a Brooklyn bodega with five other police
officers. At the time of his arrest Dowd was carrying eight ounces of cocaine. Investigators discovered more cocaine in Dowd's police locker and
$20,000 in cash at his home.[57] Dowd also took payoffs ranging from $5,000
to $10,000 from drug dealers in exchange for warning them when federal
agents were in the area, acted as an enforcer for a gang of Dominican cocaine dealers, and helped the gang commit at least one of a series of mur-
ders.[58]

At the time of his arrest the IAD had a thick folder on Dowd. For four years, Sergeant Joseph Trimboli, an IAD field investigator had brought allegations of Dowd's drug dealing to the attention of IAD officials, but the IAD failed to investigate, claiming it didn't have the resources.[59] Department insiders explained that the prevailing attitude at IAD was to avoid making big cases because they didn't want to cause another scandal like the 1987 77th precinct scandal in which 13 officers were arrested for drug-related corruption.[60]

In July 1992, Mayor David Dinkins appointed a blue-ribbon commission chaired by Deputy Mayor (and former judge) Milton Mollen to investigate the effectiveness of the IAD and police corruption. The 1992–94 Mollen Commission conducted extensive investigations and public hearings, at which Dowd was the key witness. The commission uncovered a new type of police corruption that differed from the corruption examined by previous commissions:

> While the systematic and institutionalized bribery schemes that plagued the Department a generation ago no longer exist, a new and often more invidious form of corruption has infected parts of this City, especially in high-crime precincts with an active narcotics trade. Its most prevalent form is not police taking money to accommodate criminals by closing their eyes to illegal activities such as bookmaking, as was the case twenty years ago, but police acting as criminals, especially in connection with the drug trade.[61]

The hearings made for a media extravaganza as witnesses, some testifying from behind screens or wearing black hoods, described police officers working in "crews" who stormed drug locations and stole and later sold drugs, cash, and guns. One witness alleged that Officer Alfonso Compres, known as the "Abusador," shot a drug courier in the stomach in order to rob him of drugs (p. 45). Witnesses explained how police officers stole property from the homes and bodies of deceased persons. The Mollen Commission report described an incident where Dowd responded to a call from a sixteen-year-old girl who reported her home had been burglarized:

> With theft in mind, Dowd asked her if any money had been stolen. She responded that her mother kept their savings hidden, but she did not know where. He asked her to call her mother at work to find out where she hid their cash, and offered to check it for them. The mother and daughter trustingly told Dowd where their savings—$600—was hidden. He ran to "check," slipped the money into his pocket, and reported that their savings too had been stolen, failing to mention that he was the one who stole it. (P. 24)

Witness testimony revealed that police corruption was not limited to theft, drug dealing, or selling guns, but also included brutality. According to

Dowd, brutality, or "tuning up" someone as the practice was nicknamed, was a police bonding ritual that strengthened loyalty and the code of silence among officers. Another police officer, Bernard Cawley, who was known as "the Mechanic" because of his enthusiasm for tuning people up, testified to rampant brutality at the hearing:

> Question: Did you beat up people who were arrested?
> Answer: No. We'd just beat people up in general. If they're on the street, hanging around drug locations. It was a show of force.
> Question: Why were these beatings done?
> Answer: To show who was in charge. We were in charge, the police. (P. 48)

The *Commission Report* blamed an entrenched departmental "code of silence" (comparable to Cosa Nostra's code of "omerta") and the "us against them" mentality of the officers for creating an environment in which corruption flourished. Dowd described how he initiated each of his new partners into corruption:

> Dowd told Commission investigators that each time he was assigned a new partner, he would deliberately "test" his willingness to engage in corruption by soliciting his partner to engage in minor forms of misconduct, such as taking free food and drinking on duty. Once he knew that his partner would engage in minor misconduct, he formed an express pact with him to share the proceeds of whatever corrupt acts they engaged in and to protect each other from detection. Apparently, each of his partners was willing to enter into such an agreement. (P. 18)

The Mollen Commission concluded that pervasive police corruption indicated that the Police Department's anticorruption controls, primarily the IAD and its decentralized field units, were a complete failure. It excoriated the IAD and the department for being unable and unwilling to acknowledge and uncover the scope of police corruption. That the department's anticorruption controls collapsed was, according to the commission, "no accident." The department deliberately weakened corruption controls as it became "more concerned about the bad publicity that corruption disclosures generate than the devastating consequences of corruption itself" (p. 2). Daniel Sullivan, chief of the department's Inspectional Services Bureau testified that "[t]here was a message that went out [from the top brass] to the field that maybe we shouldn't be so aggressive in fighting corruption because the Department just does not want bad press" (p. 71). The *Commission Report* set forth a list of IAD problems:

> In a Department with a budget of over one billion dollars, the basic equipment and resources needed to investigate corruption successfully were routinely de-

nied to corruption investigators; internal investigations were prematurely closed and fragmented and targeted petty misconduct more than serious corruption; intelligence gathering was minimal; . . . Internal Affairs undercover officers were often placed in precincts where corruption was least prevalent; reliable information from field associates was ignored; . . . and corruption investigators often lacked investigative experience, and almost half had never taken the Department's "mandatory" basic investigative training course. (P. 3)

Further, the commission found that IAD investigators spent over 50 percent of their time on noninvestigatory matters.

In the course of its investigation of the IAD, the Mollen Commission reviewed thousands of pages of IAD documents and discovered that IAD investigators deliberately buried evidence of police corruption by a crew of Brooklyn police known as the Morgue Boys (named for the coffin factory where they frequently met) and by officers in the 30th precinct.[62] With the help of Mr. H, an anonymous IAD insider, the commission discovered the IAD's "tickler file," which was used to bury corruption allegations involving officers who were friends or relatives of the top brass. One case buried in the tickler file detailed numerous allegations against Officer George Nova of the 30th precinct.[63] The commission confronted Officer Nova and got him to go undercover as part of a highly secretive investigation ("Operation Domino") into the 30th precinct. In order to maintain the secrecy of the investigation during the hearings in the fall of 1993, officers working undercover as part of Operation Domino testified wearing black hoods over their heads or from behind a screen.[64] After two years of undercover work, Operation Domino culminated in the arrest of twenty-nine officers in the 30th precinct, which the media quickly dubbed the "Dirty Thirty."[65] By March 1995, fourteen of the officers had pleaded guilty to drug, robbery, and conspiracy charges, and one officer was acquitted.[66]

In November 1992, when Operation Domino was heating up, Police Commissioner Raymond Kelly instituted changes in the IAD's structure and operations. Kelly expanded and centralized the IAD and the field investigative units into one bureau and renamed it the Internal Affairs Bureau (IAB). Kelly promised to direct more personnel and resources to the IAB and to provide the bureau with state-of-the-art investigative equipment.[67] While the Mollen Commission applauded Kelly's efforts, it argued that Kelly's reforms fell short of the mark. "The source of the past failures has not been eradicated, just pushed aside. As an institution, the Department will always view corruption disclosures as painful and harmful" (p. 77). The commission recommended new anticorruption strategies related to the following:

- Screening and recruitment
- Recruit education and in-service integrity training
- Attacking corruption and brutality tolerance
- Challenging other aspects of police culture and conditions that breed corruption and brutality
- Revitalizing and enforcing command accountability
- Strengthening first-line supervision
- Enhancing sanctions and disincentives for corruption and brutality
- Strengthening intelligence gathering efforts
- Soliciting police union support for anticorruption efforts

The centerpiece of the Mollen Commission's report, designed to make sure that sole responsibility for rooting out police corruption would not be the Police Department's, was the recommendation for

> [a] permanent external Police Commission, independent of the Department to: (i) perform continuous assessments and audits of the Department's systems for preventing, detecting and investigating corruption; (ii) assist the Department in implementing programs and policies to eliminate the values and attitudes that nurture corruption; (iii) insure a successful system of command accountability; and (iv) conduct, when necessary, its own corruption investigations to examine the state of police corruption. (P. 152)

According to the commission, the external police commission would (1) ensure that the department has effective methods for receiving and recording corruption allegations and analyzing corruption trends; (2) assess the sufficiency and quality of investigative resources and personnel; (3) ensure that the department employs effective methods and management in conducting corruption investigations, including abolishing the department's sole reliance on a reactive investigative system that narrowly focuses on isolated complaints and that rarely employs proactive investigative techniques; (4) ensure that the department has successful intelligence-gathering efforts, including effective undercover, field associate, integrity testing, and community outreach programs; (5) ensure that the department strengthens supervision, including the quality of first-line supervision, training of supervisors, and consideration of integrity history in determining assignments and promotions; and (6) require the department to produce reports on police corruption and corruption trends, including analyses of the number of complaints investigated and the disposition of those complaints, the number of arrests and referrals for prosecution, and the number of department disciplinary proceedings and sanctions imposed. The external police commission would also conduct performance tests and inspections of the department's anticorruption units and programs to guarantee that the department continually maximizes its capacity to police itself.

The Mollen Commission took its model of an independent police commission from the design of the Department of Investigation, but the proposed external model sounds more like the Office of the Special Prosecutor. The five members of the external board would be prominent citizens, serving pro bono, in staggered, limited terms, giving the mayor less control over the board than he has over the DOI commissioner, who serves at his pleasure.[68] As this book was going to press, Mayor Guiliani and the City Council were engaged in a heated battle over whether to implement the commission's recommendation for an external monitor. Mayor Guiliani vetoed a City Council bill that would have established such a monitor. Guiliani, who favors reviving the Office of the Special Prosecutor, opposed the external monitor because it "would dilute the mayor's ability to manage the police department."[69] The City Council overrode the veto, and Giuliani filed a law suit alleging that the council's proposed five-member monitor is illegal because the council has no authority to make appointments to a mayoral agency (the council controlled two appointments to the panel).[70] In defiance of the council's veto, Giuliani created his own external monitor, the Mayor's Commission to Combat Police Corruption, which would report directly to the mayor.[71] Nicholas Scoppetta, a former commissioner of investigation who worked with the Knapp Commission and the U.S. attorney's office on police corruption cases, was appointed to head the mayor's commission.

Meanwhile, Commissioner Kelly's successor, William Bratton, with the support of Guiliani, lobbied hard against the external monitoring agency, claiming the Police Department could police itself. To back up his claims, Bratton pointed to an internal Police Department investigation into corruption in the 109th and 48th precincts. Bratton announced that the investigation implicated between twenty and thirty officers in various corrupt practices, including shaking down drug dealers for money and drugs, stealing petty cash from grocery stores, and taking wallets from shooting and accident victims.[72] At the time Bratton made this announcement, only one officer had been arrested and two officers placed on modified duties. Prosecutors involved in the investigation blasted Bratton and Guiliani, claiming that the announcement short-circuited the investigation. One prosecutor stated,

> This appears to be good public relations over good investigations. . . . While it might appear that hurrying up is an aggressive approach, in reality, hurrying

up stalls the investigations because it lets people know about them. . . . But if
the department continues its current approach, I guarantee that by the end of
the year fewer than half a dozen [officers] will be arrested.[73]

In May 1995, sixteen officers from the 48th precinct were indicted.[74]

Even within the Police Department, anticorruption politics boiled out of
control. Commissioner Bratton fired his chief assistant in charge of corruption control, Walter Mack, and replaced him with Patrick Kelleher, a Police
Department insider. This action was criticized by the media as evidence that
Bratton was "soft on corruption." Bratton explained that Mack, as head of
the IAD, wasn't "his kind of boss"[75] and that Mack had "kept him out of the
loop."[76] While Bratton declined to explain what "loop" he meant, the media
speculated that Bratton fired him when he discovered that Mack, as a result
of an agreement with prosecutors, had been keeping secret the identity of a
30th-precinct informant.

Corruption in City Contracting

In chapter 8, we saw that the public contracting system has been subjected
to layer upon layer of anticorruption reforms. Nevertheless, it is unlikely
that an impartial observer would wish to stake his reputation on the proposition that corruption in public contracting has been significantly reduced.

Admittedly, there are no data with which to compare, for example, the
rate and average dollar value of corruption per one hundred contracts in every nth year since 1985, so it is impossible to document an increase or decrease in contracting-related corruption. Nevertheless, we can see that there
is good reason to believe that corruption continues to flourish.

Historians of nineteenth and early twentieth-century New York paint a
picture of pervasive corruption in which politicians were openly contemptuous of the law. Today's corrupt politicians are not so openly contemptuous, but the 1980s corruption scandals revealed some truly outrageous
contemptuousness. For example, according to Deputy Director of the Parking Violations Bureau Geoffrey Lindenauer, Donald Manes, Queens Borough president, once bragged to one of his protégés, "[O]nce I become
mayor, we can really make some money."[77] Operation Double Steel, an FBI
sting, conducted from 1985 to 1987 in municipalities and counties throughout New York State, uncovered rampant corruption in procurement and
contracting. Forty-four officials, including highway superintendents, parks
managers, and public works commissioners from numerous towns outside
New York City, were approached by undercover agents posing as vendors of
snowplow blades, street signs, and other products. Of 106 bribe and kick-

back offers, 105 were accepted. The one rejected bribe was refused because it was too small.[78]

Even if bribes, kickbacks, and self-dealing have declined, they nonetheless remain a basic feature of urban life in New York City and elsewhere. The regulatory reforms put in place to achieve that reduction (if reduction it be) have themselves generated corruption vulnerabilities. Undoubtedly, there has been a massive increase over time in the amount of fraud against government. In part, this corruption is a direct result of the crippling competitive bidding system that contributes to the dysfunctional relationship between the city and contractors who know how to exploit a labyrinthine, suspicion-ridden, and inefficient contracting system.

Inspectors general told the New York State Organized Crime Task Force on Corruption and Racketeering in the New York City Construction Industry that they believed there was significant fraud on every major construction project.[79] Nevertheless, the city has no way to quantify the extent (either in frequency or magnitude) to which it has been defrauded. In 1981, for example, the State Commission of Investigation received allegations of fraud and corruption in the multimillion-dollar repair program at Co-Op City, a state-financed, 15,000-unit apartment complex in the Bronx. The commission's hearings, held between 1981 and 1983, revealed that "prior to October 1981, there was widespread abuse characterized by mismanagement, waste, and corruption and that subsequent to October 1981, progress in accomplishing repairs . . . virtually ceased."[80] Emergency contracts, not subject to competitive bidding, were awarded at costs greatly exceeding the prevailing market rates. Further, inspections were inadequate and payments to contractors were not audited.

As a result of the commission's final report, twenty people were indicted and sixteen convicted. The general manager of the Co-Op City repair program, George Steiner, was convicted of extortion and tax evasion involving more than $1.2 million in kickbacks and bribes from contractors.[81] The following letter, filed at Steiner's sentencing, offers a telling commentary on the extent of corruption in public works:

> George Steiner took advantage of an environment at Co-Op City which was an incubator for corruption. The State did not provide adequate resources to protect the expenditure of its money. The [Co-Op City] Board of Directors, management and professional advisors were more interested in spending state funds first and later determining whether the expenditures were appropriate. The total lack of effective controls over state funds which were used to pay for construction defects permitted contractors to make a fortune even after having made payoffs to Steiner and others.[82]

The New York State Organized Crime Task Force and the DOI found enormous potential for corruption in the Department of Environmental Protection and that "there is reason to believe that collusive bidding, bribery, extortion, fraud, embezzlement, labor racketeering, and conflict of interest are commonplace occurrences in the agency's capital construction program."[83] Complicating the problem, New York City's five organized crime families operate, control, or influence a large number of construction and supply firms and control more than a dozen important construction unions.[84]

Conclusion

It is possible that the actual amount, frequency, or rate of corruption has declined over the course of the century, but a strong argument can be made that the anticorruption project has had a minimal impact on corruption. The New York City Department of Buildings and the New York City Police Department are perhaps the two city agencies that have been subjected to the most comprehensive anticorruption initiatives. Similarly, the New York City public contracting system has been reformed over and over again by anticorruption controllers. Nevertheless, every new scandal and investigation of the DOB and the NYPD reveals that corruption is flourishing despite layers of reforms designed to prevent it. Likewise, the public contracting process, long a highly visible target for reformers, continues to generate opportunities for corruption. We do not believe that those who assert that city government has become progressively more honest over the course of the century could support that assertion empirically.

Eleven

Public Administration: From Reform to Pathology

> Red tape tends to abound in those circumstances in which the general public
> or superiors in a bureaucratic system have lost confidence in the probity and
> judgment of the bureaucracy; the response is to attempt to control virtually
> every transaction, either by dividing it among many individuals or by insist-
> ing upon the most detailed record keeping. In many circumstances, red tape
> is a response to corruption and an attempt to control it. And yet the very
> complexities and time-consuming factors introduced by a red-tape control
> system invite enterprising people to find or bore shortcuts. In some cases, the
> remedies create new incentives for bribes.
>
> Michael Reisman, *Folded Lies: Bribery Crusades and Reforms*

It is no coincidence that the anticorruption project and public bureaucracy
have had parallel developments. Bureaucracy was the model of public administration admired by Woodrow Wilson and other Progressives precisely
because it promised to be an antidote to the corrupt spoils system.[1] To its
admirers in the late nineteenth and early twentieth centuries, bureaucracy
offered the possibility of rationalized governance by apolitical specialists
according to scientific principles, neutral rules, and fair procedures, the
very antithesis of the abhorrent spoils system.

Corruption was not supposed to occur within the properly functioning bureaucracy. Indeed, corruption was viewed as a blight on the purity of the
bureaucratic ideal. Therefore, the occurrence of a corruption scandal meant
that bureaucracy was not yet functioning properly and needed to be fine-
tuned. Thus, what we call the anticorruption project is a necessary component of the bureaucratic vision which attempts to bring actual bureaucracy
closer to the bureaucratic ideal.

From one perspective, the anticorruption project is a salve for the
wounded bureaucracy. From another perspective, however, the anticorruption project exacerbates fundamental pathologies that have always plagued
bureaucracy. Just as Wilson and the Progressives praised bureaucracy for its

rationality and efficiency, critics contended that bureaucracy was unresponsive, unaccountable, undemocratic, inefficient, and even corrupt. This
chapter recapitulates and brings together the evidence and argument of the
earlier chapters to show that the anticorruption project has contributed to
and is inextricably connected with several key bureaucratic pathologies.
Moreover, this chapter argues that anticorruption ideals and institutions
have become a major obstacle to reforming bureaucracy or replacing it with
a different model of public administration.

The Anticorruption Project
and the Pathologies of Bureaucracy

Just as the advocates of bureaucracy have always believed that bureaucracy
is the most efficient form of administration,[2] the advocates of the anticorruption project have always believed that anticorruption mechanisms and
strategies contribute to bureaucratic efficiency. We have challenged those
assumptions by illuminating the incompatibility and tension between the
anticorruption project and governmental efficiency. By making these in-
compatibilities more salient, we hope to contribute to a more sophisticated
discourse on the future of corruption control and public administration.

Decision-Making Delay

Slowness and delay are pervasive and serious failings of bureaucracy. Practically anyone who has had experience with large-scale bureaucratic government knows this only too well. For many people, government is
hopelessly slow, unwieldy, inefficient, and—bureaucratic.[3] Anyone who
has served as a government consultant and has had to wait months for reim-
bursement for travel expenses will immediately recognize this pathology.
Congressional enactments requiring government agencies to pay interest to
vendors who have had to wait an unconscionably long period to be paid is a
remarkable testament to our acceptance of and adaptation to chronic governmental delay.

Bureaucracies have been called many things—slow, inefficient, imperso-
nal,[4] ponderous, routine, overly complicated, and maladapted.[5] They have
been accused of causing "unnecessary complications, [and] stifling individual personality."[6] However, in the first half of the twentieth century,
bureaucracy was not a derogatory term. Until the 1950s, bureaucratic administration worked fairly well because

it solved basic problems. . . . It provided security. . . . It provided stability.
. . . It provided a basic sense of fairness and equity. . . . And it delivered the
basic, no-frills, one-size-fits-all services people needed and expected during
the industrial era: roads, highways, sewers, schools.[7]

What worked then doesn't work now. According to current reformers David
Osborne and Ted Gaebler, modern public administration must be flexible in
order to provide services during a technological age.

[Today's environment] demands institutions that deliver high-quality goods
and services, squeezing ever more bang out of every buck. It demands institutions that are responsive to their customers, offering choices of nonstan-
dardized services; that lead by persuasion and incentives, rather than by
commands; that give their employees a sense of meaning and control, even
ownership. It demands institutions that *empower* citizens rather than simply
serving them. [Emphasis in original][8]

Invariably, when New York City takes on a project, there are delays and
cost overruns. In the preface, we briefly mentioned New York City's failure
in renovating the Wollman Skating Rink in Central Park. The renovation
project began in 1980, and six years and $12 million later, the rink was still
unrenovated and out of service. Finally, real estate developer Donald Trump
offered to take over the project free of charge, saying the fiasco irritated
him.[9] Less than six months later, and $750,000 under the $3 million budget,
the Wollman rink opened.[10] The debacle involving the construction of
Kings County Hospital, discussed in chapter 8, is another example of city
government's inability to function effectively and efficiently.

The fact that it has taken an average of a decade to build a public school in
New York City and that this is considered normal indicates that the citizenry
has come to accept fatalistically the snail's pace of public building projects.
Similarly, for the past twenty-five years, New York City has been building a
third water tunnel to connect the city with its upstate reservoir. In 1970, contracts for the tunnel were awarded, with a completion date set for 1975. By
1974, delays and cost overruns pushed the completion date to 1978.[11] In
1989, the city, having spent close to $1.5 billion, pushed the completion
date well into the twenty-first century.[12] One project employee lamented,
"Here we are, breaking our backs in this tunnel, but we'll never live long
enough to see it finished. But hey, maybe our grandkids will drink from
it."[13]

The anticorruption project has contributed in at least two ways to the slow
and plodding style of public bureaucracies. First, the anticorruption project
demands multiple approvals for a final decision on even mundane, routine

matters to avoid any possibility that a decision might reflect conflict of interest, fraud, or thievery. Division of responsibility is a basic principle of corruption control. Decisions are not to be made intuitively, quickly, or "from the hip"; to the contrary, they are to be made "by the book," pursuant to multiple "sign-offs" up the chain of command.

Second, the anticorruption project contributes to decision-making delay by fostering an ethos of caution and even fear. Decision makers know that their decisions may be questioned by the DOI or by an audit agency at any time and that failure to dot every *i* and cross every *t* may raise suspicion and even trigger an investigation. The experienced bureaucrat, wise to the ways of self-preservation, is cautious and circumspect about committing his or her name and reputation to any decision.

Overcentralization

Overcentralization, overemphasis upon command and control, and stifling of initiative are widely recognized as some of the key pathologies of bureaucracy.[14] Bureaucracies have been characterized as

> complicated organizations that fail to allocate responsibility clearly, . . . [are rife with] rigid rules and routines that are applied with little consideration of the specific case, . . . blundering officials, . . . slow operations and buck passing, . . . conflicting directives and duplication of effort, . . . [and] concentration of control in the hands of a few.[15]

Overcentralization is pathological because it (1) causes the kind of delay discussed above; (2) distorts decision making by undervaluing or ignoring experience and judgment at the line level; and (3) negatively affects morale by disempowering subordinates. Organization theorist Michel Crozier recognized these consequences in *The Bureaucratic Phenomenon:*

> [P]ower is weak down the line, and in its absence there is relative cordiality and lack of concern. Supervisors are passive and workers tolerant. . . . However, it is important that the centralization that has occurred has caused the power of decision to be located at a level where personal influence is difficult to exercise because of the number of people involved and the lack of immediately reliable information.[16]

Public administration theorist Vincent Ostrom adds yet another charge: control in a bureaucratic administration is "law and order maintained by the commanding power of an alien force . . . in fundamental violation of the most basic precepts of democratic administration."[17]

The anticorruption project has been a key contributor to overcentralization. Indeed, the anticorruption project is practically obsessed with centralized control. Turn-of-the-century reformers associated decentralization of authority with the spoils system and ward politics. Reformers invariably sought to centralize authority because they were distrustful and suspicious of their subordinates. Further, antipatronage reformers believed that centralized government was more democratic, responsive, and accountable because its leaders were more visible. Thus, New York City government has centralized offices of personnel, contracting, and investigations, all of which sap government of the capacity to act creatively and flexibly in response to specific situations. Today, the DOI's corruption-vulnerability reports and recommendations almost always recommend more centralized control, despite the fact that decentralization is at the core of practically every modern prescription for public administration reform.[18] To the corruption controllers, decentralization means loss of control and, inevitably, corruption scandals.

Inadequate Authority

It may seem paradoxical that overcentralized public bureaucracies are also afflicted with inadequate authority. Nevertheless, this is the case. To some extent, overcentralization is the cause of inadequate authority. As authority is transferred to special agencies at the central level, the operating agencies lose the authority to carry out their responsibilities. In the parlance of organization theory, the agencies have lost control over their "environment."[19]

But the anticorruption project is very much responsible for the proliferation of "external control" agencies which significantly weaken line authority. Hundreds of auditors in specialized federal, state, and city monitoring agencies demand information, conduct investigations, and issue recommendations on agency organization, procedure, and corruption controls. In our field research we constantly heard complaints by top-level agency personnel that they had to get approvals on everything from the Department of Personnel, Bureau of the Budget, Mayor's Office on Contracts, Office of Administrative Tribunals and Hearings, and the Department of Investigation. As we saw in chapter 10, the New York City Police Department is now to be monitored by a Corruption Review Board for corruption complaints and vulnerabilities. Similarly, the New York City Department of Corrections is monitored by a Board of Correction and, for the last twenty years, by a court-appointed special master. Each time another external monitor is created, the authority of the line agencies is diminished.

The anticorruption project bears responsibility for undermining authority in a number of other ways as well. In chapter 3, we showed how civil service, the quintessential anticorruption strategy, left agency heads without the ability to motivate their employees with rewards or punishments. In chapter 5, we showed how, in an effort to encourage employees to report wrongdoing in their agencies, whistleblower laws practically assume managerial wrongdoing and leave self-proclaimed whistleblowers on the job even when their complaints of wrongdoing and retaliation are unfounded. In chapter 6, we showed how the DOI may pressure top public officials to leave a corrupt employee in place in order to improve the DOI's chances of nabbing more wrongdoers. We also showed how the role of the independent inspectors general (IGs) has made the IG a competing power center within an operating agency. The IGs, who work for and report to the Commissioner of Investigation, are authorized to attend all agency meetings, review all documents, and interject themselves into the business of agency management practically at will. In the School Construction Authority, the independent inspector general is also an agency vice-president, and arguably, with a staff of sixty, the second most powerful figure in the agency. Finally, managers in the operating agencies are constrained by masses of rules and regulations that are meant to limit their discretion. Thus, even commissioners of large agencies do not feel that they have sufficient authority to get the job done.

Defensive Management

Bureaucrats are often criticized for being cautious, unimaginative, and too concerned about "covering their ass." Crozier echoes these criticisms, arguing that the overly standardized routines, monitors, and controls imposed on public officials result in "[b]ehavioral rigidity, difficulties of adjustment to the task, and conflicts with the public."[20] One agency head we interviewed was so wary of the DOI's intentions during an investigation in another part of her agency that during the investigation she made all calls from a public phone in the corridor. Even when the DOI was not conducting an investigation, she stated that agency managers worried about where the accusing finger would point next.

The anticorruption project contributes to this pathology in the bureaucratic environment. Most commissioners and top managers take office expecting to implement their vision of the public interest. However, the values managers bring to the job are compromised, often undermined, by the demands of corruption control. While effective public administration demands flexibility, creativity, and risk-taking, concern for avoiding corruption and the appearance of corruption counsels extreme caution. Upper- and middle-level managers have to ask themselves how particular decisions will look under ex post facto scrutiny by auditors, law-enforcement investigators, and the media. If every decision may be subjected to intensive investigation, it is hardly surprising that managers adopt a defensive management style. Taking risks and "cutting through the red tape" make a manager vulnerable to corruption charges. Political scientist James Q. Wilson has described the tendency of bureaucratic managers to act defensively in the face of corruption controls:

> [M]anagers have a strong incentive to worry more about constraints than tasks, which means to worry more about process than outcomes. Outcomes are often uncertain, delayed, and controversial; procedures are known, immediate, and defined by law or rule. It is hard to hold managers accountable for attaining a goal, easy to hold them accountable for conforming to rules.[21]

Goal Displacement

Goal displacement, defined as a concern with "following the right rules rather than achieving the ultimate goal,"[22] has been widely recognized as a textbook example of bureaucratic pathology, at least since sociologist Robert Merton published his classic article, "Bureaucratic Structure and Personality," in which he observed that "adherence to the rules originally conceived as a means, becomes transformed into an end-in-itself."[23] Goal displacement frequently results in what Crozier calls the "bureaucratic vicious circle," in which the concern with following rules results in "behavioral rigidity," and difficulties in communication and in carrying out tasks.[24] As a result,

> [b]ureaucratic patterns of action, such as the impersonality of the rules and the centralization of decision-making, have been so stabilized that they have become part of the organizations' self-reinforcing equilibria. . . . [W]hen one rule prevents adequate dealing with one case, its failure will not generate pressure to abandon the rule, but, on the contrary, will engender pressure to make it more complete, more precise, and more binding.[25]

There is an obvious connection between the anticorruption project and the bureaucratic vicious circle, which reinforces goal displacement. Corruption controllers design systems to make government corruption-proof. Operating through rules, forms, and checklists, they attempt to create a decision-making process that minimizes discretion. The bureaucracy becomes absorbed in monitoring itself.

Abundant examples of goal displacement can be drawn from the organization and operation of New York City government. At the time of our field research, the Department of Buildings' assistant commissioner for operations had authority to review all operations for corruption vulnerability. Plans for decentralizing some of this authority to the department's five borough offices were put on hold while the central office implemented audit recommendations for more intensive supervision and record keeping. At the time, it seemed that the department's primary goal was to structure operations to avoid blame if corruption occurred. The information that was demanded of borough offices, the design of supervisory duties, route rotation, double checks of inspections, and the wording and review of inspection checklists were all attributable to the goal of preventing corruption. The agency's managers measured their success in terms of avoiding scandals.

Inevitably, control and monitoring functions compete for resources with management functions. Much organizational energy is expended on corruption control. For example, pursuant to the reforms mandated by the 1989 charter, each city agency must appoint an agency chief contract coordinating officer, responsible for overseeing all agency contracts and monitoring compliance with all relevant rules and laws by agency personnel and private-sector contractors and vendors. Another manager must be assigned to prepare the annual corruption-vulnerability report. Increasingly, staff designated for planning and analysis spend their time preparing for and responding to audits or recommendations of inspectors general for strengthening internal controls.

Budget cuts further reduce the resources available to agency managers for operations and services. At the same time, corruption controls are generally untouched by budget cuts because they are written into laws and regulations. Thus, the balance between the amount of discretionary funds and nondiscretionary funds is upset. Agency managers must maintain the same level of corruption controls with diminished resources, leaving even less money for operations and services. Invariably, operations and services suffer.

Internal control imposes not only direct and indirect costs, but also opportunity costs—innovation and experimentation disappear. Not only are innovation and experimentation risky from the control perspective, there are insufficient time and resources to devote to the search for new forms of management.

A good indicator of how the drive for corruption-free government stifles innovation is the number of times agency managers told us that the best way to improve their service to the public would be to transform their agency into a public authority; then, they assumed, the agency could pursue the innovations and programs that would really make a difference in the quality of service delivery.

Poor Morale

Poor employee morale is a bureaucratic pathology frequently noted by bureaucracy scholars.[26] One public employee, interviewed by Crozier in the 1960s, stated,

> It is very monotonous. . . . In the morning I have to type Series X and in the afternoon Series Y. It is quite painful. I am a sort of dreamer. . . . It is so mechanical; I am living in a different world; I never think about my work. . . . Actually, it does not have the slightest interest. Sometimes I wondered. What meaning does it have? . . . One does not have the same personality here. Here in public administration, one lose's one's own personality.[27]

Similarly, a Brookings Institute Study found that less than 30 percent of New York City employees would recommend public service as a career. The majority of New York City employees would recommend public service but only "until a better opening can be found outside," or "if it's the only position that can be found."[28]

Most readers have probably had their own experience with government agencies whose employees are indifferent, cynical, and even hostile to the agency's goals. In such agencies, avoiding work, doing as little work as possible, and even subverting formal goals is the informal norm. Fortunately, morale in all agencies is not so extremely negative, or government would hardly operate at all.[29]

In recent years, private-sector managers have come to understand the importance of empowering employees and not treating them as cogs in the organizational machine.[30] That message does not yet seem to have gotten through to public-sector managers, at least in New York City. Low morale is a problem at all levels of New York City government,[31] but especially among professionals. Engineers, lawyers, health workers, and social workers express frustration with the limitations on their discretion.

> [G]overnment personnel are greatly disserved by red tape. They would like to get on with their missions as they see them, to pursue their program goals energetically, efficiently, speedily. They chafe at the obstacles placed in their way, the restraints imposed on them, the boundaries they must observe, the procedures they must follow.[32]

In a moving account of his career in city government, one engineer explained that he gave up the opportunity to make far more money, to buy a house, and to contribute much to his children's education in order to work at a city job he considered important. However, he now finds himself so constrained by external controls and his discretion so severely limited that the work that is left to him is routine, mundane, and unfulfilling; the more interesting and challenging work has been let out to private consulting firms. In a sense, he is a victim of the anticorruption project. Another manager complained, "Once, managers could make decisions based on their experience and what they thought was right for their unit, but now the main concern is to cover yourself."

One factor that reflects and also contributes to low morale is disregard for public employees' privacy. Pressure to create an appearance of government propriety has led to the proliferation of financial disclosure requirements that treat public employees far differently from private employees. How many people would wish to reveal their finances and debts and those of their spouses and children? One public official we interviewed stated, "The financial disclosure forms are humiliating when you have a negative net worth. Working for the city is like going to the bathroom without a door on the stall." Comprehensive ethics laws and financial disclosure are meant to and do lead to continual and sometimes obsessive self-scrutiny lest one inadvertently overlook a conflict of interest or make an incomplete or inaccurate disclosure. As we discussed in chapter 4, the conflict-of-interest rules are so comprehensive (yet vague and confusing) that city employees barrage the Conflicts of Interest Board for opinions about seemingly innocuous activities. Yet another example of the erosion of privacy is the implementation of drug-testing schemes by which police, prison officers, and some transportation workers are randomly selected to provide urine samples on the spot. New York City employees, even those who are not selected for drug testing, frequently indicate that they feel as though they are under suspicion by inspectors general and the DOI. They resent the fact that they can be summoned to DOI headquarters for questioning at a moment's notice and subsequently be interrogated without ever being told the subject matter of the investigation or whether they are suspect.

This frustration and disenchantment with public service has given public service a bad reputation. A portion of the public believes that professionals would remain in public service only if they were unable to find good jobs elsewhere. One former city employee, now a high-level university administrator, told us that when he was seeking to make the switch into the private sector, he found that having served in New York City government was regarded as a blight on his résumé.

Barriers to Interorganizational Cooperation

The functional isolation of agencies is one of the classic problems of bureaucracy.[33] Once again, Michel Crozier makes an astute observation: "Bureaucracy cannot be relied on to develop imaginative solutions at this level [of operation]. . . . Governmental units that need to cooperate are unable not only to cooperate but even to consult with each other most of the time."[34]

Government bureaucracies tend to separate and compartmentalize problems that naturally go hand in hand. Ideally, the effective public manager would find ways to build bridges between government agencies, not-for-profits, foundations, universities, and private businesses in order to solve problems effectively and efficiently. Here the anticorruption project places obstacles in the way by reinforcing the separation of public and private and erecting barriers between government agencies. The conflict-of-interest rules and the chilling effect of those rules make public-sector managers shy away from building formal and informal relationships with other organizations, especially those in the private sector. Control mechanisms, requiring strict internal accounting of funds and employee time, may deter them from entering into cooperative ventures with other public-sector organizations.

Adaptive Strategies

We hesitate to speak of administrative strategies to circumvent bureaucratic pathologies as themselves being pathological. Still, it seems appropriate to mention adaptive strategies in this chapter (see chapter 3) because they are such a clear response to bureaucratic pathology, and because they themselves raise troubling issues about governing.

As early as the 1920s and 1930s, public-sector managers, frustrated with the pathologies of bureaucracy, began searching for strategies that would allow them to circumvent the bureaucracy so that they could accomplish the public's business more efficiently and effectively.[35] (Of course, other managers sought to circumvent the bureaucracy in order to line their own pockets.) In the past, the creation of public authorities to carry out tasks previously carried out by government agencies has been the most obvious and most effective end-run strategy.[36] However, in recent years, privatization has also become extremely important.[37]

The rise to prominence of public authorities and other forms of quasi-public corporations is undoubtedly a complex story, but as we saw in chapter 3, the role of the anticorruption project cannot be denied. To some government officials, like Robert Moses, it was evident that governmental objectives could not be accomplished under the constraints imposed by the government bureaucracy and civil service system generally, and the anticorruption project specifically. Therefore, these officials sought new forms of government that were less restricted by bureaucratic rules. Public authorities either are not covered by the laws that constrain other governmental units or, as in the case of civil service and competitive bidding, they have been explicitly exempted by their state-granted charters.[38] Over time, however, there has been growing pressure to apply the same anticorruption visions and associated controls to the public authorities.[39] The Feerick Commission urged that the same corruption controls, ethical standards, and oversight procedures applicable to other government agencies be applied to public authorities. According to the commission, "[t]he proliferation of these bodies, with fragmented, weak, or non-existent oversight, has important implications for the integrity of government and for how the public views government."[40] The authorities are now well within the sights of the anticorruption project's leaders and supporters.

It is surely one of the ironies of bureaucratic government that more and more often the public and government officials themselves see the creation of a public authority as the most efficient strategy for getting the job done. While not a bureaucratic pathology, the public authority might be labeled a "democratic" pathology since it is only weakly accountable to the people. In his Pulitzer-Prize-winning biography of Robert Moses, Robert Caro points out time and again that Moses implemented his own vision of the public interest, ignoring and sometimes trampling the competing visions of individual groups and sometimes whole communities.[41]

Another example of a circumvention of the anticorruption project is the invention of "fixers." The fixer's role is to grant exceptions when the bureaucratic rules bind too tight. The fixer, usually a mayoral aid or budget official, is authorized to issue exceptions to the rules that allow managers to avoid certain procedures and substantive constraints, or to expedite certain tasks. The ability to persuade the fixer that a particular situation qualifies for an exception has become one of the characteristics of a successful public-sector manager. During the Koch administration, it was widely known that one or two mayoral aides could get the Department of Buildings to issue certificates of occupancy more quickly than usual. Another aide's specialty was rapid contract approval. While these officials performed a valuable service in speeding up a cumbersome process, the existence of fixers puts a premium on personal contacts and penalizes those who must stick to the bureaucratic process.

Finally, as we pointed out in chapter 3, the growth of temporary "provisional employment" is a direct response to the constraints imposed by civil service. Hiring a provisional employee permits the manager to fill a position much more quickly than if he or she followed civil service procedures, and it allows the manager to choose a person with the necessary background and skills. What's more, if the fiscal situation deteriorates, provisional employees can be terminated expeditiously. Thus, provisional employment brings back into public administration some of the flexibility lost with the abolition of patronage, which is precisely why the Feerick Commission and the anticorruption establishment find it repugnant.[42] In any event, the anticorruption project and the reigning forces of bureaucracy are beginning to circle their wagons around provisional employment. In addition to the Feerick Commission, it has been criticized by the American Federation of State, County, and Municipal Employees.[43]

Obstacles to Public Administration Reform

The anticorruption project not only reinforces bureaucracy and its pathologies, it also poses a serious obstacle to bureaucratic reform or the replacement of bureaucracy with a different form of public administration. Over the years, numerous scholars have criticized bureaucracy and urged its reform or replacement. Lately, however, the antibureaucratic reform movement seems to be gaining support among practitioners and politicians. From our perspective, the question is whether this reform movement will be able to overcome or circumvent the anticorruption project.

Reinventing Government

Contemporary government reformers have rallied around the work of David Osborne and Ted Gaebler, whose 1992 book, *Reinventing Government*, has been embraced by mayors, governors, and even the president and vice-president of the United States.[44] Their proposals, while hailed as new, have been part of the antibureaucratic critique of big government for at least a generation. Nevertheless, Osborne and Gaebler have significantly enriched public discourse on public administration by making these ideas accessible to policy makers and the general public. They have clearly hit a responsive chord.

In their introduction, Osborne and Gaebler pull no punches in attacking outmoded public bureaucracy. They exhort us to "pick up the wreckage of our industrial-era institutions and rebuild."[45] They urge a new model of public administration, which they call "entrepreneurial government." As the name implies, the essential characteristic of such governments is that they permit the city manager, and perhaps other top decision makers, to act with substantial discretion creatively and aggressively to further the public interest, especially by means of contracting out services and creating competition for services wherever possible.

> Most entrepreneurial governments promote *competition* between service providers. They *empower* citizens by pushing control out of the bureaucracy, into the community. They measure the performance of their agencies, focusing not on inputs but on *outcomes*. They are driven by their goals—their *missions*— not by their rules and regulations. They redefine their clients as *customers* and offer them choices. . . . They *prevent* problems before they emerge, rather than simply offering services afterwards. They put their energies into *earning* money, not simply spending it. They *decentralize* authority, embracing participatory management. They prefer *market* mechanisms to bureaucratic mechanisms. And they focus not simply on providing public service, but on catalyzing all sectors—public, private and voluntary—into action to solve their community's problems. [Emphasis in original][46]

Osborne and Gaebler provide a number of illustrations of entrepreneurial government, of government officials operating quickly and effectively— the polar opposite of the horror stories often associated with bureaucratic government.

From our standpoint, the crucial test of entrepreneurial government will come with the first corruption scandal.[47] Osborne and Gaebler do not consider what is to be done about corruption and the politics of scandal and reform. However, they do note in their critique of the status quo that "in making it difficult to steal the public's money, we made it virtually impossible to *manage* the public's money."[48] Everyone is in favor of honest, clever government officials saving money and meeting, even anticipating, community needs. But what is to prevent government officials who are not subject to monitoring, auditing, and layers of control from looting the treasury? Are they just relying on the honesty of entrepreneurial administrators, the criminal justice system's deterrence threats, a scaled-down but still effective anticorruption project, or some combination of these?

New York City's experience with school decentralization illustrates the type of crisis and challenge that will inevitably confront entrepreneurial government, or at least decentralized government. In the 1960s, desiring to establish "community control" over the schools, New York City established local community school boards with significant power over hiring principals and other administrators, secretarial staffs, and special education aides.[49] While the results of this partial school decentralization have yet to be fully evaluated,[50] major corruption scandals in the decentralized school districts indicate the problems that need to be addressed.

In April 1993, the special commissioner of investigation for the New York City School District released a report describing widespread corruption in Bronx School District 12.[51] Members of the community school board had turned the district into personal patronage mills. In effect, they sold principalships and other jobs in exchange for money, political support, and sexual favors, and engaged in kickback schemes with school supply companies.[52] Members of this school board showed impressive entrepreneurialism in transforming a school system into a racketeering enterprise. Unfortunately, providing educational services was not on the board members' agenda. Former District 12 board member Randy Glenn was quoted as saying, "Nobody in their right mind is going to send their kids to District 12. I'm not sending mine . . . you're not retarding my children."[53]

We do not mean to suggest that corruption would be avoided by recentralizing authority in a single school board and reinforcing command and control. Indeed, scandals have plagued school systems through the ebb and flow of centralization and decentralization over the last several decades, not only in New York, but also in Newark, Detroit, and Chicago.[54] Our point is that the politics of scandal and reform are likely to stand in the way of more school decentralization and the decentralization of other city services unless some new model of corruption control emerges to complement a new model of public administration, or unless some new realism replaces the ideology of the anticorruption project and the politics of corruption and reform.

Osborne and Gaebler and other contemporary public administration reformers advocate, to greater or lesser extent, privatization as an answer to governmental gridlock. Privatization can mean a number things, but in general it involves private firms carrying out functions currently performed by public employees. How will corruption affect and be affected by privatization? Perhaps private firms competing for public contracts will be better able to choose, manage, and monitor employees than a government employer. If the government becomes more of a specialist in monitoring its contractors, it will be able to cancel the contracts of those firms whose performance indicates corruption. Furthermore, it is likely that corruption by employees of private firms, even when they are performing public contracts, will not have the same "scandal-value" as corruption by public employees. If that is true, then corruption, especially low-level corruption, will be less debilitating for the governing process. For these reasons, privatization may, in some cases, offer a solution to the twin crises of corruption and corruption control. But there are a lot of "ifs" here.

Conclusion

Bureaucracy requires a full-scale anticorruption project, and the anticorruption project reinforces bureaucracy as well as bureaucratic pathologies. Moreover, the anticorruption project contributes to the chronic problems of bureaucracy like decision-making delay, overcentralization, inadequate authority, goal displacement, defensive management, low morale, and inability to foster flexible solutions to problems.

These first-order bureaucratic pathologies have, in turn, stimulated end runs which circumvent the mainstream government altogether. As governing authority and responsibility are parceled out to public authorities, boards, and private-sector corporations, there is the question of "democratic pathology." Large-scale public bureaucracies are already remote from citizens' control, but the proliferation of public authorities and privatization may make government even more unaccountable and less responsive to their desires.

The anticorruption project also poses an obstacle to bureaucratic reform and a serious barrier to the replacement of bureaucracy with any other form of administration. The anticorruption project encompasses an ideology of corruption-free government that only bureaucracy promises to fulfill. It also is deeply entrenched via an establishment, including good government reformers, the media, law enforcement, investigators, inspectors general, and auditors, all of which can be counted on to oppose any turning away from the goal of corruption-free government.

TWELVE

Toward a New Discourse on Corruption Control

> Almost all of us feel . . . [that corruption] is a kind of disease which has af-
> fected the body politic. There it is to be sure; it has been there a long time.
> . . . Nevertheless, we feel that it is not supposed to be there, and that if we
> had a little more courage or sense or something we could cut away the dis-
> eased tissue and live happily ever after. The implications of this notion seem
> to me to be false, and I believe that our political thinking would be im-
> mensely more effective if we adopted an entirely opposite theory.
>
> Walter J. Lippmann, "A Theory about Corruption"

Discourse in any field consists of formal and informal communications
about professional concerns among practitioners, reflections by journalists
and scholars, and recommendations for change from many quarters. The
discourse about official corruption, which has been central to the development of American public administration, has predominantly focused on
strategies and technologies of control. The goal of this book is to stimulate a
new, public and professional discourse about corruption and corruption control. The first section of this chapter deals with the anticorruption project's
likely future if present panoptic trends continue. The second section calls
for a new more realistic discourse on corruption and corruption control. In
the third section, we offer some ideas about fine-tuning the anticorruption
project, and the fourth section examines the possibility of radical change in
the anticorruption project. Throughout the chapter we suggest how corruption control in the New York City Police Department (NYPD) might be affected by these alternative futures.

Future of Panopticon

The most likely short-term future for any social phenomenon or trend is
"more of the same." Therefore, we see no basis for predicting a reversal in
the multiplication and elaboration of corruption-control strategies and tech-

nologies. If anything, the possibility of reversal has been made even more unlikely by scandal-seeking politics, media feeding frenzies, and the entrenchment of a powerful anticorruption establishment, including investigative and prosecutorial agencies. While there are limits, especially budgetary, on the capacity of the anticorruption project to expand, we do not foresee a dismantling of the types of laws and strategies that we have examined in this book. It is entirely possible, given the institutional strength and longevity of anticorruption institutions, that discourse on corruption control will continue to downplay or ignore its costs.[1]

Unless there is radical change in public administration, we predict that the panoptic vision of corruption control will become even more firmly entrenched, more institutionalized, and further elaborated. In addition, given today's corruption-sensitive politics of scandal and reform, the anticorruption project will be propelled by the anticorruption establishment and by new technologies that make it possible to monitor people, processes, and events more thoroughly.

Information technology has vastly increased the capacity of controllers to collect information and to monitor people, processes, and transactions. While government has lagged in achieving full participation in the computer age, it is quickly catching up. More technical capacity leads naturally to an ambition to collect more information on every aspect of employees, transactions, contractors, and so forth. We have already seen the development in New York City of a database on public contractors and their officers. There is every reason to anticipate the creation of more databases on high-ranking personnel background, performance, decisions, and relationships with contractors.

Investigative technology has also advanced.[2] New miniature listening devices are far more powerful and unobtrusive than their predecessors; they can easily be used in undercover and sting operations and even in everyday monitoring of suspect employees and agencies. Some segments of the public-sector workforce are already subject to routine drug testing. For example, in New York City, police, corrections officers, and transportation personnel are required to submit to random drug testing.[3]

In addition to the use of more information and monitoring technology, if present trends continue, we can foresee other elaborations of the anticorruption project. The steady growth of criminal investigations, prosecutions, and punishment is likely to continue. On the investigative front, special anticorruption units and prosecutors are likely to be established. In New York City, the Department of Investigation may finally become fully independent of the mayor, as anticorruption reformers have long demanded. As a result of the Mollen Commission's recommendations for purging corruption from the NYPD, a new monitoring agency is already in place. The investigative apparatus used by the DOI, inspectors general, and other anticorruption players will continue professionalizing, identifying with, and borrowing heavily from the law-enforcement community. Sanctions will probably become more severe; pension forfeiture, a sanction the Mollen Commission recommended to deter and punish corrupt police officers, will probably be added to the anticorruption arsenal.[4]

The trend toward defining more kinds of conduct as corrupt shows no sign of abating. Candidates for high office, elective or appointive, are already being vetted according to extremely stringent criteria of probity in personal and professional life. The so-called Whitewater scandal, involving tax evasion and fraud allegations against President Bill Clinton and Hillary Clinton for their 1978 investment in a real estate venture company, shows that the passage of time is no barrier to the anticorruption project.[5] The high-level official's entire life is now fair game.

The open-endedness of the concept of conflict of interest, in particular, would permit more types of conduct to be circumscribed by legal prohibitions. To date, conflict of interest has focused on financial interests, which could be even more broadly defined; nonfinancial interests (romantic attachments, friendships, ethnic bonds, social clubs) could also become an issue. Integrity standards for contractors may become more stringent, and may eventually be applied to subcontractors as well.

It is hard to believe that civil service, the anticorruption strategy of almost a century ago, will continue to evolve in the directions advocated by its progenitors. Nevertheless, it is probable, at least in New York City, that more positions will be brought under the civil service umbrella, and that temporary, "provisional" positions will be reduced and more strictly regulated. It is also possible that more of the laws governing New York City government will be extended to the public authorities.[6]

Whistleblower protection seems to be a growth area. Here we see clearly the "ratchet effect" in corruption control. The response to complaints of managerial reprisals against whistleblowers calls for more protection. The absence of complaints is cited as proof that more protections are necessary to encourage more whistleblowing.

Some government reformers and contracting specialists recognize that public contracting and procurement have become crippled by the red tape generated, to a substantial extent, by the anticorruption project.[7] The growth of these corruption controls may have reached a limit, at least temporarily. However, as we have seen, New York City's vigorous effort to monitor the integrity of its public contractors is a new initiative, and in the years to come, it may take on a life of its own. It is foreseeable that this effort will lead to the creation of more databases, elevated integrity standards, new due process hearings, and the increased use of independent monitors (e.g., private investigative firms hired by private companies doing business with the government).

Public-sector auditing clearly has a bright future.[8] Auditing serves so many functions for so many interests inside and outside government that its growth in size and influence is certain. We foresee the continued proliferation of auditing entities within and external to operating agencies. There is every reason to believe that auditing will become more intensive and comprehensive as it makes greater use of the new information and monitoring technologies. Auditors themselves will become increasingly sophisticated, influential, and law-enforcement-oriented. The line between management and investigation will blur, as investigation is incorporated into routine performance assessment.

If we are correct about these trends, and if public administration remains no better able to accommodate the anticorruption project, effective administration will be even more difficult to achieve. Without wishing to sound apocalyptic, the question for the future is whether the omnibus anticorruption project will leave no room for fundamental public administration reform. If reform becomes synonymous, or nearly synonymous, with more corruption control, the future of public administration is bleak.

Police reformers have already equated corruption control with organizational reform. When the Mollen Commission talks of "transforming" the NYPD, it does not mean the quality of service or the effectiveness of *crime control:*

> We believe the Department has the leadership and commitment needed to transform the Department once again. We are confident that the current Police Commissioner has the skills and insights to accomplish his mission of driving corruption from the ranks of the Department. We have seen what appears to be a new era in the fight against police corruption. . . .The Department has begun to take its first steps in recent history to transform this culture. It is essential that these not be the last.

The language of political transformation and reform that would be familiar to the Progressives has been narrowed until it focuses only on corruption. Needless to say, the financial and administrative costs are never mentioned.

The Need for a New Discourse on Corruption Control

Before we rush to add more layers of reforms to already overburdened government processes, we need to think carefully about the problem and the tools available to solve it. We believe that for government to become more effective, it is necessary to balance more realistically the costs of corruption and corruption control. Up to this point in the history of public administration, discourse on corruption has been limited by three characteristics of the anticorruption project:

1. *The pathologies of public bureaucracy are linked to the anticorruption project.* This limits discourse, since those interested in reducing the costs and negative impacts of corruption control must confront bureaucracy.
2. *The anticorruption project is cumulative.* The momentum of anticorruption reform and its powerful moral claims limit discourse to the refinement and extension of current strategies. These strategies are enmeshed with basic administrative control, so that challenging corruption control involves challenging the structure of modern government.
3. *The anticorruption project has disconnected corruption control from government effectiveness.* Interest in efficient operation has grown in virtually every part of government, except those concerned with corruption control. No accurate assessment of corruption is possible; therefore, it has been possible to argue that corruption would be worse without current efforts and that more resources are required. Cost, efficiency, and effectiveness are submerged by the imperative of corruption-free government.

Our criticism of the anticorruption project does not ignore the importance of corruption. Corruption is not harmless. We recognize that in some societies and at some points in history, corruption has totally demoralized society, eviscerated the government's legitimacy, and led to coups, revolutions, and societal collapse, or, on occasion, simply to cynicism, alienation, and stagnation. For these reasons, corruption can hardly be legalized or ignored; it must be condemned, investigated, and punished.

While corruption is a problem for public administration, it must be placed in perspective. The inability of New York City to repair the Wollman Skating Rink in Central Park, despite years of effort, is at least as serious as any number of conflict-of-interest scandals.[9] Indeed, the paralysis of public administration merits the label "crisis." This book has argued that too many outdated and counterproductive corruption controls have contributed to that crisis, while having no significant impact on the corruption rate. We now have a corruption-control problem as well as a corruption problem.

We urge a new discourse on corruption control and public administration.

That discourse should take place in the conferences, meetings, journals, and newsletters of public administrators. It should also be cultivated and nurtured in public administration schools, where corruption needs to be brought out of the closet and placed squarely on the agenda. Public administration students should be challenged with case studies featuring trade-offs between corruption control and efficiency. Further, public administration scholars are needed for research, experimental design, evaluation, and simulations. Administrators need to share their experiences with one another: What works? What doesn't? At what cost to effectiveness and efficiency? The new discourse must be taken seriously by the media. The public must become more realistic in its demands for corruption prevention.

A more sophisticated discourse would recognize that every scandal ought not call the government's legitimacy into question. Corruption occurs even in honest administrations. Every scandal should not lead ineluctably to the creation of new agencies, wholesale reorganization of government, and new control and monitoring procedures. While corruption is never "acceptable" in a moral sense, some level of corruption is a sociopolitical fact of life in all organizations—public, private, educational, or philanthropic. Just as retailers consider some amount of "shrinkage" (theft) a cost of doing business, the public and the public sector need to realize that every instance of corruption does not require another layer of corruption-proofing.

Further, the new discourse should also recognize that not all corruption is created equal. A control that is effective in one agency or at one level of government may not be effective in another agency or level of government. Susan Rose-Ackerman has developed a complex economic model with which to analyze the probable effectiveness of corruption controls:[10]

> When corruption is uncovered at one hierarchical level, reformers often recommend a change in structure to give that level less discretion. Piecemeal reform will often fail, however, since reducing corrupt incentives at one level in a hierarchy may simply increase them someplace else. Thus, much has been made of the fact that police officers on the beat, and on-site inspectors . . . operate essentially alone without direct supervision by superiors. These jobs are conducive to corruption both because bribes can pass unobserved and because officials have broad discretion to make case-by-case determinations that cannot be easily checked by superior officials. Restricting the discretion of inferior officials may not, however, reduce corruption. Instead, its locus may simply shift to higher levels of the organization.[11]

The anticorruption project may be more effective if proposed controls are analyzed beforehand for effectiveness and possible negative impacts on public administration. Further, the new discourse should strive to prioritize different types of corruption. Perhaps it will be determined that corruption in the judiciary and prosecutors' offices (for example, bribing a judge or prosecutor) is most destructive to government legitimacy, while certain conflicts of interest in contracting are less destructive, at least when the government receives full value for its expenditures. Arguably, corruption by high-level officials is more destructive to the body politic than corruption by low-level personnel. Corruption that represents a payment for the expeditious provision of a routine service is less destructive than corruption that represents a payment to issue a license or permit which, for safety reasons, should not be issued at all. A systemic effort to prioritize corruption according to its negative consequences for society and government legitimacy would produce a hierarchical list of targets at which corruption controllers could aim.

It must be recognized that not all corruption controls impose the same direct and indirect costs on government, and that controls often involve trade-offs with effectiveness and efficiency. Each component of the anticorruption project should be periodically examined to determine whether (1) the original reasons for its creation still exist; (2) the corruption it aims to prevent and punish merits high priority; (3) there is reason to believe that it has significantly reduced the corruption it was designed to excise; (4) it has not inadvertently created new corruption vulnerabilities and spawned new forms of corruption; (5) its cost in terms of administrative efficiency is not disproportionate to its benefits in terms of reducing corruption; and (6) there is not a less costly strategy for achieving the same goal.

An enormous barrier to evaluating the efficacy of corruption controls is lack of basic data, indeed, practically any data, and an absence of indicators about the costs of corruption and the costs and benefits of corruption control. How can we rationally set policy on corruption control when we know virtually nothing about its underlying reality? Every student, scholar and public official with whom we have discussed this book has been astounded at the lack of data. The fact is, however, that we operate in a knowledge vacuum concerning both corruption and corruption control. Therefore, establishing a methodology for constructing indicators of the corruption rate and of the costs and benefits of corruption controls is absolutely vital if we are to advance policy analysis.

One way to develop an indicator of the extent of corruption would be to survey the employees and clients of government agencies. The survey might ask respondents to indicate what they know about different types of corruption and ask for "uncommon, common, very common" types of corruption, the percentage of personnel who engage in each type, and the percentage of transactions affected by each type of corruption. Of course there would be myriad problems in designing and administering such surveys, but much would be learned from pilot efforts. If the surveys, after being refined, were carried out every year or every two years in the same agencies, in time a benchmark against which to evaluate the need for more controls, enforcement, and the success or failure of particular initiatives and campaigns could be developed. There is the danger, however, that in collecting and analyzing these data, a whole new bureaucratic organization would be created.

Estimating the costs of corruption control is both harder and easier than estimating the amount of corruption itself. It is easier, in that corruption controls can be readily identified and some of their direct costs readily calculated. For example, the costs of running an inspector-general office are easily determined. It is harder, because of the importance of indirect costs like impacts on morale, appropriate levels of risk taking, and managerial effectiveness. Moreover, we should not expect to find that the same corruption controls have the same costs in different agencies. Nevertheless, our interviews with top managers in New York City government have convinced us that there are many reflective officials who, if given adequate time, resources, and assistance from evaluation-research specialists, could produce valuable case studies on the direct and indirect costs of corruption control in their agencies. After a number of those case studies were compiled, there would be a knowledge base from which we could begin to generalize. It is worth a try.

Regular corruption surveys might also stimulate and raise the consciousness of a significant percentage of government employees. Corruption control, like crime control generally, has tended to be a specialized and top-down function. Controls are created at the top and imposed upon (and frequently resented by) middle managers and the rank and file. Expanding the discourse about corruption and corruption control to all levels of an agency would certainly be a step in the right direction. It would signal agency personnel that they are regarded as part of the solution, not just part of the problem, and it would solicit ideas that can only be generated from those at the front lines. It would also contribute to a more participatory style of management, which seems now to be an accepted principle of good administration in large private-sector corporations.[12]

No agency requires a new discourse more than police departments, where reform has tended to mean the addition of layer upon layer of centralized and bureaucratic corruption controls. The benefits and costs of each of these existing controls need to be assayed, and a whole new range of ideas about police administration and policing itself needs to be generated. Arguably, we need a "policing commission" much more than a "police corruption commission." It is instructive that only a corruption scandal triggers a blue-ribbon commission; changes in the crime rate, or the conviction rate, or the cost of policing, for example, do not lead to the appointment of commissions.

It is hard to create a realistic discourse on the subject of police corruption; politically it is probably impossible, at least at the present time. Nevertheless, it seems an obvious truth that police corruption in the area of illicit drugs is an inexorable cost of our drug prohibition. As long as there is such a flourishing black market in mind-altering drugs, vast opportunities for police corruption will exist, and such opportunities will prove too tempting for a significant number of police personnel. Thus, our new discourse must begin with a hard-headed analysis of the benefits and costs of drug prohibition and an examination of a full array of policy alternatives.

Rank-and-file police officers must be key participants in the new discourse. The history of corruption reform has been one of top-down controls formulated by politicians, top brass, moral entrepreneurs, and experts without regard for social and psychological impacts on the rank and file and for administrative impacts more generally. We believe that such a style of management is highly dysfunctional and triggers resentment, itself a factor contributing to corruption.

Rank-and-file officers will undoubtedly have scores of ideas about preventing corruption, and these should be thoroughly aired and analyzed. Listening to groups of rank-and-file officers in focus groups and individual interviews is a crucial prerequisite to the development of a new discourse. Likewise, policing has been far too parochial, especially in New York City. There may be much to be learned from colleagues in other cities, in the United States and abroad, and such colleagues should become participants in the discourse.

A new discourse on police corruption must generate strategies for estimating the amount of corruption, preferably broken down by categories (i.e., accepting gifts from merchants, stealing money from drug dealers, etc.). Admittedly, it will not be easy to construct such indicators, but without them the anticorruption project is irrational and may do more harm than good. Perhaps survey researchers could devise instruments (like TV's Nielson ratings) whereby carefully constructed samples of citizens are closely questioned at periodic intervals. Perhaps samples of police themselves could be anonymously surveyed. Focus groups might be useful. Perhaps random integrity tests could be used to project baseline rates.

Generating a discourse on the costs of corruption control will be some-what easier. Managers and rank-and-file personnel will be able to identify direct and indirect costs of policies like route rotation, random drug testing, and pension forfeiture. Using focus groups and case studies would generate a mass of data that, when collated and organized, will probably provide a way to move forward with policy experiments.

Fine-Tuning The Anticorruption Project

The right level and mix of corruption controls will undoubtedly differ from governmental unit to governmental unit and from agency to agency within the same governmental unit. Moreover, the optimal level and mix may change over time. In other words, controlling corruption is a dynamic part of governing that requires constant attention. There is simply no magic list or formula of corruption control that academics, commissions, consultants, or other pundits can hand over to public administrators. Good policy will need to grow out of a sophisticated data-collecting effort, a rich discourse on the problem, the identification of alternative solutions, experimentation, evaluation, and estimates of the costs of various controls.

With the preceding caveats in mind, we offer the following ideas about fine-tuning the anticorruption project only as a contribution to getting the new discourse underway—a starting point for evaluation.

First, civil service needs to be thoroughly reformed. While it may have significantly reduced patronage and ended the practice of forcing govern-ment employees to make payoffs to the political party that "recommended" them for their jobs,[13] its costs are very high. Merit has certainly not become the centerpiece of personnel administration; paper-and-pencil civil service exams are simple, and frequently irrelevant to job requirements. Most im-portantly, civil service has severely undermined the capacity of managers to motivate their personnel through positive and negative incentives. Many scholars and commissions on civil service and personnel management have put forward thoughtful reform proposals.[14] These need to be reexamined, and the best proposals implemented. The anticorruption project and the ogre of patronage should not be allowed to stand in the way of much-needed reform.

Ethics codes and financial disclosure laws have broadened the definition of corruption. For example, awarding a contract to a firm which employs the spouse of any government employee becomes "suspicious" and presump-tively corrupt. According to Michael Reisman, this reflects the "mythical norms" of government conduct.[15] The failure to submit on time a full and accurate financial disclosure form, an aid to preventing conflict of interest, is now itself defined as corrupt. The tendency is for policy makers, who are almost never public-sector managers themselves, to define conflicts of interest too broadly. Our sense is that these laws should be curtailed. Too much effort is being expended on writing codes and blanketing public service with prohibitions, and not enough on building esprit de corps, competence, and promotional opportunities based upon proven success.

Financial disclosure has also gone too far in some jurisdictions, particularly in New York City. Too much information must be revealed, and the disclosure requirements apply too broadly. Certainly, private citizens who serve on nonpaying, voluntary boards should not have to make public their entire family finances, including debts and investments. Some specialists in ethics law advocate "transactional" disclosure rather than full disclosure. Transactional disclosure requires a public official to disclose a financial interest that might be affected by a particular decision. While this type of disclosure is not without its problems, it may be preferable to an annual "ex-ante" full personal financial disclosure.

Whistleblower protection laws have undermined the authority of public-sector managers and, on occasion, undermined the morale of a unit or agency without making any significant contribution to reducing corruption. If one cannot trust agency managers, indeed, if one presumes their venality, it is hard to see how government can possibly operate effectively. We must have confidence in top-level public-sector managers and offer the salaries necessary to get the very best people. Managers must be held accountable, but not to several different oversight bodies and not only for ensuring integrity up and down the ranks of their agency. They must be accountable to the public for getting the job done efficiently and effectively. To do that, managers need authority to manage. There must, of course, be a grievance mechanism within government and orderly procedures for reviewing disciplinary action. But a "federal case" cannot be created and the manager, in effect, placed under investigation every time disciplinary action is accompanied by a whistleblowing claim. Additionally, legitimate whistleblowing cases must be resolved quickly. It is intolerable to have whistleblowing accusations and investigations hanging over an agency and its managers for months and even years.

The DOI has rendered a valuable service to New York City. Over the course of a century, it has evolved from an agency focused on problems of efficiency and good government to a quasi-law-enforcement agency focused almost exclusively on corruption. The time may be ripe to reorient the DOI's mission. It might make sense for the DOI to focus once again on government efficiency and effectiveness. As part of the executive branch of city government, the DOI should assume some responsibility for government's performance.

The DOI's investigative strategies should also be reexamined. One might legitimately ask whether field associate programs, sting operations, and other undercover initiatives are appropriate for policing government. Those readers who are university faculty and students might want to consider their reaction to a dean's announcement that she planned to pepper the university with field associates and to run sting operations to nab buyers and sellers of student papers and exams. How would students react to being summoned before the dean and interrogated for hours without being told what the charges were and whether they were suspects? According to Gary T. Marx, the increased use and sophistication of monitoring techniques and undercover operations may have serious effects on government efficiency and effectiveness, as well as on the morale and performance of employees.

> When individuals believe that they are constantly being watched and may be tested at any point, conformity may increase as candor, spontaneity, innovation, and risk-taking decline. Organizations need to encourage flexibility and a confident encountering of their environment. But the fear that any colleague might be an informer, that any conversation might be recorded, or that secret integrity tests are rampant may encourage a pulling inward and passivity.[16]

The prosecutorial agencies may have the least impact of any of the anticorruption controls examined in this book. Prosecutors monitor agencies from a distance, and they address, or ought to address, only serious acts of criminal corruption. Until the last decade, the prosecutorial agencies had not been aggressive in investigating and prosecuting high-level officials. Pursuit of corrupt public officials has increased substantially as a result of the U.S. Department of Justice's involvement and the revitalized Manhattan district attorney's anticorruption unit. As the prosecutorial agencies devoted more resources to investigating and prosecuting corruption, so the administrative agencies might be able to devote less. If the mainstream law-enforcement and prosecutorial agencies were unable or unwilling to do so, an alternative would be the creation of a special prosecutor, provided, however, that the special prosecutor leave the prosecution of minor wrongdoing to the agencies.

The public contracting system is in need of major surgery. It is mired in red tape and multiple levels of oversight. As city governments contract for more services, an efficient procurement system is even more important. Contracting must be more expeditious, and there must be incentives for contractors to perform well. If mediocre, even incompetent, performance has no negative repercussions, and if superior performance brings no reward, contractors will perform at the lowest acceptable level. Fortunately, there is a serious and sophisticated literature on reforming government procurement that provides sound ideas to invigorate the new discourse on corruption control.[17]

Of the control mechanisms we have considered, auditing and accounting have the greatest potential to further, simultaneously, the goals of preventing corruption and of improving the efficiency and effectiveness of public administration. Strong accounting and auditing programs are essential to good management and for identifying and evaluating the costs of operations and services. Further, electronic data processing offers the possibility of tracking the flow of money through an agency with a minimum of interference to management. The negative impacts of the anticorruption project occur when auditing entities proliferate and carry out multiple audits of the same agency. Similarly, auditing may prove dysfunctional for effective administration when auditors press for government reorganization centered on corruption control. Presently, auditors feel compelled to challenge administrative practice, perceiving that their performance will be viewed negatively unless they issue critical reports and sweeping recommendations for administrative reorganization.

Returning decision-making authority and responsibility to managers is vital to establishing a better balance between corruption control and agency effectiveness. If management is reunited with control, it may be possible to return to the Progressive idea—popular with early commissioners of accounts like Raymond "Fearless" Fosdick—of addressing the corruption problem by reforming the structure and operations of agencies, rather than piling on more rules, laws, and controls.[18]

It will not be easy to fine-tune the anticorruption project. The politics of scandal and reform are indelibly impressed on the psyches of reformers and administrators. It will take imagination, creativity, and support for a new discourse on corruption and corruption control to change the current direction of the anticorruption project.

Beyond the Panopticon

At this point, the reader might understandably be wondering whether there is a different way to control government. While big city government will always require some traditional corruption controls, it is worth considering other strategies to keep government honest.

Control, or better still, compliance with norms of integrity might be predicated more on incentives and peer pressure to persuade government employees to "do the right thing"; the majority of government employees are honest, not because of rules, monitoring, or threats, but because of values and personal morality. While integrity training, education, and incentives are a step in the right direction, they are not a panacea for corruption.[19]

Our analysis brings us back to a key principle of the early Progressive platform. The Progressives believed that dedicated, "professional" civil servants, chosen on the basis of merit, would create and preside over government agencies that would be honest, efficient, and democratic. Unfortunately, it did not work out that way. Public service is not a high-status "calling," and civil service has frequently retarded professionalism and rewarded mediocrity. Out of frustration, government has increasingly relied on top-down strategies of monitoring, discipline, and control. The exercise of professional judgment and initiative are frustrated at every turn. As one New York City manager put it, "We sacrifice speed and efficiency in order to prevent corruption. But I just don't believe that corruption can be prevented by rulemaking. The only real safeguard is honesty."

How might honesty in public service be nurtured? Perhaps it has taken us a century to realize that there is no substitute for a professional public service populated by competent, committed, enthusiastic public servants who like their work and feel adequately compensated and appreciated. In short, if public employees are treated like second- or third-class citizens, they will act accordingly, and no amount of laws or controls will remedy the situation; in some cases, they will make things worse. Poorly paid, poorly treated public employees will be alienated and demoralized. Under such circumstances, corruption is easily rationalized. This is often true in police departments.

There can be no doubt about the need to invest more in our public service, especially in personnel services. The tendency these days is to "disinvest" in government; this is clearly a mistake. A necessary, albeit insufficient, precondition for honest government is that employees feel well treated, appreciated, and able to make a difference.

The problems in all ranks of government service are surely significant and difficult enough to challenge highly qualified people. Ways must be found to move toward participatory management, so that a significant portion of agency personnel identify with the agency's mission, are proud of the agency, and believe that good performance will lead to promotions. Essentially, this requires radically different personnel policies and significant bureaucratic reform.[20] Consider, once again, the police. The Police Department's human capital is its most vital resource. Cynicism and burnout are *major* problems. We must emphasize career opportunities, continuing education, nurturing leadership, and job satisfaction. Contrast the military's approach; it identifies potential leaders at every career stage and sends promising officers to training programs in military and civilian colleges.

The web of monitoring and surveillance that characterizes modern public service has replaced the expert discretion and independence of public-sector professionals. Without professionalism, however, public agencies lose the flexibility and creativity they need to respond to a changing environment. Professionals, according to the Progressive ideal, bring new knowledge into agencies and change the agencies to fit their knowledge. The strictures of corruption control have made it more likely that professionals will change to fit the agency. Donald Schon confronts the problem of professionalism in modern organizations by urging change in the education, roles, and the management of professionals, which he calls "reflective practice."[21]

The first step in reflective practice requires recognition that without independence, professionals cannot apply their training and knowledge to solve problems and make decisions. Organizations must be free from the constraints that limit experimentation and a calculated degree of risk. The anticorruption project makes no distinctions in its distrust of public employees, nor does it examine whether particular control strategies are better suited to controlling corruption among low-level, rather than high-level employees. The anticorruption project has taken a "one-size-fits-all" approach to corruption control. The great tragedy of this approach, as Schon points out, has been to neutralize the contribution of experts in favor of the routine, or what he calls "technical rationality."

Schon's portrait of the reflective practitioner is particularly well suited to the job of providing better, cheaper services in a political environment that demands both a high degree of efficiency and an institutional approach to corruption control. According to Schon,

> Reflection-in-action has a critical function, questioning the assumptional structure of knowing-in-action. We think critically about the thinking that got us into this fix or this opportunity; and we may, in the process, restructure strategies of action, understandings of phenomena, or ways of framing problems. . . . We think and try our new actions intended to explore the newly observed phenomena, test our understandings of them, or affirm the moves we have invented to change things for the better.[22]

The "assumptional structure of knowing-in-action" in American public administration is founded on and operates through the anticorruption project. Reflective practice is a necessary part of a revitalized public administration in which professionals play a central role. However, the transition from technical rationality to reflective practice remains problematic. Like the movement to reinvent government, reflective practice will founder in the first scandal attributed to "freer" professionalism. More than a century of American administrative history weighs against the success of professional discretion in the absence of corruption controls. The trick will be to insure government integrity without stifling professionalism.

It seems unlikely that big government could ever come to rely primarily on professionalism and collegial values as the main bulwark against corruption. This again forces us to face the fact that big government, dominated by bureaucracy, will always require strong external controls (i.e., an anticorruption project). Thus, a radical alternative to the contemporary anticorruption project would require a radically different model of public administration characterized by decentralization, community governance, and some privatization. While "community policing" is a somewhat vague concept that means different things to different people, it certainly points in the right direction. It requires decentralization of authority and empowerment of low-level managers and line officers. In the context of a big city police department, if properly implemented, it ought to give rank-and-file officers a sense of responsibility for the safety of the communities and neighborhoods in which they work.

The Next Stage of Reform

Neither the movement to reinvent government nor advocates of reflective practice and professionalism have grappled with the twin problems of corruption and corruption control. It seems that the logic of antibureaucratic reform leads to a model of public administration that ignores corruption, while the logic of anticorruption reform ignores public administration. It is easy to be pessimistic about the synthesis of these two models of reform. However, there is at least one approach that suggests the possibility of a synthesis.

Political scientist Vincent Ostrom has theorized about how public choice theory could be adapted both to fulfill the goals of efficiency and maintain the values of democracy. Ostrom takes as a point of departure the Nixon White House, which he found to be the apotheosis of everything wrong with the "Wilsonian," or bureaucratic, paradigm of public administration.[23] Large-scale bureaucratic administration places decision makers so far from citizens that they lose sight of their public service mission and come to focus primarily on the nourishment of their own powers as an end in itself.

A highly integrated executive structure in which the power of command is fully centralized in a single chief executive will be subject to substantial problems of institutional failure. . . . If a new executive establishment is to cope effectively with this obstacle, it will become necessary to create a Special Investigations Unit to maintain executive secrecy and exercise discipline over recalcitrant government employees. Efforts to tighten the screws of administrative control will cause bureaucratic pipelines to leak like sieves. Plumbers will be needed.[24]

The remote, power-driven form of public administration that Ostrom blames for a decline in democracy and for corruption is reinforced by the anticorruption project.

Ostrom's solution is the devolution of governing authority to a multiplicity of "communities of interest" that are specially concerned with each specialized type of governmental service. According to Ostrom, "democratic administration" characterized by competitive, community-based government would not generate "dirty tricks" and "cover-ups." The communities of interest upon which democratic administration is based may be neighborhood-based, citywide, or nongeographically organized, depending on the government service at issue. A prominent example for Ostrom is the delivery of police services. Basic patrol is delivered on a neighborhood scale; investigative services on a countywide scale; and specialized services, like forensic labs, on a regional or statewide scale. In effect, Ostrom is arguing for more than community policing. In his view, the structure of political control over public safety should be reevaluated in order to increase responsiveness to local conditions and citizen demand. These values imply a far less bureaucratic operation. A massive, hierarchically structured police agency would not survive his recommendations.

The rule for providing services under democratic administration is that the population benefiting from the service (or bearing the costs of its absence) should not only pay for it, but control *and monitor* its provision. The connection between democratic administration and corruption control grows out of the connection between citizen preferences and agency operations. According to Ostrom, bureaucracy disconnects citizens from agencies and provides no incentive for citizen vigilance. Citizens will take little interest in public administration if their preferences and demands don't count. The more citizens' demands and preferences count, the more citizen scrutiny there will be of the efficiency and integrity of government operations. The value of this kind of corruption control is that it is guided by the public directly, not by external control agencies whose budgets are dependent on the "growth" of the corruption problem. The new discourse we urge in this chapter must include the public, but this requires giving citizens a stake in the outcome.

Ostrom's vision of democratic administration suggests a way to harmonize the goals of the anticorruption and anti-bureaucratic reformers. While Osborne and Gaebler seem to avoid the question of what is to be done about corruption and the inevitable pressures for more corruption controls, Ostrom's ideas show us how we can reform public administration and control corruption at the same time. In fact, from this perspective it is impossible to control corruption effectively without public administration reforms.

A preliminary assessment must be made for each type of government service, encompassing both the interests of the community and the way that control is being exercised. New service delivery arrangements, such as decentralization, should follow from this assessment. Reformers need to match the public's demands for services with a realistic mechanism for meeting them; otherwise meaningful reform is impossible. A good illustration of how reform fails is the corruption scandal in Bronx District 12. A poor, inner-city school district, District 12 was decentralized in an attempt to improve the delivery of services. Unfortunately, decentralization has neither improved the quality of education nor decreased corruption. In fact, following decentralization, District 12 was rocked by a series of corruption scandals involving board members who purchased televisions, furniture, and personal luxury items with money earmarked for school supplies.[25]

Decentralization in District 12 failed, in part, because it did not include parental empowerment and control. It makes sense to empower parents by giving them choices among competing schools either via vouchers or some other method. Once power is firmly in the hands of those most interested in the outcome—those receiving the services—we can expect the kind of citizen involvement and vigilance that will prevent corruption. Only when citizens see a direct connection between their involvement and the quality of public services will they take an active interest in protecting the resources available to improve the quality of education for their children, the safety of their neighborhoods, or the cleanliness of their streets. Corruption might be prevented without negatively affecting administration when citizens are empowered to make decisions and have a stake in the way services are provided. Citizen participation indirectly controls corruption; citizens are not part of the decision-making and oversight process for the sole purpose of corruption control, but their stake in the outcome acts as an indirect control.

Professionals, in this scheme, are not creatures of bureaucracy, but collaborators with active citizens. Control is exerted through interaction and observation, rather than by rules and threats. Bureaucracy has managed to remove citizens from the governing process at the expense of efficiency and effectiveness, while corruption thrives. It is time to introduce into the administrative process the common sense that citizens have about public ethics and corruption control.

Conclusion

Reforming the anticorruption project is not an easy task. It is easier to continue to assert that reducing corruption requires more corruption controls. Therefore, the first priority for reformers is to create a new, more sophisticated discourse about the interrelationship of the anticorruption project and public administration. The second priority is to build a knowledge base which allows for serious evaluation of the nature and extent of corruption and the costs and benefits of corruption control. The third priority is to plan a series of careful policy experiments which would permit various anticorruption strategies to be evaluated.

In searching for solutions to the corruption problem, we must look beyond the traditional strategies of monitoring, control and punishment. We must recapture the Progressives' optimism and enthusiasm about government service and work toward creating the kind of public service that generates its own high standards, norms, and internalized controls. In short, we get the kind of government we pay for and the kind of government we deserve. Laws, rules, and threats will never result in a public administration to be proud of; to the contrary, the danger is that such an approach will create a self-fulfilling prophecy: having been placed continuously under suspicion, treated like quasi-criminals or probationers, public employees will behave accordingly.

Schon's concept of professional reflection and Ostrom's focus on citizen assessment converge in the empty space left by those rushing to destroy bureaucracy and corruption control without a clear idea of what should replace them. These alternative theories indicate that, given the right institutional setting, self-conscious professionalism might very well replace the juggernaut of routine monitoring and surveillance. Ultimately, an alternative to the status quo will require a balance between the anticorruption project and the need for efficiency and effectiveness.

The anticorruption project is the linchpin of large-scale bureaucratic government. Attacking corruption control without addressing bureaucracy is unlikely to result in any significant reforms. Bureaucracy is too well established in most governments. However, attacking bureaucracy without addressing corruption control makes it likely that future scandals will reignite the demand for strong, centralized controls. Ostrom gets us out of this predicament by presenting a technique for reforming public administration that builds citizen participation and interest in corruption prevention by dismantling bureaucracy.

Corruption and corruption control will always be with us. If we ignore the latter, the former will be close behind, looming larger than before. If we attempt to reinvent government without carefully considering, and perhaps reinventing the anticorruption project, the much-needed reform of government will be doomed from the start. An informed discourse on the relationship between public administration and the anticorruption project will help us fit the controls to the task, rather than the other way around.

Notes

Preface

1. Peter Self, *Administrative Theories and Politics* (London: Allen and Unwin, 1972), 277–78 (emphasis in original).

2. New York State Organized Crime Task Force, *Final Report on Corruption and Racketeering in the New York City Construction Industry* (New York: New York University Press, 1990).

3. Lincoln Steffins, *The Shame of the Cities* (New York: Peter Smith, 1948).

4. Larry Green, "7 More Indicted in Court Over Bribery Probe in Chicago," *Los Angeles Times,* 17 March 1988, p. 1.

5. "Public Officials for Sale," *U.S. News & World Report,* 28 Feb. 1977, p. 36.

6. Ibid.

7. David Glovin, "Weeding Out Corruption in Newark: Probes Once Every Decade," *Bergen Record,* 2 August 1994, p. A1; Clifford J. Levy, "Two Newark Politicians Found Guilty in Bribe Case," *New York Times,* 29 March 1995, p. B5; James Ahearn, "Newark's Mired in a Grim Culture of Corruption," *Bergen Record,* 19 April 1995, p. C9.

8. Gary T. Marx, "When the Guards Guard Themselves: Undercover Tactics Turned Inward," *Policing and Society* 2 (1992): 163–64.

9. Recent works that reflect the political and social significance of official corruption: Joseph Zimmerman, *Curbing Unethical Behavior in Government* (Westport, Conn.: Greenwood Press, 1994); Arnold J. Heidenheimer, Michael Johnston, and Victor T. LeVine, eds., *Political Corruption: A Handbook* (New Brunswick, N.J.: Transaction Publishers, 1989); Dennis F. Thompson, *Ethics in Congress: From Individual to Institutional Corruption* (Washington, D.C.: The Brookings Institution, 1994); Glenn R. Parker, *Congress and the Rent-Seeking Society* (Ann Arbor, Mich.: University of Michigan Press, 1996); David Burnham, *Above the Law: Secret Deals, Political Fixes, and Other Misadventures of the U.S. Department of Justice* (New York: Scribner, 1996); H. George Frederickson, ed., *Ethics and Public Administration* (Armonk, N.Y.: M. E. Sharpe, 1993); William Grieder, *Who Will Tell the People?* (New York: Simon and Schuster, 1992); and Dennis Thompson, *Political Ethics and Public Office* (Cambridge, Mass.: Harvard University Press, 1987).

10. "Public Officials for Sale," *U.S. News & World Report,* 28 February 1977, p. 36.

11. John T. Noonan, "Bribery," in *Encyclopedia of Crime and Justice* (New York: The Free Press, 1983), 1: 123.

12. Ibid.

13. See, e.g., John T. Noonan, *Bribes* (Berkeley: University of California Press, 1984); Michael Reisman, *Folded Lies: Bribery Crusades and Reforms* (New York: The Free Press, 1979).

14. Joyce Purnick, "Trump Offers to Rebuild Skating Rink," *New York Times,* 31 May 1986, p. B29.

15. Robert Fresco and Susan Bilello, "Cleaning Up Is Hard to Do," *Newsday,* 26 December 1990, p. 7; M. P. McQueen, "Agency Ripped Over Asbestos," *Newsday,* 16 September 1989, p. 3.

16. Henry Jones Ford, "Municipal Corruption," *Political Science Quarterly* 11 (1904): 678, 682–83.

17. Felix A. Nigro, *Public Personnel Administration* (New York: Henry Holt, 1959), 4.

18. Wallace S. Sayre and Herbert Kaufman, *Governing New York City: Politics in the Metropolis* (New York: W. W. Norton, 1965), 110.

19. James Fesler and Donald Kettl, *The Politics of the Administrative Process* (Chatham, N.J.: Chatham House, 1991), 321. See also Anthony Downs, *Inside Bureaucracy* (Boston: Little, Brown, 1967). Downs posits the "Law of Counter Control: the greater the effort made by sovereign or top-level officials to control the behavior of subordinate officials, the greater the efforts made by those subordinates to evade or counteract such control" (262). See also Steven Breyer, *Breaking the Vicious Circle* (Cambridge, Mass.: Harvard University Press, 1993).

20. R. Beck, C. Hoskins, and J.M. Connelly, "Rent Extraction Through Political Extortion: An Empirical Examination," *Journal of Legal Studies* 21 (Jan. 1992): 217.

21. James Buchanan and Gordon Tullock, *The Calculus of Consent: Logical Foundations of Constitutional Democracy* (Ann Arbor, Mich.: University of Michigan Press, 1965), 281.

22. Philip K. Howard, *The Death of Common Sense: How Law Is Suffocating America* (New York: Random House, 1994).

One: The Evolution of Corruption

1. For discussion of the definitions of corruption, see Daniel H. Lowenstein, "Political Bribery and the Intermediate Theory of Politics," *UCLA Law Review* 32 (April 1985): 784; V. O. Key, Jr., *The Techniques of Political Graft in the United States* (Chicago: University of Chicago Libraries, 1936), 386–401; John T. Noonan, *Bribes* (New York: Macmillan, 1984); Michael Reisman, *Folded Lies: Bribery Crusades and Reforms* (New York: Free Press, 1979).

2. See John T. Noonan, "Bribery," in *Encyclopedia of Crime and Justice,* (New York: Free Press, 1983), 1: 123; Lowenstein, "Political Bribery," 784.

3. Gary T. Marx, "When the Guards Guard Themselves: Undercover Tactics Turned Inward," *Policing and Society* 2 (1992): 166.

4. Economists speak of this manipulation of public office for private gain in terms of "rent seeking." See James M. Buchanan, "Rent Seeking and Profit Seeking," in James M. Buchanan, Robert D. Tollison, and Gordon Tullok, eds., *Toward a Theory of the Rent-Seeking Society* (Texas A&M University Press, 1980); Anne O. Krueger, "The Political Economy of the Rent-Seeking Society," *American Economic Review* 64 (June, 1974), in Buchanan, Tollison, and Tullock, eds., *Toward a Theory of the Rent-Seeking Society.*

5. Irving Welfeld illustrates this phenomenon in *HUD Scandals: Howling Headlines and Silent Fiascos* (New Brunswick, N.J.: Transaction Publishers, 1992).

6. Edward Banfield and James Q. Wilson, *City Politics* (Cambridge: Harvard University Press, 1963).

7. The three versions of the *Congressional Ethics Reform Act of 1993*, (103 H.R. 2835), (103 H.R. 2735), and (103 S. 885), would repeal the provisions of the *Ethics in Government Act of 1978*, which permitted payment of "honoraria" to members of Congress or their staffs on behalf of a charitable organization or an organization from which the member of Congress, his or her spouse, or any relative receives any financial benefit. The bill also revokes the provisions of the *Ethics Reform Act of 1989* regulating the gifts and payment of foreign travel for members of Congress and their staffs. The bills direct the House Committee on Standards of Official Conduct and the Senate Select Committee on Ethics to determine under what conditions their respective members and their staffs may accept payment for travel to attend functions relating to official duties; *The Ethics in Government Act Amendments of 1993* (103 H.R. 1095) amends the *Ethics in Government Act of 1978* by specifying the circumstances under which federal officers and employees may receive an honorarium for an article in a publication, a speech, or an appearance. The Act also prohibits the honorarium fee from exceeding $2,000 and subjects it to disclosure.

8. See Peter W. Morgan, "The Appearance of Propriety: Ethics Reform and the Blifil Paradox," *Stanford Law Review* 44 (Feb. 1992): 593.

9. Amitai Etzioni, *Capital Corruption: The New Attack on American Democracy* (New York: Harcourt Brace Jovanovich, 1984).

10. David Truman, *The Governmental Process: Political Interests and Public Opinion* (Westport, Conn.: Greenwood Press, 1981).

11. *Austin v. Michigan Chamber of Commerce*, 110 S. Ct. 1391 (1990).

12. Ibid., 1397.

13. Ibid., 1411 (Scalia, J., dissenting).

14. Bayless Manning, "The Purity Potlatch: An Essay on Conflict of Interest, American Government, and Moral Escalation," *Federal Bar Journal* 24 (3) (1964): 243.

15. This subject was touched on in Marx, "When the Guards Guard Themselves," 155 (discussing declining tolerance for white-collar crime and corruption brought about by Watergate).

16. See Morgan, "The Appearance of Propriety," 593, 595; Abraham Eisenstadt, "Political Corruption in American History," in Arnold J. Heidenheimer, Michael Johnston, and Victor LeVine, eds., *Political Corruption: A Handbook* (New Brunswick, N.J.: Transaction Publishers, 1993), 567.

17. Reisman, *Folded Lies,* chapter 1.

18. Public Law 95-521, 92 *Stat.* 1824 (1978) (codified at 2 *United States Code* §§701–709 and other scattered sections of the *United States Code*).

19. For analysis of the *Ethics in Government Act of 1978,* see "Developments in the Law—Public Employment," *Harvard Law Review* 97 (May 1984): 1669–76.

20. 5 *United States Code* §402 (app. 1988).

21. Executive Order No. 12,674, 3 *Code of Federal Regulations* 215 (1990). See

also President's Commission on Federal Ethics Law Reform, *To Serve with Honor: Report and Recommendations to the President* (Washington, D.C.: Government Printing Office, 1989).

22. Executive Order No. 12,674.

23. Since its enactment in 1978, Congress has amended the *Ethics in Government Act*. The *Ethics Reform Act of 1989*, for example, limited receipt of honoraria for officials of all three branches and placed more restrictions on revolving-door practices, requiring that members of Congress and their top staff members wait at least one year before lobbying Congress. (Public Law 101-194, 103 *Stat.* 1716 [1989]).

24. Robert N. Roberts, *White House Ethics: The History of the Politics of Conflict of Interest Regulation* (New York: Greenwood Press, 1988), 168. Ethical reforms, such as the 1978 Act, have been criticized as giving "the false impression that procedural reforms would end ethical problems in government service."

25. Suzanne Garment, *Scandal: The Culture of Mistrust in American Politics* (New York: Doubleday, 1991), 2.

26. Larry Sabato, *Feeding Frenzy* (New York: Free Press, 1991).

27. Norman J. Ornstein, "Less Seems More: What to Do about Contemporary Political Corruption," *Responsive Community* 4 (Winter 1993/94): 7. Public opinion polls reveal that the majority of people have little confidence in public officials. In December 1990, a Harris Poll found that 21 percent of the survey respondents had a "great deal of confidence" in the White House; 14 percent, 12 percent, and 10 percent of respondents had a great deal of confidence in the executive branch, Congress, and state government, respectively. See also Dennis A. Gilbert, *Compendium of American Public Opinion* (New York: Facts on File Publications, 1988): 15–19, 199–200.

28. Abraham Eisenstadt, Ari Hoogenboom, and Hans. L. Trefousse, eds., *Before Watergate: Problems of Corruption in American Society* (Brooklyn: Brooklyn College Press, 1978). See also Fred Emery, *Watergate: The Corruption of American Politics and the Fall of Richard Nixon* (New York: Times Books, 1994).

29. Ornstein, "Less Seems More," 8.

30. "In a democracy private citizens see a man of their own rank in life who rises from that obscure position in a few years to riches and power; the spectacle excites their surprise and their envy, and they are led to inquire how the person who was yesterday their equal is today their ruler. To attribute his rise to his talents or his virtues is unpleasant, for it is tacitly to acknowledge that they are themselves less virtuous or less talented than he was. They are therefore led, and often rightly, to impute his success mainly to some of his vices; and an odious connection is thus formed between the ideas of turpitude and power, unworthiness and success, utility and dishonor." Alexis de Tocqueville, *Democracy in America,* vol. 1 (New York: Vintage Books, 1945), 235.

31. See Larry L. Berg, Harlan Hahn, and John R. Schmidhauser, *Corruption in the American Political System* (Morristown, N.J.: General Learning Press, 1976); George C. S. Benson, S. A. Maaranen, and A. Heslop, *Political Corruption in America* (Lexington, Mass.: Lexington Books, 1978); Michael Johnston, *Political Corruption and Public Policy in America* (1982); Theda Skocpol, *Protecting Soldiers and Mothers* (Cambridge, Mass.: Harvard University Press, 1992), 75–77.

32. Noonan, "Bribery," 1: 123. See also Noonan, *Bribes;* and Marx, "When the Guards Guard Themselves," 158.

33. Walter Lippmann, "A Theory about Corruption," in Heidenheimer, Johnston, and LeVine, eds., *Political Corruption,* 567.

34. Senator Estes Kefauver pointed out that in the colonial period, "In a sense the whole populace engaged in the profitable process of mulcting the government—which was after all a hated tyrant—of every possible penny." See "Past and Present Standards of Public Ethics in America: Are We Improving?" *Annals of the American Academy of Political and Social Science* 280 (March 1952): 2.

35. Noonan, *Bribes,* 435–37.

36. Ibid., 447–49.

37. Ibid., 455–58.

38. Ibid., 565.

39. Ibid., 568.

40. ABSCAM refers to the FBI "sting" which led to the prosecution of one senator and a number of congressmen who took payoffs from an "Arab sheik" and promised to help him with immigration problems. See *United States v. Myers,* 527 F. Supp. 1206 (E.D.N.Y. 1981), *affirmed in part and reversed and remanded in part,* 692 F.2d 823 (2d Cir. 1982), *cert. denied,* 103 S. Ct. 2438 (1983).

Operation Greylord refers to the FBI investigation that exposed widespread bribery of Chicago judges. See James Tuoky and Rob Warden, *Greylord: Justice, Chicago Style* (New York: Putnam, 1989) and Brocton Lockwood, *Operation Greylord: Brocton Lockwood's Story* (Carbondale, Ill.: Southern Illinois University Press, 1989).

41. See Frank Lynn, "Ex-Syracuse Mayor's Schemes Detailed in Memo," *New York Times,* 7 February 1988.

42. See Peter Maas, *Marie: A True Story* (New York: Random House, 1983); John Blackmore, "Tennessee's Clemency-Selling Scheme: Could Blanton Not Have Known?" *Corrections Magazine* 5 (June 1979): 55.

43. See David Johnston, "Indictment of a Congressman," *New York Times,* 1 June 1994.

44. "Public Officials for Sale," *U.S. News & World Report,* 28 February 1977, p. 36.

45. Marx, "When the Guards Guard Themselves," 163–64.

46. In the Keating Five scandal five Senators were accused of preventing federal regulators from intervening with Charles Keating's California savings and loan association. Keating had made significant contributions to the campaigns of the Senators.

The Wedtech Scandal involved the 1988 convictions of Bronx Borough President Stanley Simon, former Bronx Congressman Mario Biaggi, and three others for transforming a small manufacturing company in the Bronx into a racketeering enterprise, using bribes in order to procure military contracts. See chapter 7.

47. At the national level, this constituency is composed of groups such as the National League of Cities and at the city level of groups like the Citizens' Budget Commission. Abraham Eisenstadt noted that "[i]n every American age, there has been a group that has sounded the cry of corruption." See "Political Corruption in American History," in Heidenheimer, Johnston, and LeVine, eds., *Political Corruption,* 539.

48. The House bank scandal involved revelations that Congressmen were allowed to

run overdrafts on their checking accounts without incurring interest charges. Since all the money in the House bank came from congressmen, in effect they were making one another no-interest loans; no taxpayer or investor money was involved. Nevertheless, the media and the public treated the matter as a scandal. See Guy Gugliotta, "Panel Says House Bank Was Abused," *Washington Post,* 28 February 1992, p. A21; Sharon LaFraniere, "Justice Presses Bank Inquiry; Report Says 'Very Few' Members, Most Out of Office, Are Involved." *Washington Post,* 17 December 1992, p. A1.

49. Geraldine Szott Moohr, "Mail Fraud and the Intangible Rights Doctrine: Someone to Watch Over Us," *Harvard Journal on Legislation* 31 (1994): 164, n. 40. See also Adam H. Kurland, "The Guarantee Clause as a Basis for Federal Prosecution at the State and Local Level," *Southern California Law Review* 62 (1989): 367; Daniel H. Lowenstein, "Political Bribery and the Intermediate Theory of Politics," *UCLA Law Review* 32 (1985): 784; Charles N. Whitaker, "Federal Prosecution of State and Local Bribery: Inappropriate Tools and the Need for a Structured Approach," *Virginia Law Review* 78 (1992): 1617.

50. See Charles Ruff, "Federal Prosecution of Local Corruption: A Case Study in the Making of Law Enforcement Policy," *Georgetown Law Journal* 65 (1977): 1171–1228.

51. Noonan, "Bribery," 120–23.

52. Ibid.

53. What would that mean? When a building inspector extorts a payment to issue a permit that is justly warranted or takes a bribe to expedite an inspection or to overlook a safety violation, there are no obvious budgetary consequences. The same is true when a politician capitalizes on insider knowledge to buy stock in a company that will get a lucrative contract. Yet these acts are clearly corrupt by today's standards.

54. Compare William Turner, "In Defense of Patronage," *Annals of the Academy of Political and Social Science,* January 1937, with James Bryce, *The American Commonwealth,* 2d ed. (London: Macmillan, 1889).

55. Federal and DOI investigations of the city's PVB led to revelations of widespread corruption, including bribery, fraud in awarding contracts, and almost total control of the agency by the Bronx, Brooklyn, and Queens party bosses.

Two: The Evolution of the Anticorruption Project

1. The statement from which the system gets it name, "To the victors belong the spoils," is credited to Senator William Marcy, around 1850. Ari Hoogenboom, *Outlawing the Spoils: A History of the Civil Service Reform Movement, 1865–1883* (Urbana, Ill.: University of Illinois Press, 1961), 6.

2. James C. Scott, "Corruption, Machine Politics, and Political Change," in Heidenheimer, Johnston, and LeVine, eds., *Political Corruption,* 276.

3. Ibid.

4. William E. Nelson, *The Roots of American Bureaucracy: 1830–1900* (Cambridge, Mass.: Harvard University Press, 1982), 121.

5. Abraham S. Eisenstadt, "Political Corruption in American History," in Heidenheimer, Johnston, and LeVine, eds., *Political Corruption,* 547.

6. Paul P. Van Riper, *History of the United States Civil Service* (White Plains, N.Y.: Row, Peterson, 1958), 7–8; Stephen Skowronek, *Building a New American State* (New York: Cambridge University Press, 1982), 47.

7. Quoted in Nelson, *The Roots of American Bureaucracy*, 121; cf. speech of Carl Schurz before the Senate, 27 January 1871, in Frederick Bancroft, ed., *Speeches, Correspondence, and Political Papers of Carl Schurz* (New York: G. P. Putnam, 1913), 3: 123.

8. Carl Schurz, "Editorial," *Harper's Weekly* 37 (1 July 1893): 614, quoted in David H. Rosenbloom, "The Inherent Politicality of Public Personnel Policy," in David H. Rosenbloom, ed., *Public Personnel Policy: The Politics of Civil Service* (Port Washington, N.Y.: Associated Faculty Press, 1985), 7.

9. Quoted in Hoogenboom, *Outlawing the Spoils*, 1; cf. Julius Bing, "Our Civil Service," *Putnam Magazine* 8 (August 1868): 233, 236.

10. Van Riper, *History of the United States Civil Service*, 84.

11. The conventional view of the Progressives as organizationally oriented is presented by Robert H. Wiebe, *The Search for Order: 1877–1920* (New York: Hill and Wang, 1967). A critique of this view holds that while organization may be the legacy of the Progressives, it is an ironic one, since their method was highly moralistic and situational. See Richard L. McCormick, "The Discovery That Business Corrupts Politics: A Reappraisal of the Origins of Progressivism," *American Historical Review* 13 (1981): 247–74.

12. Arthur S. Link, ed., *The Papers of Woodrow Wilson* (Princeton, N.J.: Princeton University Press, 1966), 370.

13. Nelson, *The Roots of American Bureaucracy*, 121.

14. Frank J. Goodnow, *Politics and Administration* (New York: Russell and Russell, 1900).

15. Ibid., 129.

16. Charles Garrett, *The LaGuardia Years: Machine and Reform Politics in New York City* (New Brunswick, N.J.: Rutgers University Press, 1961).

17. A classic argument on the enduring nature of the urban political machine and of urban political corruption holds that the machine served critical political and social functions up to the 1930s as the link between potentially disruptive immigrants needing employment, a city government embarking on epic public works, and a capital sector needing both labor and public contracts. Robert K. Merton, "Bureaucratic Structure and Personality," *Social Forces* 17 (1940): 560–68.

18. Two schools of thought developed as to the proper focus for reform efforts; one focused on economy, the other on efficiency. The primary difference between the two views was that

> either economy was a kind of virtue which "caused" efficiency, or efficiency was a kind of knowledge which produced economy; either economy or efficiency was an objective technique which could be learned and applied. Economy as an objective technique meant that bookkeeping properly handled could produce efficient, honest government. . . . Efficiency as an objective technique meant that the structure and organization of offices, responsibly arranged, would produce economical, honest government.

See Barry Dean Karl, *Executive Reorganization and Reform in the New Deal* (Cambridge, Mass.: Harvard University Press, 1963), 149.

19. Ronald L. Feinman, *Twilight of Progressivism: The Western Republican Senators and the New Deal* (Baltimore: Johns Hopkins University Press, 1981), 208.

20. Arthur Cerillo, Jr., "The Impact of Reform Ideology: Early Twentieth Century Municipal Government in New York City," in Michael H. Ebner and Eugene M. Tobin, *The Age of Urban Reform: New Perspectives on the Progressive Era* (Port Washington, N.Y.: Kennikat Press, 1977), 68–85; Charles Garrett, *The LaGuardia Years: Machine and Reform Politics in New York City* (New Brunswick, N.J.: Rutgers University Press, 1961).

21. Karl, *Reform in the New Deal,* 150.

22. Ibid., 146.

23. Leonard D. White, *The Administrative Histories: The Federalists* (New York: Macmillan, 1948); *The Jeffersonians* (New York: Macmillan, 1954); *The Republican Era, 1869–1901* (New York: Macmillan, 1958); and *Introduction to the Study of Public Administration,* rev. ed. (New York: Macmillan, 1948).

24. One study of the post-Progressive period found that "[t]he promising development of public administration as a profession during the Progressive era has dissipated. . . . The post-Progressive era was an age in which concern for the practical use and application of administrative techniques extended beyond any theoretical or normative standard for application. . . . Attention turned to more narrow technical problems rather than broader concerns." See James A. Stever, *The End of Public Administration: Problems of the Profession in the Post-Progressive Era* (Dobbs Ferry, N.Y.: Transnational, 1988), 66. See also Jordan A. Schwarz, *The New Dealers: Power Politics in the Age of Roosevelt* (New York: Alfred A. Knopf, 1993).

25. Leonard D. White, *Introduction to the Study of Public Administration,* 3d ed. (New York: Macmillan, 1948), 16.

26. Leonard D. White, *Introduction to the Study of Public Administration,* 2d ed. (New York: Macmillan, 1942), 597.

27. Luther Gulick, *The National Institute of Public Administration: An Adventure in Democracy* (New York: J.J. Little & Ives, 1928), 52.

28. Luther Gulick, "Forward," in Harold Seidman, *Investigating Municipal Administration: A Study of the New York City Department of Investigation* (New York: Columbia University Institute of Public Administration, 1941), vii–xi.

29. Michel Foucault, *Discipline and Punish: The Birth of the Prison* (New York: Vintage, 1979), 204. However, the first Panopticon, built by Jeremy Bentham's brother, was not a prison, but a Russian factory. See Scohana Zuboff, *In the Age of the Smart Machine* (New York: Basic Books, 1988), 320–22.

30. A history of the New York City Department of Investigation concluded that "the defense of democracy and the struggle for a decent life begins and continues with the fight against corruption." See Richard S. Winslow and David W. Burke, *Rogues, Rascals, and Heroes: A History of the New York City Department of Investigation* (New York: New York City Department of Investigation, 1992), 87.

31. Dennis F. Thompson argues that, in light of the scandal surrounding the Keating Five, the definition of corruption should be expanded to include "mediated corruption," which "links the acts of individual officials to effects on the democratic process" (369). Dennis F. Thompson, "Mediated Corruption: The Case of the Keating Five," *American Political Science Review* 87 (June 1993): 369–81.

32. In *The Federalist,* some of the founders argued that a plethora of rules was useless at best and possibly quite dangerous to liberty. For the relation of federalist theory to urban government, see Robert L. Bish and Vincent Ostrom, *Understanding Urban Government* (Washington, D.C.: American Enterprise Institute for Public Policy Research, 1973).

33. See Gary T. Marx, "When the Guards Guard Themselves: Undercover Tactics Turned Inward," *Policing and Society* 2 (1992): 151–72.

34. The Tenement House Committee staged a major exhibition of tenement house conditions in early 1900. The exhibition contained scores of maps and charts and five models of tenements, including a scale model of an entire block on the lower east side of Manhattan. The shocked reactions of the thousands of people who saw the exhibit helped convince the legislature and the governor to establish the Tenement House Commission. See Robert W. DeForest and Lawrence Veiller, eds., *The Tenement House Problem: Including the Report of the New York State Tenement House Commission of 1900* (New York: Macmillan, 1903), 1.

35. See DeForest and Veiller, eds., *The Tenement House Problem*, 2.

36. According to legend, after taking the oath of office, LaGuardia turned to face City Hall, shook his fist and announced, *"E finita la cuccagna"* (no more free lunch).

37. New York City Department of Investigation, *An Analysis of Corruption within the Construction Inspection Units of the Department of Buildings and the Agency's Corruption Prevention Program* (New York: New York City Department of Investigation, May 1991).

Three: Civil Service

1. Anne Freedman, *Patronage: An American Tradition* (Chicago: Nelson-Hall, 1994).

2. Arthur M. Schlesinger, *The Age of Jackson* (Boston: Little, Brown, 1945); "Developments in the Law: Public Employment," *Harvard Law Review* 97 (May 1984): 1624–26; see also Lee Benson, *The Concept of Jacksonian Democracy: New York City as a Test Case* (Princeton: Princeton University Press, 1961).

3. Lincoln Steffins, *Shame of the Cities* (New York: Hill & Wang, 1957); William Riordan, *Plunkitt of Tammany Hall* (New York: E. P. Dutton, 1983); J. Robertson, *American Myth, American Reality* (New York: Hill & Wang, 1980).

4. O. Glenn Stahl, *Public Personnel Administration*, 6th ed. (New York: Harper & Row, 1971), 30–31.

5. That the existence of a full-fledged civil service system does not necessarily spell the end of patronage is poignantly illustrated by the operation of the Nassau County Republican machine by Joseph Margiotta during the 1970s and early 1980s. See *United States v. Margiotta*, 688 F.2d 108 (2d Cir. 1982). Further, Tammany Hall maintained a foothold in New York City until the early 1970s, when Reform Democrats led by Ed Koch toppled the last Tammany boss, Carmine DeSapio. Warren Moscow, *The Last of the Big-Time Bosses: The Life and Times of Carmine DeSapio and the Rise and Fall of Tammany Hall* (New York: Stein & Day, 1976). Despite the weakening of the political machines, party bosses like Stanley Friedman, Donald Manes, and Meade Esposito continued to wield power over appointments and contracts well into the 1980s.

6. Wilbur C. Rich, *The Politics of Urban Personnel Policy: Reformers, Politicians, and Bureaucrats* (Port Washington, N.Y.: Kennikat Press, 1982), 52.

7. Joseph Schecter, "Personnel Management in the City of New York," *Public Personnel Review* (October 1957): 203.

8. Rich, *The Politics of Urban Personnel Policy*, 55–56; see also Theodore Lowi,

At the Pleasure of the Mayor: Patronage and Power in New York City (New York: Free Press of Glencoe, 1964).

9. "Developments in the Law: Public Employment," *Harvard Law Review* 97 (May 1984): 1718.

10. New York Civil Service Law §§202 and 203 (McKinney 1973).

11. John D. Feerick, "Reflections on Chairing the Commission on Government Integrity," in New York State Commission on Government Integrity, *Government Ethics Reform for the 1990s* (New York: Fordham University Press, 1991), 12.

12. Richard Levine, "Koch's Aide for Jobs Quits Amid Pressure of Integrity Inquiry," *New York Times,* 25 February 1989, p. A1.

13. New York State Commission on Government Integrity, "Playing Ball with City Hall: A Case Study of Political Patronage in New York City," in New York State Commission on Government Integrity, *Government Ethics Reform,* 498–99.

14. Freedman, *Patronage: An American Tradition,* 29.

15. New York State Commission on Government Integrity, "Playing Ball with City Hall," 505.

16. Ibid., 507.

17. Frank Lynn, "2 Koch Aides Deny Patronage in Jobs," *New York Times,* 12 January 1989, p. A1.

18. Timothy Clifford, "Ex-Koch Aid Indicted on 11 Counts," *Newsday,* 5 August 1989, p. 5.

19. New York State Commission on Government Integrity, "Playing Ball with City Hall," 545.

20. Editorial, "The Talent Bank Tale: Unfinished, Unfair," *New York Times,* 28 January 1989, p. A26.

21. Editorial, "Beneficiaries of the Talent Bank," *New York Times,* 14 January 1989, p. A27.

22. Letter to the Editor, Brooke Trent, *New York Times,* 10 February 1989, p. A34.

23. New York State Commission on Government Integrity, "Playing Ball with City Hall," 546.

24. E. S. Savas and Sigmund G. Ginsburg, "The Civil Service: A Meritless System?" *The Public Interest* 32 (Summer 1973): 70–85.

25. David T. Stanley, *Professional Personnel for the City of New York* (Washington, D.C.: The Brookings Institution, 1963).

26. Ibid., 2.

27. Ibid., 2.

28. Steven Cohen and William B. Eimicke, eds., *New York City Solutions II: Transforming the Public Personnel System,* (New York: Columbia University Program in Politics and Public Policy, February 1993).

29. Ibid., 3–5.

30. One former high-level official has written,

> [T]he city must overhaul its management of its own human resources. Changing archaic work rules would help, but it is time to move more boldly: Do city employees really need both Civil Service protection *and* the right to bargain collectively? . . . [T]he Civil Service is much less effective than the em-

ployees' own elected representatives in protecting their legitimate interests. It is not worth trying to fix; it [Civil Service] should simply be eliminated.

See Stephen Berger, "Reconstructing New York," *The City Journal* (Winter 1992): 54–60.

31. John D. Feerick, "Introduction," in New York State Commission on Government Integrity, *Government Ethics Reform*, 1–2.

32. For a detailed discussion of the 1975 Charter revision, see Rich, *The Politics of Urban Personnel Policy*, 59–65.

33. Lynn, "2 Koch Aides Deny Patronage in Jobs."

34. Kevin Flynn, "Hearings Begin on Koch's Talent Bank," *Newsday,* 9 January 1989, p. 17.

35. Editorial, "Panel Flunks Politics 101, But Aces Talent Bank Review," *Newsday,* 9 August 1989, p. 60.

36. Details of the career of Robert Moses are drawn from Robert A. Caro's authoritative biography, *The Power Broker: Robert Moses and the Fall of New York* (New York: Alfred A. Knopf, 1974).

37. In his doctoral thesis, Moses criticized the concept of open examinations for recruiting managers, a concept widely embraced by civil service reformers. According to Moses, competitive examinations could not produce a class of quality managers and "made only simple 'mathematical and palpable' distinctions between men, and that such a random selection process was too unreliable for the management needs of modern society." Moses argued that rather than selecting the best and most qualified, competitive exams would result in "uniform mediocrity." See Rich, *The Politics of Urban Personnel Policy,* 46, quoting Robert Moses, *The Civil Service of Great Britain* (Ph. D. diss., Columbia University, 1914).

38. Rich, *The Politics of Urban Personnel Policy,* 53; see Charles Garrett, *The LaGuardia Years: Machine and Reform Politics in New York City* (New Brunswick, N.J.; Rutgers University Press, 1961).

39. Wallace S. Sayre, "Merit System Progress in New York City," *Good Government* 55 (Sept.–Oct. 1938): 53.

40. Caro, *The Power Broker,* 368–73.

41. Ibid., 624–25.

42. New York State Commission on Government Integrity, "Playing Ball with City Hall," 342–43.

43. Ibid., 378.

44. Paul P. Van Riper, *History of the United States Civil Service* (Evanston, Ill.: Row, Peterson, 1958), 85.

45. William B. Munro, *Personality in Politics: Reformers, Bosses, and Leaders* (New York: Macmillan, 1924), 7.

Four: Conflicts of Interests

1. Conflict-of-interest laws are "specific, well-defined, fairly technical anticorruption laws aimed at preventing the use of public office or employment for the financial benefit or gain of oneself or another." Page E. Bigelow, "From Norms to Rules: Regulating the Outside Interests of Public Officials," in Frank J. Mauro and Gerald Benjamin, eds.,

Restructuring the New York City Government: The Reemrgence of Municipal Reform
(New York: Academy of Political Science, 1989), 141.

2. Executive Order No. 12,674, 3 *Code of Federal Regulations* 215 (1990).

3. President's Commission on Federal Ethics Law Reform, *To Serve With Honor*
(Washington, D.C.: Government Printing Office, March, 1989).

4. *United States v. Mississippi Valley Generating Co.*, 364 U.S. 520, 562 (1961).

5. "Poll: Many Say Congress 'Corrupt,'" *USA Today*, 2 June 1989, p. A1.

6. "Majority in Poll Criticize Congress," *Washington Post*, 26 May 1989, p. A8.

7. The Association of the Bar of the City of New York, Special Committee on Congressional Ethics, *Congress and the Public Trust* (1970), 39.

8. Robert C. Vaughn, "Ethics in Government and the Vision of Public Service,"
George Washington Law Review 58 (February 1990): 436, n. 90.

9. 5 *United States Code* §§201–211 (app. 1982).

10. The Association of the Bar of the City of New York, Special Committee on Congressional Ethics, *Congress and the Public Trust* (1970), 39.

11. Two earlier turn-of-the-century laws did mark the beginning of the long evolution
of ethics codes. The 1898 New York City Charter prohibited members of the city legislature, city agency heads, and their assistants and other city officials from having any direct or indirect interest in any contract with the city, the sale of any article to be purchased
with city funds, or the purchase of any property belonging to the city or sold by the city
for back taxes or assessments. The 1901 law provided that any city officer who knowingly acquired a prohibited interest in any contract or work was guilty of a misdemeanor
and forfeited office upon conviction. Payoffs to secure city employment were also misdemeanors. These laws were almost never enforced. See "How the City Charter's Conflict of Interest Provisions Evolved," *The Charter Review* (Summer 1988).

12. National Municipal League, *Model State Conflict of Interest and Financial Disclosure Law* (New York: Author, 1979), 30.

13. Vaughn, "Ethics in Government and the Vision of Public Service," 432.

14. Jack Newfield and Wayne Barrett, *City for Sale: Ed Koch and the Betrayal of New
York* (New York: Harper & Row, 1988), 248–54.

15. Ibid., 83.

16. "Moynihan Is for 'No Mercy' on Graft," *New York Times*, 13 March 1986, p. B5.

17. New York State Commission on Government Integrity, "Ethics in Government
Act: Report and Recommendations," in *Government Ethics Reform for the 1990s*, (New
York: Fordham University Press, 1991), 610–17; New York State-City Commission on
Integrity in Government, *Final Report: The Quest for an Ethical Environment* (New
York: Author, 1986), 7–10.

18. *Ethics in Government Act of 1978*, Public Law 95-521, 92 *Stat.* 1824 (1978) (codified as amended in sections of 2, 3, 18, 28, 39 *United States Code*).

19. T. J. Coffin, "The New York State Ethics in Government Act of 1987: A Critical
Evaluation," *Columbia Journal of Law and Social Problems* 22 (1989): 294–95.

20. See *Andrews v. Koch*, 528 F. Supp. 246 (E.D.N.Y. 1981), affirmed by both the
U.S. Court of Appeals for the Second Circuit and the U.S. Supreme Court: *Morris v.
Board of Estimate*, 707 F.2d 686 (2d Cir. 1983), and *Board of Estimate v. Morris*, 489
U.S. 103 (1989).

21. See *Ethics in Government Act of 1978*, Public Law 95-521, 92 *Stat.* 1824 (1978)
(codified as amended in sections of 2, 3, 18, 28, 39 *United States Code*); *Civil Service*

Reform Act of 1978, Public Law 95-454, 92 *Stat.* 1111 (1978) (codified in sections of 5, 10, 15, 28, 31, 38, 39, 42 *United States Code*); *Ethics Reform Act of 1989,* Public Law 101-194, 103 *Stat.* 1726 (1989). See also Vaughn, "Ethics in Government and the Vision of Public Service," 417–50.

22. Page E. Bigelow, "From Norms to Rules: Regulating the Outside Interests of Public Officials," in Frank J. Mauro and Gerald Benjamin, eds., *Restructuring New York City Government: The Reemergence of Municipal Reform* (New York: Academy of Political Science, 1989), 141–57.

23. New York Public Officials Laws §73(4)(b) (McKinney 1988).

24. *City Record,* 9 January 1992, New York City Conflict of Interest Board Advisory Opinion No. 92-2.

25. New York City Charter §2604(d)(2) (1989).

26. Ibid., §2604(d)(3).

27. Ibid., §2604(b)(14). For further analysis of the Charter's conflict-of-interest provisions, see Bigelow, "From Norms to Rules," 141–57.

28. New York City Charter §2604(b)(2) (1989).

29. Ibid.

30. Less than forty formal advisory opinions were issued. The majority of requests were disposed of through staff letters.

31. *City Record,* 23 November 1994, New York City Conflict of Interest Board Advisory Opinion No. 94-23.

32. *City Record,* 9 November 1992, New York City Conflict of Interest Board Advisory Opinion No. 92-29.

33. *City Record,* 20 May 1992, New York City Conflict of Interest Board Advisory Opinion No. 92-14.

34. In Advisory Opinion No. 91-5, the board ruled that a conflict of interest would arise if a public servant were hired by a private entity to teach a one- or two-day seminar concerning subject matter which directly involved official duties. The board stated that such outside employment would conflict with the proper discharge of official duties because "[i]t is likely that many people taking this one or two day course . . . would be subject to regulation by the public servant's agency." *City Record,* 29 June 1991.

35. New York City Administrative Code §12-110 (1985).

36. See New York City Administrative Code §12-110 (1985); New York City Local Law 6 (1986); New York City Local Law 9 (1990); New York City Local Law 16 (1990); Executive Orders 90-93, 99 (1986), and 109 (1987). Originally, financial disclosure was required only from elected officials, candidates for elected office, agency heads and their immediate subordinates, paid commission and board members, and city employees who belong to the management pay plan or earn more than $38,000 per year. The amendments to the 1975 Code expanded coverage to local party officials and employees "whose duties directly involve negotiation, authorization or approval of contracts, leases, franchises, variances and special permits."

37. *Ethics in Government Act,* Ch. 813, 1987, New York Laws 1404; New York Public Officials Law §§73, 73a, 76, 78; New York Executive Law §§94, 166; New York Legis. Law §80; New York General Municipal Law §§805-a, 808, 810–813; New York Judiciary Law §211 (McKinney 1988).

38. *Ethics in Government Act,* Ch. 813, 1987, New York Laws 1404; New York Public Official Law §§73, 73a, 76, 78; New York Executive Law §§94, 166; New York

Legislative Law §80; New York General Municipal Law §§805-a, 808, 810–813; New York Judiciary Law §211 (McKinney 1988).

39. According to Gene Russianoff, New York State Public Interest Research Group, New York Law School, Symposium on Municipal Corruption, 30 March 1995.

40. Joseph W. Little, "Abolishing Financial Disclosure to Improve Government," *Stetson Law Review* 14 (1987): 634.

41. New York State Commission on Government Integrity, "Campaign Financing," in *Government Ethics Reform for the 1990s* (New York: Fordham University Press, 1991), 16.

42. New York City Department of Investigation, "Report to Conflicts of Interest Board: Fleet Bank's Loan to the Liz Holtzman for Senate Committee and the Selection of Fleet Securities as a Member of the City's Underwriting Team," September 1993, 8.

43. James C. McKinley, Jr., "Underwriter Is Removed by Dinkins," *New York Times,* October 1993, p. B23.

44. New York City Conflicts of Interest Board, "Annual Report 1992," 6–7.

45. Bayless Manning, "The Purity Potlatch: An Essay on Conflict of Interest, American Government, and Moral Escalation," *Federal Bar Journal* 24 (1964): 239.

46. Todd S. Purdum, "When Life Itself is a Conflict of Interest," *New York Times,* 22 April 1990, p. E8.

47. See Alfred S. Neeley IV, "Ethics in Government Law: Are They Too Ethical?," (Washington, D.C.: American Enterprise Institute, 1984):

> During the transition from the Carter to the Reagan administration there were reports of various losses. A banker declined the job of Deputy Energy Secretary because of family oil interests. A senior vice-president of a major corporation turned down the position of Under-Secretary of the Interior because he concluded that the restrictions on the activities of a former government employee would have precluded his becoming president of his company when he returned. Another person refused the position of Secretary of the Interior because of conflicts with family grazing rights on public lands. The reader can decide whether these cases reflect a problem and constitute a loss to government. (p. 50)

48. *Hunter v. City of New York,* 58 A.D.2d 136 (1977), *affirmed,* 376 N.E.2d 928 (1978).

49. *Slevin v. City of New York,* 551 F. Supp. 917 (S.D.N.Y. 1982).

50. *Barry v. City of New York,* 712 F.2d 1554 (2d Cir. 1983); *see* Knapp Commission, *Commission Report: With Summary and Principal Recommendations* (3 August 1972); Knapp Commission, *The Knapp Commission Report on Police Corruption* (New York: Braziller, 1973).

51. *United States v. National Treasury Employees Union,* 115 S. Ct. 1003 (1995). The suit did not challenge the provision prohibiting compensation for speeches or articles relating to the public official's work.

52. See K. Sack, "New York Ethics Law Leads Local Officials to Quit Posts," *New York Times,* 18 May 1991, p. 26: "The [New York State ethics] law has generated a backlash across the state in which an effort to stop corruption is threatening to stop government instead. Officials in some municipalities fear that the resignations will paralyze

local government by making it difficult to convene quorums of zoning boards, community college boards and development agencies."

53. Joseph W. Little, "Abolishing Financial Disclosure to Improve Government," *Stetson Law Review* 16 (1987): 633.

Five: Whistleblowers

1. New York State Commission on Government Integrity, "Brave Voices: Report and Recommendations on the Need for Better Whistleblower Protection," in *Government Ethics Reform for the 1990s* (New York: Fordham University Press, 1991), 688.

2. Public Law 95-454, 92 *Stat.* 111 (1978).

3. Senate Hearings on S. 508, *Whistleblower Protection Act of 1987,* Committee on Governmental Affairs, 100th Cong., 1st sess., 20 and 31 July 1987 (statement of Senator David Pryor). Hereafter cited as *Hearings on Whistleblower Protection.*

4. *Hearings on Whistleblower Protection,* 4 (statement of Senator Carl Levin).

5. *Hearings on Whistleblower Protection,* 10–12 (statement of Harold Hipple, former Veterans Administration Hospital Police Officer).

6. Hearings on H.R. 4033, 4 (statement of William O'Connor, OSC Special Counsel).

7. H.R. 274, 100th Cong., 1st sess. 19 (1987), citing Office of Merit Systems Review and Studies, U.S. Merit Systems Protection Board, "Blowing the Whistle in the Federal Government: A Comparative Analysis of 1980 and 1983 Survey Findings" (1984), 6.

8. Hearings on H.R. 4033, 99 (statement of Stuart E. Schiffer, Deputy Assistant Attorney General, Department of Justice).

9. Public Law 101-12, 103 *Stat.* 16, §2(a) (10 April 1989).

10. H.R. 3355, 103d Cong., 2d sess. §4402 (1994).

11. See generally, Myron Glazer, *The Whistleblowers: Exposing Corruption in Government and Industry* (New York: Basic Books, 1989); Daniel Westman, *Whistleblowing: The Law of Retaliatory Discharge* (Washington D.C.: Bureau of National Affairs, 1991).

12. New York City Local Law 10; New York City Administrative Code §12-113 (1992). In 1984, the New York State Legislature passed its own whistleblower protection law, which also covers municipal employees.

13. Edward Gargan, "Koch Asks Law to Help Reveal City Corruption," *New York Times,* 13 December 1983, p. B24.

14. Michel Foucault, *Discipline and Punish: The Birth of the Prison* (New York: Vintage, 1977).

15. The city's law, in some ways, offers less comprehensive protection and encouragement than the federal law. For example, under the city's law, only certain failures to act (i.e., to appoint, to promote) are covered, while under the federal scheme *any* retaliatory action is prohibited. Furthermore, the city law does not protect whistleblowers from *threats* of retaliation, but only from actual retaliation.

16. New York City Administrative Code §12-113 (1990).

17. Admittedly, this low number would be consistent with a large number of dis-

closures, as long as there were no reprisals. However, our research does not indicate that this has been the case.

18. S. 969, 95th Cong., 2d sess. 8 (1978).

19. Ibid.

20. In the course of discussing the reasonableness of giving agency heads the first opportunity to investigate and determine the validity of a whistleblower's complaint, one law review commentator has written,

> Clearly, to give the agency head where the alleged infraction occurred the power to investigate and write up the report that will be resubmitted to the Special Counsel and which will be seen by outsiders, including Congress, the president, and the whistleblower, is to "let the fox guard the henhouse." The agency head could well be a party to the wrongdoing that is the subject of the whistleblowing. Even if the agency head were ignorant of any wrongdoing, the matter still occurred during his stewardship and as such spoke poorly of his management skills. Thus, the agency head had every incentive to "whitewash" and cover up the matter.

Bruce Fisher, "The Whistleblower Protection Act of 1989: A False Hope for Whistleblowers," *Rutgers Law Review* 43 (1991): 393.

21. New York State's statute is more sensitive than federal law to executive authority and the chain of command. It requires that before blowing the whistle to persons outside the employee's agency, the employee make a good faith effort to provide the appointing authority or a designee with the relevant information and give that person a reasonable opportunity to take appropriate action. New York Civil Service Law §75-b(2)(b).

22. Kevin M. Smith and John M. Oseth, "The Whistleblower Era: A Management Perspective," *Employee Relations Law Journal* 19 (Fall 1993): 17.

23. In a seven-year period, seven cases arising in the Department of Buildings were investigated. In five of them the DOI rejected the whistleblowers' claims of retaliation. In the two others, the DOI initially found in the whistleblower's favor, but later reversed itself.

24. Elizabeth Holtzman, "Protect Whistleblowers," *New York Times*, 30 March 1991, p. 19. The influential *Final Report on Corruption and Racketeering in the New York City Construction Industry* by the New York State Organized Crime Task Force (p. 242) also recommended strengthening the whistleblower laws. See also Gary Minda and Katie Raab, "Time for an Unjust Dismissal Statute in New York," *Brooklyn Law Review* 54 (1989): 147.

25. New York State Commission on Government Integrity, "Brave Voices: Report and Recommendations on the Need for Better Whistleblower Protection," in *Government Ethics Reform for the 1990s* (New York: Fordham University Press, 1991), 68.

26. Ibid., 697–99.

Six: Internal Government Investigation

1. Richard S. Winslow and David W. Burke, *Rogues, Rascals, and Heroes: A History of the New York City Department of Investigation* (New York: New York City Department of Investigation, 1993), 7.

2. S. J. Mandelbaum, *Boss Tweed's New York* (New York: Wiley, 1965); Alexander B. Callow, *The Tweed Ring* (Westport, Conn.: Greenwood Press, 1966).

3. The state courts later augmented the OCA's authority by allowing it to command testimony and documents from private individuals and entities with contractual or other connections to municipal government. *Matter of Edge Ho Holding Co.*, 231 A.D. 595, *revised*, 256 N.Y. 374 (1931).

4. Harold Seidman, *Investigating Municipal Administration: A Study of the New York City Department of Investigation* (New York: Institute of Public Administration, 1941), 7.

5. Winslow and Burke, *Rogues, Rascals, and Heroes*, 5.

6. Ibid., 11–13

7. Seidman, *Investigating Municipal Administration*, 41.

8. New York City Charter, ch. 466, §119 (as amended) (1901).

9. Seidman, *Investigating Municipal Administration*, 53.

10. Ibid., 8, 51–60.

11. Winslow and Burke, *Rogues, Rascals, and Heroes*, 17.

12. Seidman, *Investigating Municipal Administration*, 53.

13. *Annual Report of the Commissioner of Accounts* (1910), 7–9, quoted in Seidman, *Investigating Municipal Administration*, 53–54.

14. Winslow and Burke, *Rogues, Rascals, and Heroes*, 18–19.

15. *Annual Report of the Commissioner of Accounts* (1912), 7, quoted in Seidman, *Investigating Municipal Administration*, 55.

16. Ironically, the name change actually was precipitated by a desire to preserve the OCA's power of subpoena. The comptroller had threatened to limit the subpoena power to mayoral departments, which the OCA technically was not. The renamed DOIA, however, met that qualification. Seidman, *Investigating Municipal Administration*, 90.

17. Ibid., 41.

18. Winslow and Burke, *Rogues, Rascals, and Heroes*, 26.

19. Seidman, *Investigating Municipal Administration*, 96.

20. Ibid., quoting Norman Thomas and Paul Blanshard, *What's the Matter with New York* (New York: Macmillan, 1932), 57.

21. Herbert Mitgang, *The Man Who Rode the Tiger: The Life and Times of Judge Samuel Seabury* (Philadelphia: J.B. Lippincott, 1963), 244.

22. See Richard N. Smith, *Thomas Dewey and His Times* (New York: Simon and Schuster, 1982); Mary M. Stolberg, *Fighting Organized Crime* (Boston: Northeastern University Press, 1995).

23. Charles Garrett, *The LaGuardia Years: Machine and Reform Politics in New York City* (New Brunswick, N.J.: Rutgers University Press, 1961).

24. The 1938 Charter provided the legal basis for the predominance of the DOI's law-enforcement role. It provided a constitutional mandate for the Bureau of Complaints, shortened the name of the agency to the Department of Investigation, and transferred accounting and auditing responsibilities to the comptroller.

25. Winslow and Burke, *Rogues, Rascals, and Heroes*, 34.

26. Seidman, *Investigating Municipal Administration*, 172–73.

27. For a chronology of exposés on corruption among city building inspectors, see chapter 10; also see New York State Organized Crime Task Force, *Corruption and Racketeering in the New York City Construction Industry* (New York: New York University Press, 1990), 105–6.

28. Winslow and Burke, *Rogues, Rascals, and Heroes,* 38. The charges against Murtagh were eventually dropped.

29. New York State Temporary Commission of Investigation, Final Report of the Special Unit, *Government for Sale: A Glimpse at Waste and Corruption in the City of New York* (July 1961), 21.

30. Ibid., 30–31.

31. New York City Department of Investigation, "Preliminary Report to the Mayor on Findings of Corruption in the Construction Industry and in the Buildings Department" (7 November 1974), 2–3.

32. Interview with Stanley Lupkin, DOI Commissioner, 4 December 1991.

33. Gary T. Marx, "When the Guards Guard Themselves: Undercover Tactics Turned Inward," *Policing and Society* 2 (1992): 161.

34. Mayor Rudolph Giuliani appointed Howard Wilson as DOI commissioner. Wilson served as assistant U.S. Attorney when Giuliani was U.S. Attorney. The appointment continues the trend toward the DOI functioning as a full-fledged law-enforcement agency.

35. For an examination of the federal inspectors-general system, see Paul C. Light, *Monitoring Government: Inspectors General and the Search for Accountability* (Washington, D.C.: The Brookings Institution, 1993).

36. Mayoral Executive Order No. 21, 19 August 1970.

37. Mayor Beame adopted Lindsay's Executive Order No. 21 as his Executive Order No. 1, January 1974.

38. Executive Order No. 16, 16 July 1978.

39. City of New York Special Commission to Investigate City Contracts (September 1986).

40. Executive Order No. 105, 26 December 1986.

41. Winslow and Burke, *Rogues, Rascals, and Heroes,* 61.

42. Ibid.

43. Executive Order No. 105, 26 December 1986.

44. New York City Department of Investigation, "Annual Report to the Mayor: The City-Wide Anti-Corruption Program," (October 1991), 5.

45. Jack Newfield and Wayne Barrett, *City for Sale: Ed Koch and the Betrayal of New York* (New York: Harper & Row, 1988), 204; see also Marx, "When the Guards Guard Themselves," 157.

46. "Use immunity" means that anything the interviewee says cannot be used against her in a criminal proceeding. "Derivative use immunity" means that any leads or other incriminating evidence derived from what the interviewee says likewise cannot be used against her in a criminal proceeding.

47. Committee on Legal Affairs, Association of the Bar of the City of New York, "Report on the New York City Department of Investigation," *The Record* 43 (1988): 948–86.

Seven: State and Federal Prosecutors

1. John T. Noonan, "Bribery," in *Encyclopedia of Crime and Justice* (New York: Free Press, 1983), 1: 123.

2. Gary T. Marx, "When the Guards Guard Themselves: Undercover Tactics Turned Inward," *Policing and Society* 2 (1992): 158.

3. Ibid., 156.

4. In the mid-1970s, New York State Governor Hugh Carey fired Special Prosecutor Maurice Nadjari because of an alleged "decline in public confidence" in Nadjari due to his "dubious methods of collecting evidence." Nadjari accused the governor of firing him because his investigations were getting too close to him. Dennis Williams and Phyllis Malamud, "Sacking of a Supercop," *Newsweek,* 5 January 1976, p. 17. An excellent contemporary example is the dismantling of the twenty-six-year-old Pennsylvania Crime Commission by the state attorney general after the Commission pressed forward with its investigation into improprieties by the state attorney general. "PA Crime Commission Closing," *Lancaster Intelligencer Journal,* 27 June 1994, p. A1.

5. Marx, "When the Guards Guard Themselves," 156.

6. Ibid., 157; Jack Newfield and Wayne Barrett, *City for Sale: Ed Koch and the Betrayal of New York* (New York: Harper & Row, 1988), 170.

7. However, prosecutors did catch some big fish. In the mid-1960s, Carmine DeSapio, "the strongest Tammany boss since the 1920s," was sentenced to two years for his role in a bribery and bid-rigging scheme involving Con Edison. See Newfield and Barrett, *City for Sale,* 108; Jack Newfield and Paul Du Brul, *The Abuse of Power: The Permanent Government and the Fall of New York* (New York: Viking Press, 1977), 269–74. Meade Esposito, retired Brooklyn party boss, and Mario Biaggi, a Bronx congressman, were convicted on charges of bribery, conspiracy, illegal gratuities, and interstate travel in aid of racketeering, and sentenced to two years probation and a $500,000 fine, and thirty months in prison, respectively. Newfield and Barrett, *City for Sale,* 338, 342.

8. See New York City Charter, §801.

9. Richard S. Winslow and David W. Burke, *Rogues, Rascals, and Heroes: A History of the New York City Department of Investigation* (New York: New York City Department of Investigation, 1993), 1, n. 3.

10. Lawrence Fleischer, "Thomas E. Dewey and Earl Warren: The Rise of the Twentieth Century Urban Prosecutor," *California Western Law Review* 28 (1991): 6.

11. Alan A. Block, *Lepke, Kid Twist, and the Combination: Organized Crime in New York City 1930–1944* (unpublished Ph.D. diss.) quoted in Fleischer, "Thomas E. Dewey and Earl Warren," 11.

12. Charles Whitman (1868–47) is the best example of a progressive reformer who was swept into office as Manhattan district attorney. Whitman emphasized police corruption aligned with illegal gambling interests. See Andy Logan, *Against the Evidence: The Becker Rosenfeld Affair* (New York: McCall, 1970).

13. Norman Thomas and Paul Blanshard, *What's the Matter with New York* (New York: Macmillan, 1932), 11–12.

14. Herbert Mitgang, *The Man Who Rode the Tiger: The Life and Times of Judge Samuel Seabury* (New York: J.B. Lippincott Co., 1963); Mary M. Stolberg, *Political Justice: Thomas Dewey and the Anatomy of a Crime Wave* (unpublished Ph.D. diss., Department of History, University of Virginia, 1991).

15. Stolberg, *Political Justice,* 55.

16. For an excellent account of Mayor Walker's political rise and fall, see Milton Mackaye, *The Tin Box Parade* (New York: Robert M. McBride 1934), and William B. Northrop and John B. Northrop, *The Insolence of Office* (New York: G. P. Putnam's Sons, 1932).

17. Thomas and Blanshard, *What's the Matter with New York,* 331–49, Appendix I.

18. Ibid., 342–43.

19. Stolberg, *Political Justice,* 56.

20. Northrop and Northrop, *The Insolence of Office,* 121–22.

21. Richard N. Smith, *Thomas E. Dewey and His Times* (New York: Simon & Schuster, 1982), 147–50.

22. For an excellent account of Dewey's tenure as a prosecutor, see Stolberg, *Political Justice;* see also Smith, *Thomas E. Dewey and His Times.*

23. Smith, *Thomas E. Dewey and His Times.*

24. Barry Cunningham and Mike Pearl, *Mr. District Attorney* (New York: Mason/Charter, 1977).

25. Of course, there were exceptions in these offices too. One of the most salient was Burton Roberts, a Hogan protégé, who served for a time as Bronx chief assistant district attorney.

26. There was a flurry of prosecutorial activity in the late 1940s aimed at corruption at the top levels of Mayor William O'Dwyer's administration. James J. Moran, the deputy fire commissioner, a close friend of the mayor's, was exposed as a major grafter. O'Dwyer resigned and became ambassador to Mexico. Hogan, with the support of Tammany boss Carmine DeSapio, ran unsuccessfully for the U.S. Senate.

27. Commission to Investigate Allegation of Police Corruption and the City's Anti-Corruption Procedures (The Knapp Commission) *Commission Report* (26 December 1972).

28. Milton S. Gould, "A Requiem for Andy Tyler," *New York Law Journal* 20 November 1989, p. 1.

29. See Maurice Nadjari, "New York State's Office of the Special Prosecutor: A Creation Born of Necessity," *Hofstra Law Review* 2 (1974): 102.

30. Ibid.

31. Tom Goldstein, "The Nadjari Record: Rights Sometimes Were Ignored," *New York Times,* 1 November 1976, p. D8.

32. *Rao v. New York,* 74 A.D.2d 964, 425 N.Y.S.2d 888 (3d Dept. 1980).

33. Ibid.

34. *People v. Rao, Jr.,* 73 A.D.2d 88, 425 N.Y.S.2d 122 (2d Dept. 1980) (reversing conviction of Judge Rao's son); *Nigrone v. Murtagh,* 46 A.D.2d 343, 362 N.Y.S.2d 513 (2d Dept. 1974) (reversing convictions of Judge Rao and his son's law partner).

35. *Nigrone v. Murtagh,* 46 A.D.2d 343, 347, 362 N.Y.S.2d 513, 516 (2d Dept. 1974).

36. Ibid., 347, 362 N.Y.S.2d 517. But see *People v. Archer,* 68 A.D.2d 441, 417 N.Y.S.2d 507 (2d Dept. 1979). In *Archer,* a former Queens assistant district attorney and head of the Indictments Bureau was convicted of bribe receiving and

official misconduct for fixing cases before the grand jury. Archer was nabbed when undercover agents put a phony case before the grand jury. In contrast to the *Rao, Jr.* and *Nigrone* cases, the appellate division did not blast the prosecution for putting fictitious cases before the grand jury. The court stated that Archer's "participation in this corruption scheme was not the product of active encouragement or instigation by the government." The court reasoned that the government simply manufactured a setting for a crime that would have occurred anyway.

37. Leslie Maitland, "A Second Nadjari Indictment against Goldman Is Dismissed," *New York Times,* 23 March 1977, p. 1.

38. *People v. Mackell,* 47 A.D.2d 209, 220, 366 N.Y.S.2d 173, 184 (2d Dept. 1975), *affirmed,* 40 N.Y.2d 59, 351 N.E.2d 684 (1976).

39. Ibid., 220, 366 N.Y.S.2d 184.

40. Marcia Chambers, "Goldman Charge Dropped; Murtagh Upbraids Nadjari," *New York Times,* 11 November 1975, p. 1.

41. Marcia Chambers, "Nadjari's Perjury Case against Lawyer Dismissed," *New York Times,* 18 November 1975, p. 61.

42. Marcia Chambers, "Merola Questions Legality of Investigations By Nadjari," *The New York Times,* 1 January 1976, p. 1.

43. Tom Goldstein, "Merola Says Nadjari Has 'Ability to Smear,'" *New York Times,* 28 January 1976, p. 1.

44. Selwyn Raab, "The Nadjari Years: There Were Also Ups," *New York Times,* 28 December 1975, p. 7.

45. Dennis A. Williams and Phyllis Malamud, "Sacking of a Supercop," *Newsweek,* 5 January 1976, p. 17.

46. Ibid., 17.

47. *People v. DiFalco,* 44 N.Y.2d 482, 377 N.E.2d 732, 406 N.Y.S.2d 279 (1978); Dena Kleiman, "Court Ready to Kill Saypol's Indictment," *New York Times,* 21 December 1976, p. 1; Leslie Maitland, "A Second Nadjari Indictment Against Goldman Dismissed," *New York Times,* 23 March 1977, p. 1 (discussing dismissal of indictment against DeSapio).

48. *People v. Cunningham,* 88 Misc. 2d 1065; 390 N.Y.S.2d 547 (Sup. Ct. 1976)

49. *Dondi v. Jones,* 40 N.Y.2d 8, 18, 351 N.E.2d 650, 658, 386 N.Y.S.2d 4, 11 (1976).

50. Tom Goldstein, "Grumet Upholds Carey's Motives in Nadjari Action," *New York Times,* 23 June 1976, p. 1.

51. The State of New York Temporary Commission of Investigation, *The Nadjari Office and the Press* (1976).

52. Tom Goldstein, "Debate Is Intense on Nadjari's Effectiveness in Special Prosecutor Post," *New York Times,* 28 March 1977, p. 57.

53. Leonard Buder, "Staff of Anticorruption Chief Will Be Cut a Third on Jan. 1," *New York Times,* 13 December 1981, p. 64.

54. Jeffrey Schmalz, "A 'Temporary' Office Gets Its 5th Occupant," *New York Times,* 23 June 1985, p. D8.

55. Selwyn Raab, "State to End New York City Corruption Office," *New York Times,* 14 January 1990, p. A28.

56. Ibid.

57. Friedman was convicted of perjury, racketeering, conspiracy, and mail fraud, and sentenced to twelve years in prison. *United States v. Friedman,* 854 F.2d 535 (2d Cir. 1988).

58. Esther Pessin, "Perjury Trial of Ex-City Transportation Chief Begins," *United Press International,* 1 July 1987.

59. Michael Oreskes, "A Yearlong Look at Government's Underside," *New York Times,* 4 January 1987, p. D6.

60. Philip Shenon, "U.S. Officials See Sweeping Effort to Combat Municipal Corruption," *New York Times,* 30 March 1986, p. A1.

61. John T. Noonan, *Bribes* (Berkeley: University of California Press, 1984), 584–87.

62. 18 *United States Code* §§1341 and 1343 (1988 and Supp. IV 1992).

63. See Arthur Maass, "Public Policy By Prosecution," *The Public Interest* 89 (Fall 1987): 107–27.

64. Marx, "When the Guards Guard Themselves," 156.

65. One of the most famous precedent-setting cases was *U.S. v. Margiotta,* 688 F.2d 108 (2d Cir. 1982), involving the conviction of the Republican boss of Nassau County.

66. James Touhy and Rob Warden, *Greylord: Justice, Chicago Style* (New York: Putnam, 1989).

67. Oreskes, "A Yearlong Look at Government's Underside," p. D6.

68. Ibid.

69. Marianne Yen, "Who's Who in New York City Corruption Scandals," *Washington Post,* 26 August 1987, p. A14.

70. *People v. Nussbaum,* 142 A.D.2d 739, 531 N.Y.S.2d 122 (2d Dept. 1988).

71. Maass, "Public Policy By Prosecution," 110.

72. Ibid., 111.

73. Mark A. Uhlig, "Wedtech's Story: From Symbol of Hope to Emblem of Greed," *New York Times,* 5 August 1988, p. B4.

74. Josh Barbanel, "Wedtech: Portrait of An American Scheme," *New York Times,* 7 August 1988, p. D6. See also Larry Sabato, *Feeding Frenzy* (New York: Free Press, 1991); Marilyn W. Thomson, *Feeding the Beast: How Wedtech Became the Most Corrupt Little Company in America* (New York: Charles Scribner's Sons, 1990).

75. Merril Perlman, "The Crimes and Punishments of Wedtech," *New York Times,* 22 October 1989, p. D5.

76. *United States v. Biaggi,* 909 F.2d 662, 669 (2d Cir. 1990).

77. Ibid., 670.

78. *United States v. Biaggi,* 909 F.2d 669 (2d Cir. 1990), *cert. denied sub nom. Simon v. United States,* 499 U.S. 904 (1991).

79. Ibid.

80. Newfield and Barrett, *City for Sale,* 204.

81. The appellate courts, however, continue to find defects in corruption trials requiring reversal of convictions. See, for example, *People v. Ohrenstein,* 77 N.Y.2d 38, 565 N.E.2d 493 (1990) (reversing conviction of Democratic state senate minority leader for funding no-show jobs).

Eight: Purging Corruption from Public Contracting

1. Technically, contracts awarded by the city can be divided into five categories: (1) capital construction and major equipment; (2) supplies, materials, property, equipment, and related services and charges; (3) program operations, primarily concerned with the purchase of health and human services; (4) architectural, engineering, and construction management services; and (5) other professional services.

Prior to the 1989 charter, the first two categories of contracts were subject to competitive bidding requirements. The remaining three were not, although in many instances the contract award is subject to a competitive "request for proposals" procedure that was quasi-competitive. All noncompetitive contracts required approval by the Board of Estimate, which was abolished by the 1989 charter.

2. See Alexander Callow, *The Tweed Ring* (New York: Oxford University Press, 1966); Alfred Connawe and Edward Silberfarb, *Tigers of Tammany: Nine Men Who Ran New York* (New York: Holt Rinehart & Winston, 1967); Gustavs Myers, *The History of Tammany Hall* ([1901] New York: Dover, 1971); Jerome Mushkat, *Tammany: The Evolution of a Political Machine, 1789–1865* (Syracuse, N.Y.: Syracuse University Press, 1971); Warren Moscow, *The Last of the Big-Time Bosses: The Life and Times of Carmine DeSapio and the Rise and Fall of Tammany Hall* (New York: Stein & Day, 1976).

3. James F. Nagle, *Federal Procurement Regulations: Policy, Practice, and Procedures* (Chicago: American Bar Association, 1987), 12–13, and *A History of Government Contracting* (Washington, D.C.: George Washington University Press, 1992).

4. Jack Newfield and Wayne Barrett, *City for Sale: Ed Koch and the Betrayal of New York* (New York: Harper & Row, 1988), 244–49.

5. Statement to the New York City Charter Revision Commission By Edward V. Regan, Comptroller, the State of New York, 15 October 1987.

6. New York City Charter (1994), §315 and §312(a)(2).

7. The other stated goals follow:

> (1) To simplify, clarify, and modernize the law governing procurement; (2) To permit the continued development of procurement policies and practices; (3) To make as consistent as possible the uniform application of these policies throughout New York City agencies; (4) To provide for increased public confidence in New York City's procurement procedures; (5) To ensure the fair and equitable treatment of all persons who deal with the procurement system of the City of New York; (6) To provide for increased efficiency, economy and flexibility in City procurement activities and to maximize to the fullest extent the purchasing power of the City; (7) To foster effective broad-based competition from all segments of the vendor community, including small businesses, women, and minority-owned and operated enterprises; . . . (9) To ensure appropriate public access to contracting information; (10) To foster equal employment opportunities in the policies and practices of contractors and subcontractors wishing to do businesses with the City.

Procurement Policy Board Rules, 1 August 1990, Rule 111(b).

8. Procurement Policy Board Rules, 1 August 1990, Rule 111(c).

9. Ibid.

10. Procurement Policy Board Rule 521.

11. Procurement Policy Board Rule 521(b)(2)(vi).

12. Procurement Policy Board Rule 521(e)(1).

13. Douglas Feiden, "New Turn of Phrase Scares Off Vendors," *Crain's New York Business,* 2 March 1992, p. 3.

14. For a description of VENDEX (Vendor Information Exchange System), see New York City Mayor's Office of Contracts, "VENDEX: Policies and Procedure," (March 1990).

15. Feiden, "New Turn of Phrase Scares Off Vendors," p. 3. Rather than ensuring that city contracts are awarded to competent, honest contractors, in practice, "VENDEX is essentially blackballing legitimate companies and adding reams of red tape and onerous paperwork."

16. New York City Charter and Administrative Code, New York City Local Law 5 (1991 Amendments).

17. New York City Mayor's Office of Contracts, "VENDEX: Policies and Procedures Manual," (March 1990), 30.

18. Feiden, "New Turn of Phrase Scares Off Vendors," p. 3.

19. See New York State Organized Crime Task Force, *Corruption and Racketeering in the New York City Construction Industry* (New York: New York University Press, 1990).

20. See Thomas D. Thacher II, "Institutional Innovation in Controlling Organized Crime," in Cyrille Fijnaut and James Jacobs, eds., *Organized Crime and Its Containment: A Transatlantic Initiative* (Amsterdam: Kluwer Academic Publishers, 1991), 169–82; see also "Schools for Scandal: A Staff Report on the New York City Board of Education's Mismanagement of School Construction, Repair, and Renovation," New York State, Senate Committee on Investigations, Taxation, and Government Operations (Sept. 23, 1987).

21. New York State School Construction Authority, "Prequalification Application: Construction Contractors," (November 1990), 26, 29.

22. Francis K. McArdle, Managing Director of the New York City General Contractors Association, warned against arbitrary action by contracting agencies and called for the creation of an appeals board to protect contractors from the use of "subjective reasons" in the exclusion of bidders. See Selwyn Raab, "52 Companies Banned from School Construction Bids," *New York Times,* 27 August 1991, p. B1.

23. See Office of Inspector General, New York City School Construction Authority, Press Release, July 29, 1991.

24. Selwyn Raab, "New York Halts Contract With Gotti Son-in-Law," *New York Times,* 19 November 1991, p. B1.

25. The controversy over the emergency jail construction contract is documented in an internal Comptroller's Office Memorandum from David Eichenthal, Counsel for Special Projects, and Elizabeth Lang, Special Counsel for Investigations, to Comptroller Elizabeth Holtzman, "Re: Contract Award to Leon DeMatteis Construction," (August 23, 1991).

26. Selwyn Raab, "New York Cancels Builder's Contract, Citing Reports on Mob Ties," *New York Times,* 26 December 1991, p. B11.

27. "Termination of City Contract is Overturned as Unreasonable," *New York Law Journal,* 16 October 1992, p.21.

28. *DeMatteis Construction Corp. v. Dinkins,* 190 A.D.2d 621, 594 N.Y.S.2d 167 (1st Dept. 1993).

29. 298 N.E.2d 105 (Court of Appeals 1973).

30. Selwyn Raab, "Housing Agency Contractor Named in Fraud Indictment," *New York Times,* 28 February 1992, p. B3.

31. A trenchant critique of the lowest responsible bidder system and suggestions for its reform are in Steven Kelman, *Procurement and Public Management: The Fear of Discretion and the Quality of Government Performance* (Washington, D.C.: AEI Press, 1990).

32. Office of the Comptroller, City of New York, "Second Interim Report on Diversified Products of New York, Ltd." (December 1990).

33. David Firestone, "New York Hospitals Chief Calls Brooklyn Plan a Failure," *New York Times,* 11 February 1994, p. A1.

34. Alan Finder, "Managing to Fail: How a Hospital Wasn't Built," *New York Times,* 3 April 1994, p. A1.

35. David Firestone, "New York Hospitals Chief Calls Brooklyn Plan a Giant Failure," *New York Times,* 11 February 1994, p. A1.

36. William Bunch, Mitchell Moss, and Gale Scott, "Costly Oops: Bid Fiasco Just Latest Hospital Woe," *Newsday,* 19 February 1994, p. 3.

37. David Firestone, "Manager Says New York Let Hospital Fail," *New York Times,* 12 February 1994, p. 21.

38. James C. McKinley, Jr., "Payments to Consulting Firm Frozen in Kings Hospital Work," *New York Times,* 12 March 1994, p. 24.

39. New York State Commission on Government Integrity, "A Ship Without a Captain: The Contracting Process in New York City," in *Government Ethics Reform for the 1990s* (New York: Fordham University Press, 1991), 1. Just three years earlier, the State-City Commission on Integrity in Government (Sovern Commission) conducted an overview of the city's contracting problems and warned that failure to address the fragmentation and complexity of contracting operations was an open invitation to corruption. See State-City Commission on Integrity in Government, *Report and Recommendations Relating to City Procurement and Contracts* (November 19, 1986), 67.

40. New York State Commission on Government Integrity, "A Ship without a Captain," 471.

41. Ibid., 472.

42. Ibid., 469.

43. Ibid., 464–65.

44. Interviews with Joseph DeLuca, assistant inspector general, New York City School Construction Authority, 25 September and 18 November 1992. Investigation costs are adapted from private-sector estimates.

45. Meyer S. Frucher, former president of the Battery Park City Authority, was able to save several million dollars in construction costs by using a labor consultant who persuaded the teamsters on the job to forego their usual gateway charges on nonunion haulers. It turned out later that the labor consultant had been implicated in, but acquitted of, charges related to a gangland murder. Frucher's achievement in completing the project and raising money through the Authority for low-income housing elsewhere was impugned by a report of the State Investigation Commission, because of his use of the tainted labor consultant. The effect of such criticism may be to deter public entrepreneurship. See State of New York Commission of Investigation, "Investigation of the Build-

ing and Construction Industry: Report of Conclusions and Recommendations" (1986), 2738.

46. In the winter of 1994, a year of particularly bad snow storms, the media blasted New York Mayor Rudolph Guliani for inefficiently plowing and removing snow from city streets. The problem was not that the city was overcharged when it awarded these emergency contracts, but that eleven of the companies hired had "checkered pasts, ranging from suspected mob ties to criminal conviction." Kevin Flynn, "Plow Now Anyhow, Buried City Hired Tainted Contractors," *Newsday,* 28 February 1994, p. 7.

Nine: Auditing and Accounting Controls

1. Bureau of Municipal Research, "What Should New York's Next Comptroller Do?" (October 1909), 3.

2. Ibid., 7.

3. "Some Results and Limitations of Central Financial Control," *Municipal Research Bulletin* 81 (January 1917): 3.

4. For example, during the heyday of the Tweed ring, the mayor and the comptroller conspired to loot the public coffers:

> The main reliance of the brazen robbers was contract padding. The figures on bills of City contractors were raised, sometimes it is said even by adding ciphers. Then the amounts were allowed by Comptroller Connolly and, after the contractor had been given an extra sum for his trouble, the surplus went into the pockets of the ring.

Alexander Flick, ed., *History of the State of New York* (New York: New York Historical Association, 1935), 7: 148.

5. Leonard D. White, *Trends in Public Administration* (New York: McGraw-Hill, 1933), 162.

6. As noted by William Lafferty in 1933, this was part of a general trend at the time:

> Older charters usually gave the local finance officers only responsibility for the records in their own offices. Recent charters tend to place responsibility for all accounting and accounting procedures on one city finance officer. Where the responsibilities for all city accounting [are] put on one person, it is possible to work all departmental accounts and records into one accounting system.

William A. Lafferty, Jr. *The Auditing of Municipal Accounts in New York State* (Albany, N.Y.: New York State Conference of Mayors and Other Officials, 1933), 23.

Despite this continually repeated aspiration, New York City was not able to achieve a unified accounting system until the 1980s.

7. New York State Commission on Governmental Operations of the City of New York, "Background Research on the Top Structure of the Government of the City of New York," *Finance Management* 3 (February 1961): 116–17. See also Edward F. Marek, *The Historical Development and Administrative Role of the Comptroller in New York City Government* (Ph.D. diss., Columbia University, 1966), 146–47.

8. See Suzanne Garment, *Scandal: The Culture of Mistrust in American Politics* (New York: Doubleday, 1991).

9. Roger Starr, *The Rise and Fall of New York* (New York: Basic Books, 1985), 225; James L. Chan, "The Birth of the Governmental Accounting Standards Board: How?

Why? What Next?" in James L. Chan, ed., *Research in Governmental and Non-Profit Accounting* (Greenwich, Conn.: JAI Press, 1985) 1: 6.

10. Starr, *The Rise and Fall of New York,* 225; Jack Newfield and Paul Du Brul, *The Abuse of Power: The Permanent Government and the Fall of New York* (New York: Viking Press, 1977), 177–79.

11. According to the Bureau of Labor Statistics, the average number of accountants and auditors in the public sector in 1991 was 217,000, of which 90,000 were federal, 88,000 were state, and 39,000 were local. This compares with 161,000 in 1983. (Interview with Philip Rones, U.S. Bureau of Labor Statistics, 14 June 1992).

12. For an explanation of EDP, see James O. Hicks, Jr., *Information Systems in Business: An Introduction,* 2d ed. (St. Paul, Minn.: West Publishing, 1990); GAO, "Assessing the Reliability of Computer-Processed Data," (September 1990).

13. The Port Authority of New York and New Jersey has established a goal of carrying out at least 20 percent of internal audits by EDP. Audit Division, Port Authority of New York and New Jersey, "Audit Plan, 1992" (13 January 1992).

14. Warren Moscow, *The Last of the Big-Time Bosses: The Life and Times of Carmine DeSapio and the Rise and Fall of Tammany Hall* (New York: Stein & Day, 1976), 169–70.

15. New York City Charter §93(c)(e) (1989).

16. New York City Comptroller, "Comptroller's Internal Control and Accountability Directives" (15 April 1985), 1.

17. Ibid., 1–4.

18. Ibid.

19. City of New York, Office of the Comptroller, Special Investigations Unit, "Social Clubs," SPIN 90-005 (8 April 1991), 4.

20. Ibid., 25.

21. Ibid., 26.

22. Under GAGAS, financial statement audits must determine: (1) whether the financial statements of an audited entity present fairly the financial position, results of operations, and cash flows or changes in financial position in accordance with generally accepted accounting principles; and (2) whether the entity has complied with laws and regulations for those transactions and events that may have a material effect on the financial statements. "Financial related audits include determining: (1) whether financial reports and related items, such as elements, accounts, or funds are fairly presented; (2) whether financial information is presented in accordance with established or stated criteria; and (3) whether the entity has adhered to specific financial compliance requirements."

See Comptroller General of the United States, "Government Auditing Standards, Standards For Audit of Governmental Organizations, Programs, Activities, and Functions" (1988 revision).

23. Ibid.

24. The *Budget and Accounting Act* of 1921 gave the comptroller the power to investigate "all matters relating to the receipt, disbursement and application of public funds," and in reports to Congress "to make recommendations looking to greater economy or efficiency in public expenditures." 31 *United States Code* §312.

25. The General Accounting Office conducts audits of "government organizations, programs, activities, and functions, and of government funds received by contractors,

nonprofit organizations, and other nongovernment organizations." U.S. General Accounting Office, *Government Auditing Standards: Standards For Audit of Government Organizations, Programs, Activities, and Functions* (Washington, D.C.: Government Printing Office, 1988), 1.

26. U.S. General Accounting Office, "Report to Selected Members of Congress: Mass Transit Grants, Noncompliance, and Misspent Funds by Two Grantees in UMTA's New York Region" (January 1992).

27. New York State Constitution, art. 5, §1; General Municipal Law, art. 3.

28. The comptroller registers contracts. The Procurement Policy Board sets contracting policy and tracks the volume of city contracting. The Mayor's Office of Contracts attempts to resolve problems that arise in the contracting process. Each agency's chief contracting officer is responsible for ensuring agency adherence to the comprehensive and complex contracting regime. Collectively, these "reforms" centralize and expand control over the agency-level contracting process.

29. New York City Department of Investigation, Corruption Prevention and Management Review Bureau, "An Analysis of the Corruption Risks in the Management and Control Systems within the Department of General Services, Bureaus of Leasing and Design, in Leasing Private Space for City Use" (January 1989), 7.

30. New York City Department of Investigation, Corruption Prevention and Management Review Bureau, "An Analysis of Corruption within the Construction Inspection Units of the Department of Buildings and the Agency's Corruption Prevention Program" (May 1991), 55–58.

31. See Richard Winslow and David Burke, *Rogues, Rascals, and Heroes: A History of the New York City Department of Investigation* (New York: New York City Department of Investigation, 1992).

32. Auditing also has become an important investigative tool in the federal government. Congress mandated a deputy IG for audit and a deputy IG for investigation. For a legislative history of the federal *Inspector-General Act of 1978*, see Margorie Knowles, "The Inspector General in the Federal Government: A New Approach to Accountability," *Alabama Law Review* 36 (Winter 1985): 475–513. See also Mark H. Moore and Margaret Jane Gates, *Inspectors-General: Junkyard Dogs or Man's Best Friend?* (New York: Russell Sage Foundation, 1986); Paul Light, *Monitoring Government: Inspectors General and the Search For Accountability* (The Brookings Institution, 1993).

33. Keith Hoskin and Richard H. Macve, "Accounting and the Examination: A Genealogy of Disciplinary Power," *Accounting, Organization, and Society* 11 (1986): 134.

34. In a criticism of public administration scholarship, James Q. Wilson noted, "To my knowledge no one has systematically compared the cost of all the inspectors, rules, and auditors with the savings that are achieved to see if all the checking and reviewing is worth it." See James Q. Wilson, *Bureaucracy: What Government Agencies Do and Why They Do It* (New York: Basic Books, 1989), 323.

35. J. D. Dermer and R. G. Lucas, "The Illusion of Managerial Control," *Accounting, Organization, and Society* 11 (1986): 471.

36. Eric G. Flamholtz, T. K. Das, and Anne S. Tsui hypothesize the ways in which measurement influences work behavior:

First, it serves as a criterion function by operationally defining the goals and standards of activities. The criterion becomes the decision premise . . . or the constraint . . . that guides behavior or action . . . [measurements] also induce the manager to engage in systematic planning. This is the catalytic function. . . . A third way in which the act of measurement can influence behavior is through affecting perception. . . . Thus, decision and behavioral alternatives tend to be limited to the set of information produced by the measurement system. This is called the set function. Lastly, the motivational function refers to the attention-focusing property of the information system, i.e., individuals concentrate efforts where results are measured . . . and ignore those aspects that are not being measured or recorded.

See Eric G. Flamholtz, T. K. Das, and Anne S. Tsui, "Toward an Integrative Framework of Organizational Control, *Accounting, Organization, and Society* 10 (1985): 40–41.

37. Robert Klitgaard, *Controlling Corruption* (Berkeley: University of California Press, 1988), 25–27 (emphasis in original) citing Herman B. Leonard, "Measuring and Reporting the Financial Condition of Public Organizations," in Chan, ed., *Research in Governmental and Non-Profit Accounting*, 1: 120–21.

38. National Academy of Public Administration, *Revitalizing Federal Management: Managers and Their Overburdened Systems* (November 1983), 3.

Ten: Waging War against the Inevitable

1. "26 City Inspectors Face Graft Trials," *New York Times*, 9 November 1940, p. 19.

2. "City Drops 32 Men on Graft Charges," *New York Times*, 9 March 1942, p. 21.

3. "Clerk Is Accused of Stealing Data on Housing; Graft Inquiry Is Seen," *New York Times*, 11 June 1947, p. 1.

4. "City Housing Official Indicted for Perjury," *New York Times*, 27 October 1950, p. 6; "$10,000 in 4 Banks, City Employee Out," *New York Times*, 1 January 1951, p. 42.

5. Charles G. Bennett, "Buildings Inquiry Pursued by State," *New York Times*, 6 November 1957, p. 37.

6. "City Maps Reforms in Realty Agencies," *New York Times*, 17 March 1958, p. 1; "Hidden Accounts Linked to City Aides," *New York Times*, 20 March 1958, p. 19.

7. Charles G. Bennett, "City Reorganizes Buildings Office," *New York Times*, 8 January 1959, p. 1.

8. "Buildings Graft Hunted in Kings," *New York Times*, 3 February 1959, p. 26.

9. Jack Roth, "Jury Sees Wide Disorder in City's Building Agency," *New York Times*, 10 March 1959, p. 1.

10. "Building Chief Reports on Graft," *New York Times*, 1 January 1961, p. 52; Edith Evans Asbury, "Graft Is Charged in Buildings Unit," *New York Times*, 11 January 1961, p. 1.

11. "Police Shifted in Building Case," *New York Times*, 3 February 1962, p. 22; "Watch to Be Kept on Building Aides," *New York Times*, 9 February 1961, p. 16.

12. "Moerdler Transferring 18 on S. I. after Inquiry into Housing Graft," *New York Times,* 7 May 1966, p. 1.

13. David K Shipler, "Study Finds $25 Million Yearly in Bribes Is Paid by City's Construction Industry," *New York Times,* 26 June 1972, p. 1; David K. Shipler, "City Construction Grafters Face Few Legal Penalties," *New York Times,* 27 June 1972, p. 1.

14. New York City Department of Investigation, "A Preliminary Report on Corruption in the Department of Buildings and in the Construction Industry" (1974), 3.

15. Richard S. Winslow and David W. Burke, *Rogues, Rascals, and Heroes: A History of the New York City Department of Investigation* (New York: New York City Department of Investigation, 1993), 56.

16. *United States v. DeMeo,* 86 C.R. 703 (S.D.N.Y. 1986).

17. *People v. Emmolo,* Ind. No. 6037/89 (New York County 1989).

18. New York City Department of Investigation, "Report to the Mayor, 1990–1993" (December 1993), 14.

19. Selwyn Raab, "Extortion Tied to Lax Supervision," *New York Times,* 23 October 1993, p. A27.

20. Ibid.

21. A study of the politics and administration of inspectional service in Chicago can be found in Bryan Jones, *Governing Buildings and Building Governments* (University of Alabama Press, 1985).

22. Antony E. Simpson, *The Literature of Police Corruption* (New York: John Jay Press, 1977), 79.

23. *Report and Proceedings of the Senate Committee Appointed to Investigate the Police Department of the City of New York* (18 January 1895), 17–30.

24. Ibid., 43–44.

25. *Report of the Special Committee of the Board of Aldermen of the City of New York to Investigate the Police Department* (10 June 1913), 1.

26. Ibid.

27. Ibid., 3.

28. Ibid., 3–4.

29. Samuel Seabury, *The Investigation of the Magistrates' Courts in the First Judicial Department and the Magistrates Thereof, and of Attorneys-at-Law Practicing in Said Courts,* (28 March 1932), 22.

30. Ibid.

31. Richard N. Smith, *Thomas E. Dewey and His Times* (New York: Simon & Schuster, 1982); Lawrence W. Sherman, "Police Corruption Control: New York, London, Paris," in Lawrence W. Sherman, ed., *Police Corruption: A Sociological Perspective* (Garden City, N.Y.: Anchor Books, 1974), 221.

32. Thomas Kessner, *Fiorello H. LaGuardia and the Making of Modern New York* (New York: McGraw-Hill, 1989), 358–60.

33. Ibid., 364.

34. Ibid., 363.

35. Kessner, *Fiorello H. LaGuardia,* 363–64.

36. Ibid., 365.

37. Ibid., 364.

38. Commission to Investigate Alleged Police Corruption and the City's Anti-Corruption Procedures (Knapp Commission), *Commission Report* (26 December 1972), 63. Cited hereafter as Knapp Commission, *Report.*

39. Ibid.

40. Institute of Public Administration, "The New York Police Survey: A Report for the Mayor's Committee on Management Survey" (1952), pp. iii–iv.

41. Lawrence W. Sherman, "Police Corruption Control: New York, London, Paris," in Sherman, ed., *Police Corruption,* 225.

42. Jack Newfield and Paul Du Brul, *The Abuse of Power: The Permanent Government and the Fall of New York* (New York: Viking Press, 1977), 158.

43. Ibid., 158–59.

44. David Burnham, "Graft Paid to Police Here Said to Run Into Millions," *New York Times,* 25 April 1970, p. 1.

45. Ibid.

46. Knapp Commission, *Report,* i.

47. Ibid., 204.

48. Ibid., 43–45.

49. Those officers were Patrolmen William Phillips, Waverly Logan, Edward Droge, Alfonso Janotta, and Detective Robert Leuci. Leuci and Janotta did not testify at the hearings. Janotta became too ill to testify, and Leuci was working for the federal government as an undercover agent in an investigation of corruption in the department's elite narcotics division, the Special Investigations Unit. Knapp Commission, *Report,* 48–60. Hereafter cited parenthetically in text by page number.

50. Barbara Gelb, "The Hard Code of the Super Chiefs," *New York Times Magazine,* 9 October 1983, p. 23.

51. Ibid.

52. Ibid.

53. James Lardner, "Murphy's Law," *Washington Post,* 12 February 1978, p. G3.

54. Maurice Punch, *Conduct Unbecoming: The Social Construction of Police Deviance and Control* (New York: Tavistock Publications, 1985), 27.

55. Maurice Nadjari, "New York State's Office of the Special Prosecutor: A Creation born of Necessity," *Hofstra Law Review* 2 (1974): 102.

56. Joseph B. Treaster, "Knapp Commission Reunion Has Unexpected Currency," *New York Times,* 28 June 1992, p. A25.

57. Mitch Gelman, "Tagging a Cop: IAD Had Paper Trail on Officer Busted for Dealing Drugs," *Newsday,* 13 May 1992, p. 6.

58. Ibid.

59. David Kocieniewski and Leonard Levitt, "Feds Bypass IAD," *Newsday,* 16 June 1992, p. 20.

60. Ibid., 2.

61. Commission to Investigate Allegations of Police Corruption and the Anti-Corruption Procedures of the Police Department (Mollen Commission), *Commission Report* (7 July 1994), 24–25. Hereafter cited parenthetically in text by page number.

62. Eric Pooley, "Untouchables: Police Corruption in the New York Police Department," *New York Magazine,* 11 July 1994, p. 16.

63. Ibid.

64. Ibid.

65. David Kocieniewski, "Dirty 30 Precinct: 12 of City's Finest Accused of Out-crooking Crooks," *Newsday,* 16 April 1994, p. 5; David Kocieniewski, "Pushers Bid on Cop Coke, Virtually Every Drug Dealer Knew," *Newsday,* 17 April 1994, p. 5; Editorial, "Corruption in the Dirty 30," *New York Times,* 1 October 1994, p. A22.

66. David Kocieniewski, "Jury Finds Dirty 30 Cop Clean," *Newsday,* 2 March 1995, p. 3.

67. Robert D. McFadden, "Commissioner Orders an Overhaul in Fight against Police Corruption," *New York Times,* 17 November 1992, p. A1.

68. The 1989 City Charter requires the mayor to report to the City Council reasons for removing the Investigations Commissioner.

69. Sydney H. Schanberg, "Knives Are Out for Cop Watchdog," *Newsday,* 13 December 1994, p. 35.

70. Jonathan P. Hicks, "Giuliani's Panel on Police Gets Off to a Running Start," *New York Times,* 1 March 1995, p. B2.

71. Bob Liff, "Rudy's Power Play," *Newsday,* 28 February 1995, p. 17.

72. Clifford Krauss, "Hunting Rogues: Police Corruption Signals Abound," *New York Times,* 6 February 1995, p. B1.

73. Leonard Levitt, "Confidential: DA's Graft Probe Kept Bratton Out of Loop," *Newsday,* 6 February 1995, p. 18.

74. Clifford Krauss, "16 Officers Indicted in a Pattern of Brutality in a Bronx Precinct," *New York Times,* 4 May 1995, p. B1.

75. Editorial, "Why Mug Mack? Let Him Run New Cop Watchdog Unit," *Newsday,* 31 January 1995, p. 24.

76. Leonard Levitt, "Confidential: DA's Graft Probe Kept Bratton Out of Loop," *Newsday,* 6 February 1995, p. 18.

77. Jack Newfield and Wayne Barrett, *City for Sale: Ed Koch and the Betrayal of New York* (New York: Harper & Row, 1980).

78. Ralph Blumenthal, "FBI Says Public Officials Accepted 105 of 106 Bribes Offered in 2-Year Operation," *New York Times,* 12 August 1987, p. A1; see also, U.S. Department of Justice, Law Enforcement Assistance Administration, National Institute of Law Enforcement and Criminal Justice, *Corruption in Land Use and Building Regulation: An Integrated Report of Conclusions,* vol. 1 (Washington, D.C.: Government Printing Office, 1979).

79. New York State Organized Crime Task Force, *Corruption and Racketeering in the New York City Construction Industry* (New York: New York University Press, 1990).

80. New York State Commission of Investigation, "The Co-Op City Repair Program" (March 1983), 3.

81. *United States v. Steiner,* 86 C.R. 507 (S.D.N.Y. 1986).

82. New York State Organized Crime Task Force, *Corruption and Racketeering in the New York City Construction Industry,* 132.

83. Ibid., 129.

84. Ibid., 259.

Eleven: Public Administration

1. Henry Jacoby, *The Bureaucratization of the World* (Berkeley: University of California Press 1973); Ralph Humel, *The Bureaucratic Experience* (New York: St. Martin's Press, 1987); David Nachmias and David H. Rosenbloom *Bureaucratic Government USA* (New York: St. Martin's Press, 1980); Victor A. Thompson, *Bureaucracy and the Modern World* (Morristown, N.J.: General Learning Press, 1976); Philip B. Heymann, *The Politics of Public Management* (New Haven, Conn.: Yale University Press, 1987); Herbert Kaufman, *Red Tape: Its Origins, Uses, and Abuses* (Washington, D.C.: The Brookings Institution, 1977).

2. See Peter Wilenski, *Public Power and Public Administration* (Sydney: Hale and Iremonger, 1986).

3. David Osborne and Ted Gaebler, *Reinventing Government: How the Entrepreneurial Spirit Is Transforming the Public Sector* (Reading, Mass.: Addison-Wesley, 1992), 14. This point is also made in William T. Gormley, Jr., *Taming the Bureaucracy* (Princeton, N.J.: Princeton University Press, 1989).

4. Ibid.

5. Michel Crozier, *The Bureaucratic Phenomenon* (Chicago: University of Chicago Press, 1964), 3.

6. Ibid., 1.

7. Osborne and Gaebler, *Reinventing Government,* 14.

8. Ibid., 15.

9. William E. Geist, "Pssst, Here's a Secret: Trump Rebuilds Ice Rink," *New York Times,* 15 November 1986, p. A35.

10. Ibid.

11. Letter to the Editor, "Tunnel Falls Short of a Triumph," *New York Times,* 27 February 1985, p. A22.

12. Bill Breen, "New York Thirsts for Third Water Tunnel," *Christian Science Monitor,* 3 October 1989, p. 13.

13. Ibid.

14. Crozier, *The Bureaucratic Phenomenon,* 178–79; "Bureaucracy," in *Encyclopedia of the Social Sciences* (New York: Free Press, 1968) 2: 206.

15. "Bureaucracy," in *Encyclopedia of the Social Sciences,* 206.

16. Crozier, *The Bureaucratic Phenomenon,* 108.

17. Vincent Ostrom, *The Intellectual Crisis in American Public Administration,* 2d ed. (Tuscaloosa, Ala.: University of Alabama Press, 1989), 104.

18. Melvin J. Dubnick, "Administrative Reform: Prospects for Debureaucratizing," paper delivered at the Annual Meeting of the Southwestern Political Science Association (17–20 March 1993); Michael Barzelay, *Breaking Through Bureaucracy: A New Vision For Managing in Government* (Berkeley: University of California Press, 1992); Walter G. Farr, Lance Liebman, and Jeffrey S. Wood, *Decentralizing City Government: A Practical Study of a Radical Proposal for New York City* (New York: Praeger Publishers, 1972); Steven Berger, "Reconstructing New York," *City Journal* (Winter 1992): 54; Bernard Helmut Baum, *Decentralization of Authority in a Bureaucracy* (Englewood Cliffs, N.J.: Prentice-Hall, 1961); Judith E. Gruber, *Controlling Bureaucracies: Dilemmas in Democratic Governance* (Berkeley: University of California Press, 1987); Bruce L. R.

Smith and James D. Carroll, eds., *Improving the Accountability and Performance of Government* (Washington, D.C.: The Brookings Institution, 1982).

19. Victor A. Thompson, *Modern Organization* (Tuscaloosa, Ala.: University of Alabama Press, 1977); Victor A. Thompson, *Bureaucracy and the Modern World* (Morristown, N.J.: General Learning Press, 1976).

20. Crozier, *The Bureaucratic Phenomenon,* 179.

21. James Q. Wilson, *Bureaucracy: What Government Agencies Do and Why They Do It* (New York: Basic Books, 1989), 131.

22. Ibid., 69.

23. Robert Merton, "Bureaucratic Structure and Personality," *Social Forces* 17 (1940): 560–68, reprinted in Robert Merton, ed., *Reader in Bureaucracy* (New York: Free Press, 1952), 361–71.

24. Crozier, *The Bureaucratic Phenomenon,* 185–87.

25. Ibid., 1987.

26. Ibid., 199–200.

27. Ibid., 27.

28. David T. Stanley, *Higher Skills for the City of New York: Study of Professional, Technical, and Managerial Manpower Needs of the City of New York* (Washington, D.C.: The Brookings Institution, 1963), 72–73.

29. Even Max Weber, who extolled the efficiency and general superiority of bureaucracy as a form of administration, painted a fairly grim picture of the bureaucrat's predicament: "The individual bureaucrat cannot squirm out of the apparatus in which he is harnessed. . . . [T]he professional bureaucrat is chained to his activity by his entire material being and ideal existence. In the great majority of cases, he is only a single cog in an ever-moving mechanism which prescribes to him an essentially fixed route of march." See H. H. Gerth and C. Wright Mills, trans., *From Max Weber: Essays in Sociology* (New York: Oxford University Press, 1946), 228.

30. See Douglas Murray McGregor, *The Human Side of Enterprise* (New York: McGraw-Hill, 1985); Osborn and Gaebler, *Reinventing Government,* 114–15.

31. Steven Cohen and William B. Eimicke, eds., *New York City Solutions II: Transforming the Public Personnel System* (New York: Columbia University Program in Politics and Public Policy, February 1993); Stanley Hill, "New York's Unhappy Employees," *New York Times,* 25 July 1987, p. A31.

32. Herbert Kaufman, *Red Tape: Its Origins, Uses, and Abuses* (Washington, D.C.: The Brookings Institution, 1977), 25.

33. Crozier, *The Bureaucratic Phenomenon,* 190–92.

34. Michel Crozier, "The Ungovernability of Democracy," *The American Enterprise* 4 (November/December 1993): 33.

35. Robert A. Caro, *The Power Broker: Robert Moses and the Fall of New York* (New York: Vintage Books, 1975).

36. William J. Quirk and Leon E. Wein, "A Short Constitutional History of Entities Commonly Known as Public Authorities" *Cornell Law Review* 56 (April 1971): 521.

37. Steven Lee Myers, "Guiliani Moving Ahead to Put City Services in Private Hands," *New York Times,* 5 December 1994, p. A1; James Krohe, Jr., "Why Reform Government? Replace It, Privatizing Government Services" *Across the Board* 29 (December 1992): 40.

38. New York State Commission on Government Integrity, "Underground Government: Preliminary Report on Authorities and Other Public Corporations," in *Government Ethics Reform for the 1990s* (New York: Fordham University Press, 1991), 342.

39. Ibid., 334–47, 378; Donald Axelrod, *Shadow Governments: The Hidden World of Public Authorities* (New York: John Wiley & Sons, 1992); Editorial, "Public Authorities, Public Competence," *New York Times,* 22 May 1988, p. D28.

40. New York State Commission on Government Integrity, "Underground Government: Preliminary Report on Authorities and Other Public Corporations," in *Government Ethics Reform for the 1990s,* 342.

41. Caro, *The Power Broker,* 499–698.

42. New York State Commission on Government Integrity, "Playing Ball with City Hall: A Case Study of Political Patronage in New York City," in *Government Ethics Reform for the 1990s,* 547.

43. Stanley Hill, "New York City's Unhappy Employees," *New York Times,* 25 July 1987, p. A31.

44. The National Performance Review, chaired by Vice-President Albert Gore, adapted most of the ideas from *Reinventing Government* for use in the federal government. See National Performance Review, *From Red Tape to Results: Creating Government That Works Better and Costs Less* (New York: Times Books, 1993).

45. Osborne and Gaebler, *Reinventing Government,* 16.

46. Ibid., 19–20.

47. Corruption is not the only scandal attributable to inadequate controls on decision makers. The recent Orange County bankruptcy arising from a single government entrepreneur's reckless investment strategy on behalf of the county is another example. This kind of scandal also triggers calls for increased controls over decision makers. See James Sterngold, "Orange County Noteholders' Anger Grows," *New York Times,* 3 June 1995, p. A31.

48. Osborne and Gaebler, *Reinventing Government,* 14 (emphasis in original).

49. See Joseph Viteritti, *Across the River: Politics and Education in the City* (New York: Holmes & Meier, 1983); David Rogers and Norman H. Chung, *110 Livingston Street Revisited: Decentralization in Action* (New York: New York University Press, 1983), xvi; Lydia Siegal, "Who Really Runs the Schools?" *The City Journal* 5, no. 1 (Winter): 3.

50. There is a limited body of literature evaluating school decentralization in New York City. See Viteritti, *Across the River;* Rogers and Chung, *110 Livingston Street Revisited;* Segal, *A Proposal for a Study of Corruption in the New York City Public Schools;* Marilyn Gittell, "School Governance," in Charles Brecher and Raymond D. Horton, eds., *Setting Municipal Priorities* (Montclair, N.J.: Allenheld Osman, 1981), 181–212.

51. Special Commissioner of Investigation for the New York City School District, "Power, Politics, and Patronage: Education in Community School District 12" (April 1993).

52. Ibid.; Siegal, "Who Really Runs the Schools?" 4–5; Liz Willen, "School Scam: 6 Ed Board Employees Charged in Slush Fund Scheme," *Newsday,* 5 October 1994, p. 5.

53. Alair A. Townsend, "Velella Should Ask Dad about NY School Reform," *Crain's New York Business,* 1 August 1994, p. 9.

54. Siegal, "Who Really Runs the Schools," 4, n. 1.

Twelve: Toward a New Discourse on Corruption Control

1. See Neil Skene, "Assault on Bureaucracy Never Materialized," *Congressional Quarterly Weekly Report* (7 November 1992) 50: 3608.

2. See Gary T. Marx, "When the Guards Guard Themselves: Undercover Tactics Turned Inward," *Policing and Society* 2 (1992): 151–72.

3. James B. Jacobs and Lynn Zimmer, "Drug Testing and Workplace Drug Testing: Politics, Symbolism, and Organizational Dilemmas," *Behavioral Science and the Law* 9 (1991): 345–60.

4. Commission to Investigate Allegations of Police Corruption and the Anti-Corruption Procedures of the Police Department, *Commission Report* (7 July 1994), 142–44.

5. Howard Schneider and Charles R. Babcock, "Clintons' Arkansas Land Venture Losses Disputed," *Washington Post,* 19 December 1993, p. A1; Jeff Gerth, "Records Show Clintons Lost Less in Venture Than Partner," *New York Times,* 25 March 1992, p. A19.

6. New York State Commission on Government Integrity, "Underground Government: Preliminary Report on Authorities and Other Public Corporations," in *Government Ethics Reform for the 1990s* (New York: Fordham University Press, 1991), 345.

7. New York State Commission on Government Integrity, "A Ship without a Captain: The Contracting Process in New York City," in *Government Ethics Reform for the 1990s,* 460–91.

8. See H. Thomas Johnson, "Managing by Remote Control: Recent Management Accounting Practice in Historical Perspective," in Peter Temin, ed., *Inside the Business Enterprise: Historical Perspectives on the Use of Information* (Chicago: University of Chicago Press, 1991).

9. Joyce Purnick, "Trump Offers to Rebuild Skating Rink," *New York Times,* 31 May 1986, at B29.

10. Susan Rose-Ackerman, *Corruption: A Study in Political Economy* (New York: Academic Press, 1978).

11. Susan Rose-Ackerman, "Which Bureaucracies Are Less Corruptible?," in Arnold J. Heidenheimer, Michael Johnston, and Victor LeVine, eds., *Political Corruption: A Handbook* (New Brunswick, N.J.: Transaction Publishers, 1993), 809.

12. Thomas C. Kohler, "Models of Worker Participation: The Uncertain Significance of Section 8 (a) (2)" *Boston College Law Review* 27 (May 1986): 499; John R. McLain, "Participatory Management Under Sections 2 (5) and 8 (a) (2) of the National Labor Relations Act," *Michigan Law Review* 83 (June 1985): 1736.

13. Even this claim must be qualified. See *United States v. Margiotta,* 688 F.2d 108 (2d Cir. 1982) (Republican political boss controlled all governmental hiring in Nassau County despite the existence of civil service).

14. Steven Cohen and William B. Eimicke, eds., *New York City Solutions II: Transforming the Public Personnel System,* (New York: Columbia University Program in Politics and Public Policy, February 1993). See also John J. DiIulio, Jr., Gerald Garvey, and Donald F. Kettl, *Improving Government Performance: An Owner's Manual* (Washington, D.C.: The Brookings Institution, 1993); James L. Heskett, W. Earl Sasser, and Chrisopher W. L. Hart, *Service Breakthroughs: Break-*

ing the Rules of the Game (New York: Free Press, 1990); Martin A. Levin and Mary Bryna Sanger, *Making Government Work: How Entrepreneurial Executives Turn Bright Ideas into Real Results* (San Francisco: Jossey-Bass, 1994).

15. Michael Reisman, *Folded Lies: Bribery Crusades and Reforms* (New York: Free Press, 1979), 100.

16. Marx, "When the Guards Guard Themselves," 169.

17. See Steven Kelman, "Deregulating Federal Procurement," in John J. DiIulio, Jr., ed., *Deregulating the Public Service: Can Government Be Improved?* (Washington, D.C.: The Brookings Institution, 1994); Steven Kelman, *Procurement and Public Management: The Fear of Discretion and the Quality of Government Performance* (Washington, D.C.: AEI Press, 1990); and *Service Delivery in the 1990s: Alternative Approaches for Local Government* (Washington, D.C.: International City Management Association, 1989).

18. The consequences of rule-oriented solutions are considered in Walter K. Olson, *The Litigation Explosion* (New York: Penguin Books, 1991). Prospects for alternative control models are assessed by Charles E. Lindblom, *Inquiry and Change: The Troubled Attempt to Understand and Shape Society* (New Haven, Conn.: Yale University Press, 1990); Donald F. Kettl and John J. DiIulio, Jr., eds., *Inside the Reinvention Machine: Appraising Governmental Reform* (Washington, D.C.: The Brookings Institution, 1995); and W. Richard Scott, *Institutions and Organizations* (Thousand Oaks, Calif.: Sage, 1995).

19. Both the Knapp Commission and the Mollen Commission found that peer pressure and the desire for continued comradery with and acceptance by fellow police officers created a culture in which bribery and other types of corruption were tolerated. Commission to Investigate Allegations of Police Corruption and the City's Anti-Corruption Procedures (Knapp Commission), *Commission Report* (26 December 1972), 4–7. Commission to Investigate Allegations of Police Corruption and the Anti-Corruption Procedures of the Police Department (Mollen Commission), *Commission Report* (7 July 1994), 51–65.

20. See Mark H. Moore, *Creating Public Value: Strategic Management in Government* (Cambridge, Mass.: Harvard University Press, 1995); Richard N. Haass, *The Power to Persuade: How to Be Effective in Government, the Public Sector, or Any Unruly Organization* (Boston: Houghton Mifflin, 1994); Steven Cohen and Ronald Bran, *Total Quality Management in Government: A Practical Guide for the Real World* (San Francisco: Jossey-Bass,1993); William G. Ouchi, *Theory Z: How American Business Can Meet the Japanese Challenge* (Reading, Mass.: Addison-Wesley, 1981); Richard T. Pascale and Anthony G. Athos, *The Art of Japanese Management* (New York: Simon & Schuster, 1981); Marshall Sashkin, *A Manager's Guide to Participatory Management* (New York: American Management Association, 1982); see above, note 12.

21. Donald A. Schon, *Educating the Reflective Practitioner: Toward a New Design for Teaching and Learning in the Professions* (San Francisco: Jossey-Bass, 1987); see also John Kotter, *A Force for Change: How Leadership Differs from Management* (New York: Free Press, 1990); John P. Burke, *Bureaucratic Responsibility* (Baltimore: Johns Hopkins University Press, 1986); Laurence E. Lynn, Jr., *Managing the Public's Business: The Job of the Government Executive* (New York: Basic Books, 1981).

22. Ibid., 28.

23. Vincent Ostrom, *The Intellectual Crisis in American Public Administration,* 2d ed. (Tuscaloosa, Ala.: University of Alabama Press, 1989), 116–19.

24. Ibid., 124–25.

25. Liz Willen, "School Scam: 6 Board of Ed Employees Charged in Slush Fund Scheme," *Newsday,* 5 October 1994, p. A5; Alair Townsend, "Velella Should Ask Dad about NY School Reform," *Crain's New York Business,* 1 August 1994, p. 9.

Bibliography

Ahearn, James. 1995. "Newark's Mired in a Grim Culture of Corruption." *Bergen Record*, 19 April.

Annual Report of the Commisioners of Accounts of New York City, 1900.

Annual Report of the Commissioner of Accounts, 1912.

Asbury, Edith Evans. 1961. "Graft Is Charged in Buildings Unit." *New York Times*, 11 January.

The Association of the Bar of the City of New York, Special Committee on Congressional Ethics. 1970. *Congress and the Public Trust*, 39.

Audit Division, Port Authority of New York and New Jersey. 1992. "Audit Plan, 1992." 13 January.

Axelrod, Donald. 1992. *Shadow Governments: The Hidden World of Public Authorities.* New York: John Wiley and Sons.

Banfield, Edward C. 1985. "Corruption as a Feature of Governmental Organization." *The Journal of Law and Economics* 18: 599.

Banfield, Edward, and James Q. Wilson. 1963. *City Politics.* Cambridge: Harvard University Press.

Barbanel, Josh. 1988. "Wedtech: Portrait of an American Scheme." *New York Times*, 7 August.

Barnard, Chester. 1939. *The Functions of the Executive.* Cambridge, Mass.: Harvard University Press.

Barzelay, Michael. 1992. *Breaking Through Bureaucracy: A New Vision for Managing in Government.* Berkeley: University of California Press.

Baum, Bernard Helmut. 1961. *Decentralization of Authority in a Bureaucracy.* Englewood Cliffs, N.J.: Prentice-Hall.

Beck, R., C. Hoskins, and J. M. Connolly. 1992. "Rent Extraction through Political Extortion: An Empirical Examination." *Journal of Legal Studies* 21 (January): 217–24.

Benson, George C. S., S. A. Maaranen, and A. Heslop. 1978. *Political Corruption in America.* Lexington, Mass.: Lexington Books.

Bennett, Charles G. 1959. "City Reorganizes Buildings Office." *New York Times*, 8 January.

Benson, Lee. 1961. *The Concept of Jacksonian Democracy: New York City as a Test Case.* Princeton: Princeton University Press.

Berg, Larry, Harlan Hahn, and John R. Schmidhauser. 1976. *Corruption in the American Political System.* Morristown, N.J.: General Learning Press.

Berger, Stephen. 1992. "Reconstructing New York." *The City Journal* (Winter): 54–60.

Bergman, Bruce C. 1975. "Reletting the Abandoned or Defaulted Public Works Project in New York—To Bid or Not to Bid?" *Fordham Urban Law Journal* 3: 451–73.

———. 1985. "Public Contracts: Rejecting the Irresponsible Bidder, Part I." *New York State Bar Journal* 57 (July): 22–27.

———. 1985. "Public Contracts: Rejecting the Irresponsible Bidder, Part II." *New York State Bar Journal* 57 (October): 43–49.

Bigelow, Page E. 1989. "From Norms to Rules: Regulating the Outside Interests of Public Officials." In *Restructuring New York City Government: The Reemergence of Municipal Reform,* edited by Frank J. Mauro and Gerald Benjamin, 141–57. New York: Academy of Political Science.

Bing, Julius. 1868. "Our Civil Service." *Putnam Magazine* 2(8): 233

Bish, Robert L., and Vincent Ostrom. 1973. *Understanding Urban Government.* Washington, D.C.: American Enterprise Institute for Public Policy Research.

Blackmore, John. 1979. "Tennessee's Clemency-Selling Scheme: Could Blanton Not Have Known?" *Corrections Magazine* 5 (June): 55.

Blumenthal, Ralph. 1987. "FBI Says Public Officials Accepted 105 of 106 Bribes Offered in 2-year Operation." *New York Times,* 12 August.

Bollens, John C., and Henry J. Schmandt. 1979. *Political Corruption: Power, Money, and Sex.* Pacific Palisades, Calif.: Palisades Publishers.

Breen, Bill. 1989. "New York Thirsts for Third Water Tunnel." *The Christian Science Monitor.*

Breyer, Steven. 1993. *Breaking the Vicious Circle.* Cambridge, Mass.: Harvard University Press.

Brooks, Robert C. 1910. *Corruption in American Politics and Life.* New York: Dodd, Mead.

Bruere, Henry. 1914. *A Proposed Division of Administration in the Mayor's Office: A Plan for Reorganizing the Office of the Commissioner of Accounts.* Quoted in Harold Seidman, *Investigating Municipal Administration: A Study of the New York City Department of Investigation.* New York: Institute of Public Administration, Columbia University, 1941, 64.

———. 1915. *Administrative Reorganization and the Constructive Work in the Government of the City of New York.* New York: Office of the New York City Chamberlain.

Bryce, James. 1889. *The American Commonwealth.* 2d ed. London: Macmillan.

Buchanan, James. 1980. "Rent Seeking and Profit Seeking." In *Toward a Theory of the Rent-Seeking Society,* edited by James M. Buchanan, Robert D. Tollison, and Gordon Tullok. College Station, Tex.: Texas A&M University Press.

Buchanan, James, and Gordon Tullock. 1965. *The Calculus of Consent: Logical Foundations of Constitutional Democracy.* Ann Arbor, Mich.: University of Michigan Press.

Buder, Leonard. 1981. "Staff of Anticorruption Chief Will Be Cut a Third on January 1." *New York Times,* 13 December.

"Building Chief Reports on Graft." 1961. *New York Times,* 1 January.

"Buildings Graft Hunted in Kings." 1959. *New York Times,* 3 February.

Bunch, William, Mitchell Moss, and Gale Scott. 1994. "Costly Oops: Bid Fiasco Just Latest Hospital Woe." *Newsday,* 19 February.

Bureau of Municipal Research. 1909. "What Should New York's Next Comptroller Do?"

Burke, John P. 1986. *Bureaucratic Responsibility.* Baltimore: Johns Hopkins University Press.

Burnham, David. 1970. "Graft Paid to Police Here Said to Run into Millions." *New York Times,* 25 April.

———. 1996. *Above the Law: Secret Deals, Political Fixes, and Other Misadventures of the U.S. Department of Justice.* New York: Charles Scribner and Sons.

Callow, Alexander B. 1966. *The Tweed Ring.* Westport, Conn.: Greenwood Press.

Caro, Robert A. 1974. *The Power Broker: Robert Moses and the Fall of New York.* New York: Alfred A. Knopf.

Cerillo, Arthur, Jr. 1977. "The Impact of Reform Ideology: Early Twentieth Century Municipal Government in New York City." In *The Age of Urban Reform: New Perspectives on the Progressive Era,* edited by Michael H. Eisner and Eugene M. Tobin. Port Washington, NY: Kennikat Press.

Chambers, Marcia. 1975. "Goldman Charge Dropped; Murtagh Upbraids Nadjari." *New York Times,* 11 November.

———. 1975. "Nadjari's Perjury Case Against Lawyer Dismissed." *New York Times,* 18 November.

———. 1976. "Merola Questions Legality of Investigations by Nadjari." *New York Times,* 1 January.

Chan, James L. 1985. "The Birth of the Governmental Accounting Standards Board: How? Why? What Next?" In *Research in Governmental and Non-Profit Accounting,* edited by James L. Chan. Greenwich, Conn.: JAI Press.

Chandler, Alfred D. 1977. *The Visible Hand: The Managerial Revolution in American Business.* Cambridge, Mass.: Belknap Press.

"City Drops Thirty-Two Men on Graft Charges." 1942. *New York Times,* 9 March.

"City Housing Official Indicted for Perjury." 1950. *New York Times,* 27 October.

City of New York. 1986. *Special Commission to Investigate City Contracts.* September.

City of New York, Department of Investigation. 1989. *City-Wide Anti-Corruption Program.*

———. 1991. *Annual Report to the Mayor: The City-Wide Anti-Corruption Program.*

———. 1993. *Report to the Conflicts of Interest Board: Fleet Bank's Loan to the Liz Holtzman for Senate Committee and the Selection of Fleet Securities as a Member of the City's Underwriter Team.*

City of New York Office of the Comptroller. 1990. *Second Interim Report on Diversified Products on New York, Ltd.*

City of New York Office of the Comptroller, Special Investigations Unit. 1991. "Social Clubs." *SPIN* 90-005.

City of New York, Mayor's Office of Contracts. 1990. "VENDEX: Policies and Procedures Manual." March.

"Clerk Is Accused of Stealing Data on Housing: Graft Inquiry Is Seen." 1947. *New York Times,* 11 June.

Clifford, Timothy. 1989. "Ex-Koch Aide Indicted on Eleven Counts." *Newsday,* 5 August.

Coffin, Tristram J. 1989. "The New York State Ethics in Government Act of 1987: A Critical Evaluation." *Columbia Journal of Law and Social Problems* 22: 269–305.

Cohen, Steven, and Ronald Bran. 1993. *Total Quality Management in Government: A Practical Guide for the Real World.* San Francisco: Jossey-Bass.

Cohen, Steven, and William B. Eimicke, eds. 1993. *New York City Solutions II: Transforming the Public Personnel System*. New York: Columbia University Program in Politics and Public Policy.

Commission to Investigate Allegations of Police Corruption and the Anti-Corruption Procedures of the New York City Police Department. 1983. *Interim Report and Principal Recommendations*.

Committee on Legal Affairs of the Association of the Bar of the City of New York. 1980. "Report on the New York City Department of Investigation." *The Record* 43 (10): 948–80.

Comptroller General of the United States. 1988. *Government Auditing Standards, Standards for Audit of Governmental Organizations, Programs, Activities, and Functions*.

Comptroller's Office Memorandum from David Eichenthal, Counsel for Special Projects, and Elizabeth Lang, Special Counsel for Investigations to Comptroller Elizabeth Holtzman. 1991. "Re: Contract Award to Leon DeMatteis Construction." 23 August.

Connawe, Alfred, and Edward Silberfarb. 1967. *Tigers of Tammany: Nine Men Who Ran New York*. New York: Holt Rinehart and Winston.

Croly, Herbert. 1914. *Progressive Democracy*. New York: Macmillan.

Crozier, Michel. 1964. *Bureaucratic Phenomenon*. Chicago: University of Chicago Press.

———. 1968. "Bureaucratic Phenomenon." In *Encyclopedia of the Social Sciences*. Vol. 2, 206. New York: MacMillan and Free Press.

———. 1993. "The Ungovernability of Democracy." *The American Enterprise* 4 (Nov./Dec.): 33.

Cunningham, Barry, and Mike Pearl. 1977. *Mr. District Attorney*. New York: Mason/-Charter.

De Tocqueville, Alexis. 1945. *Democracy in America*. Vol. 1. New York: Vintage Books.

DeForest, Robert W., and Lawrence Veiller, eds. 1903. *The Tenement House Problem: Including the Report of the New York State Tenement House Commission of 1900*. Vol. 2. New York: MacMillan.

Dermer, J. D., and R. G. Lucas. 1986. "The Illusion of Managerial Control." *Accounting, Organization, and Society* 11 (6): 471–82.

"Developments in the Law: Public Employment." *Harvard Law Review 97* (May 1984).

DiIulio, John J., Jr., Gerald Garvey, and Donald F. Kettl. 1993. *Improving Government Performance: An Owner's Manual*. Washington, D.C.: The Brookings Institution.

Downs, Anthony. 1967. *Inside Bureaucracy*. Boston: Little, Brown.

Dubnick, Melvin J. 1993. "Administrative Reform: Prospects for Debureaucratizing." Paper delivered at the Annual Meeting of the Southwestern Political Science Association, 17–20 March .

Eichenthal, David, and Elizabeth Lang. 1991. "Comptroller's Office Memorandum to Comptroller Elizabeth Holtzman, 23 August."

Eisenstadt, Abraham. 1993. "Political Corruption in American History." In *Political Corruption: A Handbook,* edited by Arnold J. Heidenheimer, Michael Johnston, and Victor Levine. New Brunswick, N.J.: Transaction Publishers.

Eisenstadt, Abraham, Ari Hoogenboom, and Hans L. Trefousse, eds. 1978. *Before Wa-*

tergate: Problems of Corruption in American Society. Brooklyn, N.Y.: Brooklyn College Press.

Emery, Fred. 1994. *Watergate: The Corruption of American Politics and the Fall of Richard Nixon.* New York: Times Books.

Epstein, Edward. 1992. "Corruption and the Three Arbitraries." *China News Analysis* 1457: 2–9.

Etzioni, Amitai. 1984. *Capital Corruption: The New Attack on American Democracy.* New York: Harcourt Brace Jovanovich.

Farr, Walter G., L. Liebman, and J. S. Wood. 1972. *Decentralizing City Government and a Practical Study of a Radical Proposal for New York City.* New York: Praeger Publishers.

Feerick, John D. 1991. "Reflections on Chairing the Commission on Government Integrity." In *Government Ethics Reform for the 1990s: The Collected Reports of the New York State Commission on Government Integrity,* edited by Bruce A. Green. New York: Fordham University Press.

Feider, Douglas. 1992. "New Turn of Phrase Scares off Vendors." *Crain's New York Business,* 2 March.

Feinman, Ronald L. 1981. *Twilight of Progressivism: The Western Republican Senators and the New Deal.* Baltimore: Johns Hopkins University Press.

Fesler, James W., and D. F. Kettl. 1991. *The Politics of the Administrative Process.* Chatham, N.J.: Chatham House.

Finder, Alan. 1994. "Managing to Fail: How a Hospital Wasn't Built." *New York Times,* 3 April.

Finder, Alan, and Albert Scardino. 1985. "Fourteen Charged in Housing Bribes." *New York Times,* 22 September.

Firestone, David. 1994. "New York Hospitals Chief Calls Brooklyn Plan a Failure." *New York Times,* 11 February.

———. 1994. "Manager Says New York Let Hospital Fail." *New York Times,* 12 February.

Fisher, Bruce. 1991. "The Whistleblower Protection Act of 1989: A False Hope For Whistleblowers." *Rutgers Law Review* 43 (Winter): 355–416.

Flamholtz, Eric G., T. K. Das, and A. S. Tsui. 1985. "Toward an Integrative Framework of Organizational Control." *Accounting, Organization, and Society* 10 (1): 35–50.

Fleisher, Lawrence. 1991. "Thomas E. Dewey and Earl Warren: The Rise of the Twentieth-Century Urban Prosecutor." *California Western Law Review* 28: 1–50.

Flick, Alexander, ed. 1935. *History of the State of New York.* Vol. 7. New York: New York Historical Association.

Flynn, Kevin. 1989. "Hearings Begin on Koch's Talent Bank." *Newsday,* 9 January.

———. 1994. "Plow Now Anyhow. Buried City Hired Tainted Contractors." *Newsday,* 28 February.

Ford, Henry Jones. 1904. "Municipal Corruption." *Political Science Quarterly* 19 (December): 678.

Foucault, Michel. 1979. *Discipline and Punish: The Birth of the Prison.* New York: Vintage.

Frederickson, H. George, ed. 1993. *Ethics and Public Administration.* Armonk, N.Y.: M. E. Sharpe.

Freedman, Anne. 1994. *Patronage: An American Tradition.* Chicago: Nelson-Hall.

Fresco, Robert, and Susan Bilello. 1990. "Cleaning Up Is Hard to Do." *Newsday,* 26 December.

Gardiner, John. 1974. *Theft of the City.* Bloomington: Indiana University Press.

Gargan, Edward. 1983. "Koch Asks Law to Help Reveal City Corruption." *New York Times,* 13 December.

Garment, Suzanne. 1991. *Scandal: The Culture of Mistrust in American Politics.* New York: Doubleday.

Garrett, Charles. 1961. *The LaGuardia Years: Machine and Reform Politics in New York City.* New Brunswick, N.J.: Rutgers University Press.

Geist, William E. 1986. "Pssst, Here's a Secret: Trump Rebuilds Ice Rink." *New York Times,* 15 November.

Gelb, Barbara. 1983. "The Hard Code of the Super Chiefs." *New York Times,* 9 October.

Gelman, Mitch. 1992. "Tagging a Cop: IAD Had Paper Trail on Officer Busted for Dealing Drugs." *Newsday,* 13 May.

Gerth, H. H., and C. W. Mills. 1946. From *Max Weber: Essays in Sociology.* New York: Oxford University Press.

Gerth, Jeff. 1992. "Records Show Clintons Lost Less in Venture Than Partner." *New York Times,* 25 March.

Gilbert, Dennis A. 1988. *Compendium of American Public Opinion.* New York: Facts on File.

Gittell, Marilyn. 1981. "School Governance." In *Setting Municipal Priorities,* edited by Charles Brecher and Raymond D. Horton. Montclair, N.J.: Allenheld Osman.

Gladden, E. N. 1972. "Development of Modern Systems of Public Administration: 1815–1971." In *A History of Public Administration.* Vol. 2. London: Frank Cass, 307–64.

Glazer, Myron. 1989. *The Whistleblowers: Exposing Corruption in Government and Industry.* New York: Basic Books.

Glovin, David. 1994. "Weeding Out Corruption in Newark: Probes Once Every Decade." *The Bergen Record,* 2 August.

Goldstein, Tom. 1976. "Merola Says Nadjari Has 'Ability to Smear.'" *New York Times,* 28 January.

———. 1976. "Grumet Upholds Carey's Motives in Nadjari Action." *New York Times,* 23 June.

———. 1976. "The Nadjari Record: Rights Sometimes Were Ignored." *New York Times,* 1 November.

———. 1977. "Debate Is Intense on Nadjari's Effectiveness in Special Prosecutor Post." *New York Times,* 28 March.

Goodnow, Frank J. 1900. *Politics and Administration.* New York: Russell and Russell.

Gormley, William T., Jr. 1989. *Taming the Bureaucracy.* Princeton, N.J.: Princeton University Press.

———. 1991. *Privatization and Its Alternatives.* Madison, Wis.: University of Wisconsin Press.

Gould, Milton S. 1989. "A Requiem for Andy Tyler." *New York Law Journal,* 20 November.

Green, Bruce, and John D. Feerick. 1991. *Government Ethics Reform for the 1990s: The Collected Reports of the New York State Commission on Government Integrity.* New York: Fordham University Press.

Green, Larry. 1988. "7 More Indicted in Court Over Bribery Probe in Chicago." *Los Angeles Times,* 17 March.

Grieder, William. 1992. *Who Will Tell the People?* New York: Simon and Schuster.

Gruber, Judith E. 1987. *Controlling Bureaucracies: Dilemmas in Democratic Governance.* Berkeley: University of California Press.

Gugliotta, Guy. 1992. "Panel Says House Bank Was Abused." *Washington Post,* 28 February.

Gulick, Luther. 1928. *The National Institute of Public Administration: An Adventure in Democracy.* New York: J. J. Little and Ives.

———. 1941. "Forward." In *Investigating Municipal Administration: A Study of the New York City Department of Investigation,* edited by Harold Seidman. New York: Columbia University Institute of Public Administration.

Guy, Dan M., and D. R. Carmichael. 1986. *Audit Sampling: An Introduction to Statistical Sampling in Auditing.* 2d. ed. New York: John Wiley and Sons.

Haass, Richard N. 1994. *The Power to Persuade: How to Be Effective in Government, the Public Sector, or Any Unruly Organization.* Boston: Houghton Mifflin.

Harvard Law Review Association. 1984. "Developments in the Law: Public Employment." *Harvard Law Review* 97 (May): 1611–1800.

Heidenheimer, Arnold J., Michael Johnston, and Victor T. LeVine, eds. 1989. *Political Corruption: A Handbook.* New Brunswick, N.J.: Transaction Publishers.

Herlands, William. 1941. Preface to *Investigating Municipal Corruption: A Study of the New York City Department of Investigation,* by Harold Seidman. New York: Institute of Public Administration, Columbia University.

Heskett, James L. W., Earl Sasser, and Christopher W. L. Hart. 1990. *Service Breakthroughs: Breaking the Rules of the Game.* New York: Free Press.

Heymann, Philip B. 1987. *The Politics of Public Management.* New Haven, Conn.: Yale University Press.

Hicks, James O., Jr. 1990. *Information Systems in Business: An Introduction.* 2d ed. St. Paul, Minn.: West Publishing.

Hicks, Jonathan P. 1995. "Giuliani's Panel on Police Gets Off to a Running Start." *New York Times,* 1 March.

Hill, Stanley. 1987. "New York City's Unhappy Employees." *New York Times,* 25 July.

Holtzman, Elizabeth. 1991. "Holtzman Says City Agencies Refuse to Provide Records; Stymies Audit Report." *Press Release no. 48.* New York: New York City Office of the Comptroller, 7 March.

———. 1991. Letter to Mayor David Dinkins, 28 October.

———. 1991. "Protect Whistleblowers." *New York Times,* 30 March.

Hoogenboom, Ari. 1961. *Outlawing the Spoils: A History of the Civil Service Reform Movement, 1865–1883.* Urbana, Ill.: University of Illinois Press.

Hoskin, Keith, and Richard H. Macve. 1986. "Accounting and the Examination: A Genealogy of Disciplinary Power." *Accounting, Organization, and Society* 11 (2): 105–36.

"How the City Charter's Conflict of Interest Provisions Evolved." *The Charter Review* (Summer 1988).

Howard, Philip K. 1994. *The Death of Common Sense: How Law Is Suffocating America.* New York: Random House.

Humel, Ralph. 1987. *The Bureaucratic Experience.* New York: St. Martin's Press.

Institute of Public Administration. 1952. *The New York Police Survey: A Report for the Mayor's Committee on Management Survey.*

————. 1987. *Contracting in New York City Government: Final Report and Recommendation.*

Jacobs, James B., and Lynn Zimmer. 1991. "Drug Testing and Workplace Drug Testing: Politics, Symbolism, and Organizational Dilemmas." *Behavioral Science and the Law* 9: 345–60.

Jacoby, Henry. 1973. *The Bureaucratization of the World.* Berkeley: University of California Press.

Johnson, H. Thomas. 1991. "Managing by Remote Control: Recent Management Accounting Practice in Historical Perspective." In *Inside the Business Enterprise: Historical Perspectives on the Use of Information,* edited by Peter Temier. Chicago: University of Chicago Press.

Johnston, Michael. 1982. *Political Corruption and Public Policy in America.* Monterey, Calif.: Brooks/Cole.

Johnston, David. 1994. "Indictment of a Congressman." *New York Times,* 1 June.

Joint Commission on Integrity in the Public Schools. 1990. *Investigating the Investigators: A Report on the Inspector General of the NYC Board of Education.*

Jones, Bryan. 1985. *Governing Buildings and Building Governments.* Tuscaloosa, Ala.: University of Alabama Press.

Karl, Barry Dean. 1963. *Executive Reorganization and Reform in the New Deal.* Cambridge, Mass.: Harvard University Press.

Kaufman, Herbert. 1963. *Politics and Policies in State and Local Governments.* Englewood Cliffs, N.J.: Prentice-Hall.

————. 1977. *Red Tape: Its Origins, Uses, and Abuses.* Washington, D.C.: The Brookings Institution.

Kefauver, Estes. 1952. "Past and Present Standards of Public Ethics in America: Are We Improving?" *Annals of the American Academy of Political and Social Science.* 280 (March).

Kelman, Steven. 1989. *Service Delivery in the 1990s: Alternative Approaches for Local Government.* Washington, D.C.: International City Management Association.

————. 1990. *Procurement and Public Management: The Fear of Discretion and the Quality of Government Performance.* Washington, D.C.: AEI Press.

————. 1994. "Deregulating Federal Procurement." In *Deregulating the Public Service: Can Goverment Be Improved?* edited by John J. DiIulio, Jr. Washington, D.C.: The Brookings Institution.

Kessner, Thomas. 1989. *Fiorello H. LaGuardia and the Making of Modern New York.* New York: McGraw-Hill.

Kettl, Donald F., and John J. DiIulio, Jr., eds. 1995. *Inside the Reinvention Machine: Appraising Governmental Reform.* Washington, D.C.: The Brookings Institution.

Key, V. O., Jr. 1936. *The Techniques of Political Graft in the United States.* Chicago: University of Chicago Libraries.

Kleiman, Dena. 1976. "Court Ready to Kill Saypol's Indictment." *New York Times,* 21 December.

Klitgaard, Robert. 1988. *Controlling Corruption.* Berkeley: University of California Press.

Knapp Commission. 1973. *The Knapp Commission Report on Police Corruption.* New York: Braziller.

Knowles, Marjorie. 1985. "The Inspector General in the Federal Government: A New Approach to Accountability." *Alabama Law Review* 36 (Winter).

Kocieniewski, David. 1994. "Pushers Bid on Cop Coke; Virtually Every Drug Dealer Knew." *Newsday,* 17 April.

———. 1994. "Dirty 30 Precinct: 12 of City's Finest Accused of Outcrooking Crooks." *Newsday,* 16 April.

———. 1995. "Jury Finds Dirty 30 Cop Clean." *Newsday,* 2 March.

Kocieniewski, David, and Leonard Levitt. 1992. "Feds Bypass IAD." *Newsday,* 16 June.

Kohler, Thomas C. 1986. "Models of Worker Participation: The Uncertain Significance of Section 8 (a) (2)." *Boston College Law Review* 27 (May): 499.

Kotter, John. 1990. *A Force for Change: How Leadership Differs from Management.* New York: Free Press.

Krauss, Clifford. 1994. "More Officers Caught in Stings, Police Say." *New York Times,* 6 July.

———. 1995. "16 Officers Indicted in a Pattern of Brutality in a Bronx Precinct." *New York Times,* 4 May.

———. 1995. "Hunting Rogues: Police Corruption Signals Abound." *New York Times,* 6 February.

Krohe, James, Jr. 1992. "Why Reform Government? Replace It, Privatizing Government Services." *Across the Board* 29 (December): 40.

Krueger, Anne O. 1974. "The Political Economy of the Rent-Seeking Society." *American Economic Review* 64 (June). Reprinted in *Toward a Theory of the Rent-Seeking Society,* edited by James Buchanan, Robert D. Tollison, and Gordon Tullock. College Station, Tex.: Texas A&M University Press, 1980.

Kurland, Adam H. 1989. "The Guarantee Clause as a Basis for Federal Prosecution at the State and Local Level." *University of Southern California Law Review* 62 (January): 367–491.

Lafferty, William A., Jr. 1933. *The Auditing of Municipal Accounts in New York State.* Albany, N.Y.: New York State Conference of Mayors and Other Officials.

LaFraniere, Sharon. 1992. "Justice Presses Bank Inquiry; Report Says 'Very Few' Members, Most Out of Office, Are Involved." *Washington Post,* 17 December.

Lardner, James. 1978. "Murphy's Law." *Washington Post,* 12 February.

Levin, Martin A., and Mary Bryna Sanger. 1994. *Making Government Work: How Entrepreneurial Executives Turn Bright Ideas into Real Results.* San Francisco: Jossey-Bass.

Levine, Richard. 1989. "Koch's Aide for Jobs Quits Amid Pressure of Integrity Inquiry." *New York Times,* 25 February.

Levitt, Leonard. 1995. "Confidential: DA's Graft Probe Kept Bratton Out of Loop." *Newsday,* 6 February.

Levy, Clifford J. 1995. "Two Newark Politicians Found Guilty in Bribe Case." *New York Times,* 29 March.

Lewinson, Edwin R. 1965. *John Purroy Mitchel: The Boy Mayor of New York.* New York: Astra Books.

Lewis, Eugene. 1980. *Public Entrepreneurship: Toward a Theory of Bureaucratic Polit-*

ical Power: The Organizational Lives of Hyman Rickover, J. Edgar Hoover, and Robert Moses. Bloomington, Ind.: Indiana University Press.

Liff, Bob. 1995. "Rudy's Power Play." *Newsday,* 28 February.

Light, Paul C. 1993. *Monitoring Government: Inspectors General and the Search for Accountability.* Washington, D.C.: The Brookings Institution.

Lindbom, Charles E. 1990. *Inquiry and Change: The Troubled Attempt to Understand and Shape Society.* New Haven, Conn.: Yale University Press.

Link, Arthur S., ed. 1966. *The Papers of Woodrow Wilson.* Princeton, N.J.: Princeton University Press.

Lippman, Walter. 1989. "A Theory about Corruption." In *Political Corruption: A Handbook,* edited by Arnold J. Heidenheimer, Michael Johnston, and Victor T. LeVine. New Brunswick, N.J.: Transaction Publishers.

Lipsky, Michael. 1980. *Street-Level Bureaucracy: Dilemmas of the Individual in Public Services.* New York: Russell Sage Foundation.

Little, Joseph W. 1987. "Abolishing Financial Disclosure to Improve Government." *Stetson Law Review* 16 (Summer): 633–79.

Lockwood, Brocton. 1989. *Operation Greylord: The Brocton Lockwood Story.* Carbondale, Ill.: Southern Illinois University Press.

Logan, Andy. 1970. *Against the Evidence: The Becker-Rosenfeld Affair.* New York: McCall.

Lowenstein, Daniel H. 1985. "Political Bribery and the Intermediate Theory of Politics." *UCLA Law Review* 32: 705–806.

Lowi, Theodore. 1964. *At the Pleasure of the Mayor: Patronage and Power in New York City, 1898–1958.* New York: Free Press of Glencoe.

Lynn, Frank. 1988. "Ex-Syracuse Mayor's Schemes Detailed in Memo." *New York Times,* 7 February.

———. 1989. "Two Koch Aides Deny Patronage in Jobs." *New York Times,* 12 January.

Lynn, Laurence E., Jr. 1981. *Managing the Public's Business: The Job of the Government Executive.* New York: Basic Books.

Maas, Peter. 1983. *Marie: A True Story.* New York: Random House.

Maass, Arthur. 1987. "Public Policy By Prosecution." *The Public Interest* 89: 107.

MacKaye, Milton. 1934. *The Tin Box Parade.* New York: Robert M. McBride.

Maitland, Leslie. 1977. "A Second Nadjari Indictment against Goldman Is Dismissed." *New York Times,* 23 March.

"Majority in Poll Criticize Congress." 1989. *Washington Post,* 26 May.

Mandelbaum, S. J. 1965. *Boss Tweed's New York.* New York: John Wiley and Sons.

Manning, Bayless. 1964. "The Purity Potlatch: An Essay on Conflict of Interest, American Government, and Moral Escalation." *Federal Bar Journal* 24 (3): 239–56.

Marek, Edward F. 1966. *The Historical Development and Administrative Role of the Comptroller in New York City Government.* Ph.D. diss., Department of Public Administration, New York University, New York.

Marx, Gary. 1988. *Undercover Police Surveillance in America.* Berkeley: University of California Press.

———. 1992. "When the Guards Guard Themselves: Undercover Tactics Turned Inward." *Policing and Society* 2: 151–72.

McBride, Anne. 1990. "Ethics in Congress: Agenda and Action." *George Washington Law Review* 53: 451–87.

McCormick, Richard L. 1981. *From Realignment to Reform: Political Change in New York State, 1893–1910.* Ithaca, N.Y.: Cornell University Press.

———. 1981. "The Discovery That Business Corrupts Politics: A Reappraisal of the Origins of Progressivism." *American Historical Review* 13 (3): 247–74.

McElroy, Jerome E. 1993. *Community Policing: The CPOP in New York.* Newbury Park, Calif.: Sage Publications.

McFadden, Robert D. 1992. "Commissioner Orders an Overhaul in Fight against Police Corruption." *New York Times,* 17 November.

McGregor, Douglas Murray. 1985. *The Human Side of Enterprise.* New York: McGraw-Hill.

McKinley, James C., Jr. 1993. "Underwriter Is Removed by Dinkins." *New York Times,* 8 May.

———. 1994. "Payments to Consulting Firm Frozen in Kings Hospital Work." *New York Times,* 12 March.

McLain, John R. 1985. "Participatory Management Under Sections 2 (5) and 8 (a) (2) of the National Labor Relations Act." *Michigan Law Review,* 83 (June): 1736.

McQueen, M. P. 1989. "Agency Ripped over Asbestos." *Newsday,* 16 September.

Meacham, Michael. 1989. "'Ill Wind' Guilty Pleas Show Pattern of Basic Corruption." *Aviation Week and Space Technology* 130 (April 3): 24.

Merton, Robert K. 1940. "Bureaucratic Structure and Personality." *Social Forces* 8: 18.

———. 1957. *Social Theory and Social Structure.* Glencoe, Ill.: Free Press.

Minda, Gary, and Katie Raab. 1989. "Time for an Unjust Dismissal Statute in New York." *Brooklyn Law Review* 54 (Winter): 1137–1214.

Mitgang, Herbert. 1963. *The Man Who Rode the Tiger: The Life and Times of Judge Samuel Seabury.* Philadelphia: J. B. Lippincott.

Mollen Commission. 1994. *Commission Report: Commission to Investigate Allegations of Police Corruption and the Anti-Corruption Procedures of the Police Department.* 7 July.

Moohr, Geraldine Szott. 1994. "Mail Fraud and the Intangible Rights Doctrine: Someone to Watch over Us." *Harvard Journal on Legislation* 31 (Winter): 153–209.

Moore, Mark H. 1995. *Creating Public Value: Strategic Management in Government.* Cambridge, Mass.: Harvard University Press.

Moore, Mark H., and Margaret Jane Gates. 1986. *Inspectors-General: Junkyard Dogs or Man's Best Friend?* New York: Russell Sage Foundation.

Morgan, Peter W. 1992. "The Appearance of Propriety: Ethics Reform and the Blifil Paradoxes." *Stanford Law Review* 44 (February): 593–621.

"Moynihan Is for 'No Mercy' on Graft." 1986. *New York Times,* 13 March.

Moscow, Warren. 1976. *The Last of the Big-Time Bosses: The Life and Times of Carmine DeSapio and the Rise and Fall of Tammany Hall.* New York: Stein and Day.

Munro, William B. 1924. *Personality in Politics: Reformers, Bosses, and Leaders: What They Do and How They Do It.* New York: Macmillan.

Mushkat, Jerome. 1971. *Tammany: The Evolution of a Political Machine, 1789–1865.* Syracuse: Syracuse Univ. Press.

Myers, Gustavus. [1901]. 1971. *The History of Tammany Hall.* New York: Dover.

Myers, Steven Lee. 1994. "Giuliani Moving Ahead to Put City Services in Private Hands." *New York Times,* 5 December.

Nachmias, David, and David H. Rosenbloom. 1980. *Bureaucratic Government U.S.A.* New York: St. Martin's Press.

Nadjari, Maurice. 1974. "New York State's Office of the Special Prosecutor: A Creation Born of Necessity." *Hofstra Law Review* 2: 97–128.

Nagle, James F. 1987. *Federal Procurement Regulations: Policy, Practice, and Procedures.* Chicago: American Bar Association.

———. 1992. *A History of Government Contracting.* Washington, D.C.: George Washington University Press.

National Municipal League. 1979. *Model State Conflict of Interest and Financial Disclosure Law.*

National Performance Review. 1993. *From Red Tape to Results: Creating Government That Works Better and Costs Less.* New York: Times Books.

Neeley IV, Alfred S. 1984. "Ethics in Government Law: Are They Too Ethical?" Washington, D.C.: American Enterprise Institute.

Nelson, William E. 1982. *The Roots of American Bureaucracy: 1830–1900.* Cambridge, Mass.: Harvard University Press.

"New York City Solutions II: Transforming the Public Personnel System." 1993. In *Columbia University Program in Politics and Public Policy,* edited by Steven Cohen and William B. Eimicke. New York: Columbia University.

New York City Department of Investigation. 1974. *Preliminary Report to the Mayor on Findings of Corruption in the Construction Industry and in the Buildings Department.*

———. 1989. *City-Wide Anti-Corruption Program, Report to the Mayor, December 31.*

———. 1993. *Report to Conflicts of Interest Board: Fleet Bank's Loan to the Liz Holtzman for Senate Committee and the Selection of Fleet Securities as a Member of the City's Underwriting Team.* September.

New York City Department of Investigation, Corruption Prevention and Management Review Bureau. 1989. *City-wide Anti-Corruption Program, Report to the Mayor, December 31, 1989.*

———. 1989. *An Analysis of the Corruption Risks in the Management and Control Systems within the Department of General Services, Bureaus of Leasing and Design in Leasing Private Space for City Use.*

———. 1991. *An Analysis of the Corruption within the Construction Inspection Units of the Department of Buildings and the Agency's Corruption Prevention Program.*

New York City Comptroller. 1985. *Comptroller's Internal Control and Accountability Directives, April 15.*

New York City Conflicts of Interest Board. 1992. *Annual Report 1992.*

New York City Mayor's Office of Contracts. 1990. *VENDEX: Policies and Procedures.* March.

New York City School Construction Authority. 1990. *Prequalification Application: Construction Contractors.*

New York City School Construction Authority, Office of Inspector General. 1991. Press Release, 29 July.

New York State-City Commission on Integrity in Government. 1986. *Report and Recommendations Relating to City Procurement and Contracts, 19 November.*

———. 1986. *Final Report: The Quest for an Ethical Environment.*

New York State Commission on Integrity in Government. 1986. *Report and Recommen-*

dations on Whistleblowing Protection in New York. Albany: New York State General Services Administration.

———. 1991. "'Playing Ball' with City Hall: A Case Study of Political Patronage in New York City." In *Government Ethics Reform For the 1990s*. New York: Fordham University Press.

———. 1991. "Campaign Financing: Preliminary Report." In *Government Ethics Reform for the 1990s*. New York: Fordham University Press.

———. 1991. "Ethics in Government Act: Report and Recommendations." In *Government Ethics Reform for the 1990s*. New York: Fordham University Press.

———. 1991. "Underground Government: Preliminary Report on Authorities and Other Public Corporations." In *Government Ethics Reform for the 1990s*. New York: Fordham University Press.

———. 1991. "A Ship without a Captain: The Contracting Process in New York City." In *Government Ethics Reform for the 1990s*. New York: Fordham University Press.

New York State Organized Crime Task Force. 1990. *Corruption and Racketeering in the New York City Construction Industry*. New York: New York University Press.

New York State Commission on Governmental Operations of the City of New York. 1961. "Background Research in the Top Structure of the Government of the City of New York." *Finance Management* 3 (February): 116–17.

New York State, Senate Committee on Investigations, Taxation, and Government Operations, 1987. "School for Scandal: A Staff Report on the New York City Board of Education's Mismanagement of School Construction, Repair, and Renovation." 23 September.

New York State Temporary Commission of Investigation. 1961. *Final Report of the Special Unit: Government for Sale: A Glimpse at Waste and Corruption in the City of New York, July, 1961.*

———. 1976. *The Nadjari Office and the Press.*

New York Times. 1988. "Public Authorities, Public Competence." Editorial, 22 May.

New York Times. 1989. "The Talent Bank Tale: Unfinished, Unfair." Editorial, 28 January.

New York Times. 1989. "Beneficiaries of the Talent Bank." Editorial, 14 January.

New York Times. 1994. "Corruption in the Dirty 30." Editorial, 1 October.

Newfield, Jack, and Wayne Barrett. 1977. *The Abuse of Power*. New York: Viking Press.

———. 1988. *City for Sale: Ed Koch and the Betrayal of New York*. New York: Harper and Row.

Newsday. 1989. "Panel Flunks Politics 101, But Aces Talent Bank Review." Editorial, 9 August.

Newsday. 1995. "Why Mug Mack? Let Him Run New Cop Watchdog Unit." Editorial, 31 January.

Nigro, Felix A. 1959. *Public Personnel Administration*. New York: Henry Holt.

Noonan, John T. 1983. "Bribery." In *Encyclopedia of Crime and Justice*. New York: Macmillan and Free Press.

———. 1984. *Bribes*. New York: Macmillan.

Northrop, William B., and John B. Northrop. 1932. *The Insolence of Office*. New York: G. P. Putnam and Sons.

Office of Inspector General, New York City School Construction Authority, 1991. Press release, 29 July.

Olson, Mancur. 1971. *The Logic of Collective Action.* Rev. ed. New York: Schocken.

Olson, Walter K. 1991. *The Litigation Explosion.* New York: Penguin Books.

Oreskes, Michael. 1987. "A Yearlong Look at Government's Underside." *New York Times,* 4 February.

Ornstein, Norman J. 1994. "Less Seems More: What to Do about Contemporary Political Corruption." *Responsive Community* 4 (Winter): 7.

Osborne, David, and Ted Gaebler. 1992. *Reinventing Government: How the Entrepreneurial Spirit Is Transforming the Public Sector from Schoolhouse to Statehouse, City Hall to the Pentagon.* Reading, Mass.: Addison-Wesley.

Ostrom, Elinor, Roger B. Parks, and Gordon P. Whitaker. 1977. *Policing Metropolitan America.* Washington, D.C.: National Science Foundation.

Ostrom, Vincent. 1987. *The Political Theory of a Compound Republic: Designing the American Experiment.* 2d ed. Lincoln, Neb.: University of Nebraska Press.

———. 1989. *The Intellectual Crisis in American Public Administration.* 2d ed. Tuscaloosa, Ala.: University of Alabama Press.

Ouchi, William G. 1981. *Theory Z: How American Business Can Meet the Japanese Challenge.* Reading, Mass.: Addison-Wesley.

"PA Crime Commission Closing." 1994. *Lancaster Intelligencer Journal,* 27 June.

Parker, Glenn R. 1996. *Congress and the Rent-Seeking Society.* Ann Arbor, Mich.: University of Michigan Press.

Pascale, Richard T., and A. G. Athos. 1981. *The Art of Japanese Management.* New York: Simon and Schuster.

Perlman, Merril. 1989. "The Crimes and Punishments of Wedtech." *New York Times,* 22 October.

Pessin, Esther. 1987. "Perjury Trial of Ex-City Transportation Chief Begins." *United Press International,* 1 July.

"Police Shifted in Buildings Case." 1961. *New York Times,* 3 February.

Policy Procurement Board. 1990. *Procurement Policy Board Rules,* 1 August.

"Poll: Many Say Congress 'Corrupt.'" *USA Today,* 2 June.

Pooley, Eric. 1994. "Untouchables: Police Corruption in the New York Police Department." *New York Magazine,* 11 July.

Port Authority of New York and New Jersey, Audit Division. 1992. *Audit Plan, 1992.*

President's Commission on Federal Ethics Law Reform. 1989. *To Serve with Honor: Report and Recommendations to the President.* Washington, D.C.: Government Printing Office.

"Public Officials for Sale." 1977. *U.S. News and World Report,* 28 February.

Punch, Maurice. 1985. *Conduct Unbecoming: The Social Construction of Police Deviance and Control.* New York: Tavistock Publications.

Purdum, Todd S. 1990. "When Life Itself Is a Conflict of Interest." *New York Times,* 22 April.

Purnick, Joyce. 1986. "Koch Concedes His Ties to Party Were Too Close." *New York Times,* 25 February.

———. 1986. "Trump Offers to Rebuild Skating Rink." *New York Times,* 31 May.

Quirk, William J., and L. E. Wein. 1971. "A Short Constitutional History of Entities Commonly Known as Public Authorities." *Cornell Law Review* 56 (April): 521.

Raab, Selwyn. 1975. "The Nadjari Years: There Were Also Ups." *New York Times,* 28 December.

————. 1985. "Housing Officials Divulge Secrets on Inquiry." *New York Times*, 26 October.

————. 1990. "State to End New York City Corruption Office." *New York Times*, 14 January.

————. 1991. "New York Halts Contract With Gotti Son-in-Law." *New York Times*, 19 November.

————. 1991. "New York Cancels Builder's Contract, Citing Reports on Mob Ties." *New York Times*, 26 December.

————. 1991. "Fifty-two Companies Banned for School Construction Bids." *New York Times*, 27 August.

————. 1992. "Housing Agency Contractor Named in Fraud Indictment." *New York Times*, 28 February.

————. 1993. "Extortion Tied to Lax Supervision." *New York Times*, 23 October.

Rainey, Hal G. 1990. "Public Management: Recent Developments and Current Prospects." In *Public Administration: The State of the Discipline*, edited by Naomi B. Lynn and Aaron Wildavsky. Chatham, N.J.: Chatham House Publishers.

Regan, Edward V., New York State Comptroller. 1987. Statement to the New York City Charter Revision Commission, 15 October.

Reisman, Michael. 1979. *Folded Lies: Bribery Crusades and Reforms*. New York: Free Press.

"Report on the New York City Department of Investigation. 1980." *The Record* 43 (10): 948–80.

Rich, Wilbur. 1982. *The Politics of Urban Personnel Policy: Reformers, Politicians, and Bureaucrats*. Port Washington, N.Y.: Kennikat Press.

Riordan, William L. 1963. *Plunkitt of Tammany Hall*. New York: Dutton.

Roberts, Robert N. 1988. *White House Ethics: The History of the Politics of Conflict of Interest Regulation*.

Robertson, James O. 1980. *American Myth, American Reality*. New York: Hill and Wang.

Rogers, David, and N. H. Chung. 1983. *110 Livingston Street Revisited: Decentralization in Action*. New York: New York University Press.

Rogow, Arnold, and Harold Lasswell. 1963. *Power, Corruption and Rectitude*. Englewood Cliffs, N.J.: Prentice Hall.

Rones, Phillip. Interview by author. 14 June 1992. United States Bureau of Labor Statistics.

Rose-Ackerman, Susan. 1978. *Corruption: A Study in Political Economy*. New York: Academic Press.

————. 1989. "Which Bureaucracies Are Less Corruptible?" In *Political Corruption: A Handbook*, edited by Arnold J. Heidenheimer, Michael Johnston, and Victor T. LeVine. New Brunswick, N.J.: Transaction Publishers.

Rosenbaum, Dennis P., ed. 1994. *The Challenge of Community Policing: Testing the Promises*. Thousand Oaks, Calif.: Sage Publications.

Rosenbloom, David H. 1985. "The Inherent Politicality of Public Personnel Policy." In *Public Personnel Policy: The Politics of Civil Service*, edited by David H. Rosenbloom. Port Washington, N.Y.: Associated Faculty Press.

Roth, Jack. 1959. "Jury Sees Wide Disorder in City's Building Agency." *New York Times*, 10 March.

Ruff, Charles. 1977. "Federal Prosecution of Local Corruption: A Case Study in the Making of Law Enforcement Policy." *Georgetown Law Journal* 65: 1171–1228.

Russianoff, Gene. 1995. New York State Public Interest Research Group, New York Law School Symposium on Municipal Corruption, March 30.

Sabato, Larry. 1991. *Feeding Frenzy: How Attack Journalism Has Transformed American Politics.* New York: The Free Press.

Sack, Kevin. 1991. "New York Ethics Law Leads Local Officials to Quit Posts." *New York Times,* 18 May.

Sashkin, Marshall. 1982. *A Manager's Guide to Participatory Management.* New York: American Management Association.

Savas, E. S. 1977. "An Empirical Study of Competition in Municipal Service Delivery." *Public Administration Review* 37 (November–December).

Savas, E. S., and Sigmund G. Ginsburg. 1973. "The Civil Service: A Meritless System?" *The Public Interest* 32 (Summer): 70.

Sayre, Wallace S. 1938. "Merit System Progress in New York City." *Good Government* 55 (Sept./Oct.): 53.

Sayre, Wallace S., and Herbert Kaufman. 1965. *Governing New York City: Politics in the Metropolis.* New York: W. W. Norton.

Schanberg, Sydney H. 1994. "Knives Are Out for Cop Watchdog." *Newsday,* 13 December.

Schecter, Joseph. 1957. "Personnel Management in the City of New York." *Public Personnel Review* (October): 203.

Schlesinger, Arthur M. 1945. *The Age of Jackson.* Boston: Little, Brown.

Schmalz, Jeffrey. 1985. "A 'Temporary' Office Gets Its Fifth Occupant." *New York Times,* 23 June.

———. 1985. "Fourteen Charged in Kickbacks in City Housing Projects." *New York Times,* 20 September.

Schmitt, Eric. 1991. "Guilty Plea By Unisysis Expected: Military Contractor Would Admit Fraud and Pay $190 Million." *New York Times,* 6 September.

Schneider, Howard, and C. R. Babcock. 1993. "Clintons' Arkansas Land Venture Losses Disputed." *Washington Post,* 19 December.

Schon, Donald A. 1987. *Educating the Reflective Practitioner: Toward a New Design for Teaching and Learning in the Professions.* San Francisco: Jossey-Bass.

Schurz, Carl. 1893. Editorial. *Harper's Weekly,* 1 July, 614.

Schurz, Carl. 1913. "Speech Before the Senate, 27 January 1871." In *Speeches, Correspondence, and Political Papers of Carl Schurz,* edited by Frederick Bancroft. Vol. 3. New York: G. P. Putnam.

Schwarz, Jordan A. 1993. *The New Dealers: Power Politics in the Age of Roosevelt.* New York: Alfred A. Knopf.

Scott, James C. 1993. "Corruption, Machine Politics, and Political Change." In *Political Corruption: A Handbook,* edited by Arnold J. Heidenheimer, Michael Johnson, and Victor T. LeVine. New Brunswick, N.J.: Transaction Publishers.

Scott, W. Richard. 1995. *Institutions and Organizations.* Thousand Oaks, Calif.: Sage.

Seidman, Harold. 1941. *Investigating Municipal Administration: A Study of the New York City Department of Investigation.* New York: Institute of Public Administration, Columbia University.

Self, Peter. 1972. *Administrative Theories and Politics*. London: Allen and Unwin.

Shafritz, Jay, and Albert Hyde. 1992. *Classics of Public Administration*. 3rd ed. Pacific Grove, Calif.: Brooks/Cole.

Sherman, Lawrence W. 1974. "Police Corruption Control: New York, London, Paris." In *Police Corruption: A Sociological Perspective*, edited by Lawrence W. Sherman. Garden City, N.Y.: Anchor Books.

Shenon, Philip. 1986. "U.S. Officials See Sweeping Effort to Combat Municipal Corruption." *New York Times*, 30 March.

Shipler, David K. 1972. "Study Finds $25 Million Yearly in Bribes Is Paid by City's Construction Industry." *New York Times*, 26 June.

———. 1972. "City Construction Grafters Face New Legal Penalties." *New York Times*, 27 June.

Siegal, Lydia. 1995. "Who Really Runs the Schools?" *City Journal* 5, no. 1 (Winter): 3.

Simpson, Anthony E. 1977. *The Literature of Police Corruption*. New York: John Jay Press.

Skene, Neil. 1992. "Assault on Bureaucracy Never Materialized." *Congressional Quarterly Weekly Report* 50 (7 November): 3608.

Skocpol, Theda. 1992. *Protecting Soldiers and Mothers*. Cambridge, Mass.: Harvard University Press.

Skowronek, Stephen. 1982. *Building a New American State*. New York: Cambridge University Press.

Smith, Bruce L. R., and James D. Carroll, eds. 1982. *Improving the Accountability and Performance of Government*. Washington, D.C.: The Brookings Institution.

Smith, Kevin M., and Oseth, John M. 1993. "The Whistleblower Era: A Management Perspective." *Employee Relations Law Journal* 19 (Fall): 17.

Smith, Richard N. 1982. *Thomas E. Dewey and His Times*. New York: Simon and Schuster.

"Some Results and Limitations of Central Financial Control." 1917. *Municipal Research Bulletin* 81 (January): 3.

Sperry, Roger L., Timothy D. Desmond, Kethi F. McGraw, and Barbara Schmitt. 1981. *GAO 1966–1981: An Administrative History*. Washington, D.C.: U.S. General Accounting Office.

Stahl, O. Glenn. 1971. *Public Personnel Administration*. 6th ed. New York: Harper and Row.

Stancik, Edward F. 1993. *A Report of the Special Commissioner of Investigation for the NYC School District: Power Politics and Patronage: Education in Community School District 12*.

Stanley, David T. 1963. *Higher Skills for the City of New York: Study of Professional, Technical, and Managerial Manpower Needs of the City of New York*. Washington, D.C.: The Brookings Institution.

———. 1963. *Professional Personnel for the City of New York*. Washington, D.C.: The Brookings Institution.

Starr, Roger. 1985. *The Rise and Fall of New York*. New York: Basic Books.

State of New York, Commission of Investigation. 1983. *The Co-op City Repair Program*. March.

———. 1986. *Investigation of the Building and Construction Industry: Report of Conclusions and Recommendations*.

Steffins, Lincoln. 1948. *Shame of the Cities.* New York: Peter Smith.

Sternberg, William, and Matthew C. Harrison. 1989. *Feeding Frenzy.* New York: Henry Holt.

Sterngold, James. 1995. "Orange County Noteholders' Anger Grows." *New York Times,* 3 June.

Stever, James A. 1988. *The End of Public Administration: Problems of the Profession in the Post-Progressive Era.* Dobbs Ferry, N.Y.: Transnational.

Stolberg, Mary M. 1991. *Fighting Organized Crime.* Boston: Northeastern University Press.

Taylor, Frederick. 1967. *The Principles of Scientific Management.* New York: W. W. Norton.

TerHorst, J. F. 1978. "Civil Service: It's Time for Reform." *The Pittsburgh Press,* April 12.

"Termination of City Contract Is Overturned as Unreasonable." 1992. *New York Law Journal,* 16 (October): 21.

Thacher, Thomas D. 1991. "Institutional Innovation in Controlling Organized Crime." In *Organized Crime and Its Containment: A Transatlantic Initiative,* edited by Cyrille Fijnaut and James B. Jacobs. Amsterdam: Kluwer Academic Publishers, 169–82.

Thomas, Norman, and Paul Blanshard. 1932. *What's the Matter with New York: A National Problem.* New York: Macmillan.

Thompson, Dennis F. 1987. *Political Ethics and Public Office.* Cambridge, Mass.: Harvard University Press.

———. 1993. "Mediated Corruption: The Case of the Keating Five." *American Political Science Review* 87 (2): 369–81.

———. 1995. *Ethics in Congress: From Individual to Institutional Corruption.* Washington, D.C.: The Brookings Institution.

Thompson, Victor A. 1976. *Bureaucracy and the Modern World.* Morristown, N.J.: General Learning Press.

———. 1977. *Modern Organization.* Tuscaloosa, Ala.: University of Alabama Press.

Thomson, Marilyn W. 1990. *Feeding the Beast: How Wedtech Became the Most Corrupt Little Company in America.* New York: Charles Scribner and Sons.

Touhy, James, and Rob Warden. 1989. *Greylord: Justice, Chicago Style.* New York: G. P. Putnam.

Townsend, Alair A. 1994. "Velella Should Ask Dad about NY School Reform." *Crain's New York Business,* 1 August.

Treaster, Joseph B. 1992. "Knapp Commission Reunion Has Unexpected Currency." *New York Times,* 28 June.

Trent, Brooke. 1989. Letter to the Editor. *New York Times,* 10 February.

Truman, David. 1981. *The Governmental Process: Political Interests and Public Opinion.* Westport, Conn.: Greenwood Press.

Turn, William. 1937. "In Defense of Patronage." *Annals of the Academy of Political and Social Science.* 189 (January): 22.

"Twenty-six City Inspectors Face Graft Trials." 1940. *New York Times,* 9 November.

Uhlig, Mark A. 1988. "Wedtech's Story: From Symbol of Hope to Emblem of Greed." *New York Times,* 5 August.

United States Department of Justice, Law Enforcement Assistance Administration, National Institute of Law Enforcement and Criminal Justice. 1979. *Corruption in Land Use and Building Regulation: An Integrated Report of Conclusions.* Vol. 1. Washington, D.C.: Government Printing Office.

United States General Accounting Office. 1988. "Government Auditing Standards: Standards for Audit of Government Organizations, Programs, Activities, and Functions." Washington, D.C.: Government Printing Office.

———. 1990. *Assessing the Reliability of Computer-Processed Data.* Washington, D.C.: GAO.

———. 1992. *Report to Selected Members of Congress: Mass Transit Grants, Noncompliance and Misspent Funds by Two Grantees in UMTS's New York Region.* Washington, D.C.: Government Printing Office.

Van Riper, Paul P. 1958. *History of the United States Civil Service.* Evanston, Ill.: Row, Peterson.

Vaughn, Robert G. 1990. "Ethics in Government and the Vision of Public Service." *George Washington Law Review* 58 (February): 417–50.

Viteritti, Joseph. 1983. *Across the River: Politics and Education in the City.* New York: Holmes and Meier.

Warren, Robert O. 1970. "Federal-Local Development Planning: Scale Effects in Representation and Policy Making." *Public Administration Review* 30 (November–December)

"Watch to Be Kept on Building Aides." 1961. *New York Times,* 9 February.

Welfeld, Irving. 1992. *HUD Scandals: Howling Headlines and Silent Fiascos.* New Brunswick, N.J.: Transaction Publishers.

Westman, Daniel. 1991. *Whistleblowing: The Law of Retaliatory Discharge.* Washington D.C.: Bureau of National Affairs.

Whitaker, Charles N. 1992. "Federal Prosecution of State and Local Bribery: Inappropriate Tools and the Need for a Structured Approach." *Virginia Law Review* 78 (October): 1617–54.

White, Leonard D. 1933. *Trends in Public Administration.* New York: McGraw-Hill.

———. 1948. *The Administrative Histories: The Federalists.* New York: Macmillan.

———. 1948. *Introduction to the Study of Public Administration.* 3d ed. New York: Macmillan.

———. 1954. *The Jeffersonians.* New York: Macmillan.

———. 1958. *The Republican Era 1869–1901.* New York: Macmillan.

Wiebe, Robert H. 1967. *The Search for Order: 1877–1920.* New York: Hill and Wang.

Wilenski, Peter. 1986. *Public Power and Public Administration.* Sydney: Hale and Iremonger.

Willen, Liz. 1994. "School Scam: 6 Ed Board Employees Charged in Slush Fund Scheme." *Newsday,* 5 October.

Williams, Dennis, and Phyllis Malamud. 1976. "Sacking of a Supercop." *Newsweek,* 5 January.

Wilson, Woodrow. 1887. "The Study of Administration." *Political Science Quarterly* 2 (June): 197.

Wilson, James Q. 1989. *Bureaucracy: What Government Agencies Do and Why They Do It.* New York: Basic Books.

———. 1994. "Can Bureaucracy Be Deregulated?" In *Deregulating the Public Service:*

Can Government Be Improved? edited by John J. DiIulio, Jr. Washington, D.C.: The Brookings Institution.

Winslow, Richard S., and David W. Burke. 1993. *Rogues, Rascals, and Heroes: A History of the New York City Department of Investigation.* New York: New York City Department of Investigation.

Yen, Marianne. 1987. "Who's Who in New York City Corruption Scandals." *Washington Post,* 26 August.

Zimmerman, Joseph. 1994. *Curbing Unethical Behavior in Government.* Westport, Conn.: Greenwood Press.

Zuboff, Scohana. 1988. *In the Age of the Smart Machine.* New York: Basic Books.

Table of Cases

Index

Department of Environmental Protection, New York City, 172
Department of Investigation (DOI), New York City: administrative reform role, 87; during Beame administration, 81–82, 85; Bureau of Complaints in, 79; Corruption Prevention and Management Review Bureau, 147; Corruption Prevention Bureau (CPB), 87–88; criticism of, 81; effects of, 88–91; enforcement by, 57, 81–84, 92; evolving role of, 27–28; inspectors-general (IG) system, 84–87, 89, 92, 148; investigation of contractors, 128; investigation of official corruption, 147; during Koch administration, 84, 85–86; during LaGuardia administration, 79–80; Operation Ampscam, 83–84; post-LaGuardia era, 80–81; proposed reexamination of, 199–200; role in whistleblower protection, 67–69; during Tammany administrations, 78
Department of Justice. *See* U.S. Department of Justice
DeSapio, Carmine, 100, 142
DeVincenzo, Joseph, 34–36
Dewey, Thomas E., 96, 158
DiFalco, Samuel, 100
Dinkins, David N. (mayor, 1990–94), 59, 130, 165
District attorneys, New York City: Manhattan corruption prosecutions (1992–94), 102, 108–13; Manhattan's handling of corruption cases, 102; post-OSPC corruption cases, 101–2
Dodge, William Copeland, 96
DOI. *See* Department of Investigation (DOI), New York City
Dowd, Michael, 164–66
Durk, David, 160–61

Electronic data processing, 201
Enforcement: in corruption control, 13–14; of ethics laws, 57; federal role in local corruption, 103–6; by New York City DOI, 81–84
Entrepreneurial government, 186
Ethics Code [Chapter 68] (1989), New York City, 50–53, 59–60
Ethics codes, New York City, 48–49
Ethics in Government Act (1978), federal, 8, 211n.7
Ethics in Government Act (1987), New York State, 49, 51, 53–54, 61

Ethics law (1991), New York State, 61
Ethics laws: Commission on Federal Ethics Law Reform, 46–47; New York State, 48–49; perceived requirement for, 47–48; role and effect of, 56–62. *See also* Conflict-of-interest laws; Financial disclosure
Extortion: New York City Department of Buildings (1940–93), 154–57; New York City police department, 157–58

Federal Bureau of Investigation (FBI), 103, 170
Federal Civil Service Act (1883), 32
Feerick Commission: on campaign finance, 55; critique of, 42–44; on impact of corruption controls, 134–35; recommendations and views of, 49, 184–85; Talent Bank investigation, 34–37; on whistleblower rules, 63, 71–72
Fesler, James, xvi
Financial controls: effect in New York City of expansion, 149; evolution of public sector, 140–42. *See also* Accounting; Auditing
Financial disclosure: application and function of laws, 45–48, 56–58; for candidates for elected office in New York, 55; laws of, New York State, 53–55; laws of, New York City, 48
Ford, Gerald, 103
Ford, Henry Jones, xv
Fosdick, Raymond "Fearless," 77–78, 80
Foucault, Michel, 24
Friedman, Stanley, 48, 51, 102–4, 124–25

Gaebler, Ted, 175, 185–86
Garment, Suzanne, 8, 14
Giuliani, Rudolph, 102, 104, 169
Goal displacement, 179–80
Goldman, Irving, 99
Goodnow, Frank, 21
Gross, Harry, 159
Gross Committee (1954), 157
Gulick, Luther, 23

Health and Hospitals Corporation (HHC), New York City, 133–34
Hein, James G., 35–36
Herlands, William, 27, 75, 79, 80
Hines, Jimmy, 96, 158
Hogan, Frank, 96–97
Holtzman, Elizabeth, 55–56, 71, 127, 130